G000155133

Keeping Children Safe

Keeping Children Safe

*Child Abuse, Child Protection
and the Promotion
of Welfare*

Harry Ferguson
and
Máire O'Reilly

A. & A. Farmar

First published 2001
by
A. & A. Farmar
Beech House
78 Ranelagh Village
Dublin 6
Ireland
Tel: +353-1-496-3625
Fax: +353-1-497-0107
Email: afarmar@iol.ie
Web: farmarbooks.com

Index by Helen Litton
Designed and typeset by A. & A. Farmar
Printed and bound by GraphyCems

ISBN 1-899047-72-7

To
Ellen Niamh Ferguson
born 6 June 2000

Contents

Foreword

Public discourse regarding child abuse, and child protection systems in particular, tends to be influenced by disclosures regarding the 'failure' of services and systems to protect children. Much of the work of childcare professionals occurs in private and consequently little is known of the day to day work which is undertaken with families and children.

This comprehensive study outlines the reality of how services respond to the complexities involved when issues regarding the care and protection of children arise. The focus is on individual and organisational practices and processes and the outcome of professional interventions.

The commissioning of this research is part of the overall commitment of the Mid-Western Health Board to develop services and practices based an evidence and to strive continuously towards best practices.

The longitudinal approach was taken in order to allow the progress of cases to be tracked and to establish outcomes. Clearly such an exhaustive study identified areas in which improvements must be made and also identified gaps in service provision. It is heartening, however, to note that it has also been possible to identify many examples of good practice from which we can also learn and enhance effective interventions.

The research which analyses the findings goes beyond a limited concern with child protection issues to consider responses to children in domestic violence cases and those where control and behaviour problems and other special needs arise. The result is a book which clearly has relevance to deepening understandings of child care protection practices and systems, not only in the Mid-Western Health Board region but indeed nationally

The study is particularly timely in that it provides a vital picture on which to assess how the Health Board is fulfilling its new obligations under the Child Care Act (1991) which was fully implemented immediately prior to the initiation of this study.

The research findings have already assisted the Mid-Western Health Board in introducing a number of changes in its child care and protection services. In addition to strengthening service provision, management structures and practices and training resources have also been strengthened.

The phased implementation of the 1999 'Children First' National Guidelines for the Protection and Welfare of Children is also being implemented throughout the region and associated information systems are being improved.

I wish to pay tribute to the Health Board's child care professionals and our partner organisations who work so hard to keep children safe and who gave so willingly of their time and energy in supporting this research.

In a time when childcare is increasingly being defined as a 'high-risk' professional activity it is of enormous pride to this Board that the child care professionals co-operated so willingly in opening their practices to such a comprehensive evaluation.

The Health Board is committed to learning the lessons from this evaluation and working to ensure the safety and well being of children and families in the Mid-West.

S. de Búrca
Príomh Oifigeach Foidhmeacháin
Mid-Western Health Board

Acknowledgements

Keeping Children Safe is the culmination of some five years work which began in 1995 when the Mid-Western Health Board (MWHB) commissioned Professor Harry Ferguson, then of the Department of Applied Social Studies, University College Cork, to carry out an evaluation of its child care and protection services. Máire O'Reilly began working as Research Officer on the project in October 1996. The gathering of the research data commenced in April 1996 and lasted until 1998. The research report was submitted to the MWHB in June 1999, following which substantial discussions took place with senior managers and front-line practitioners and the implications of the findings absorbed. We are deeply grateful to the MWHB for allowing us the academic freedom to substantially revise the original report and publish the findings in this book.

The book would not have been possible without the help and support of many people. We are deeply grateful to Michèle Croke who acted as Research Assistant for all her hard work, intellectual contributions and support. Patsy Devoy completed the huge task of transcribing the interviews and did so with great professionalism. The project benefited from discussions with Dr Kieran McKeown in the early days of research design, and with Fergus Hogan and Marian Murphy at various points in the lifetime of the project. Professor Fred Powell, Head of the Department of Applied Social Studies, University College Cork, gave invaluable support and encouragement. We are grateful to our publishers, Anna and Tony Farmar for their assistance and commitment in producing the book.

It takes a great deal of courage—as well as extra work—for professionals to allow their practice to be scrutinised by researchers and we would like to thank the staff of the Mid-Western Health Board and Clare Care from whom we could not have received more co-operation and support. We are deeply grateful to the social workers who put a huge amount of work into the completion of the survey forms, made themselves freely available for interviews and helped us to gain the participation of the parents and children who contributed so much to this study. We are also indebted to all the other professionals, both within the Health Board and outside it, who agreed to be interviewed and who made time in their busy schedules to assist us in the research. Particular thanks go to Jacquie Deevey, Gildas Gordon, Jackie Hogan, Margaret Lee, Phil Mortell, Kerstin Murray, Ita O'Brien, Kevin O'Farrell and Colette Quinlivan for their assistance in gathering the data. Meanwhile, back at HQ, Finola Downes, Carol Murray and other colleagues too numerous to mention made us very welcome and we really appreciated their hospitality while we took up residence for several months. We are very grateful to Fr Ger Nash, Director of Clare Care, the voluntary organisation which provides child care and protection services alongside the Health Board in County Clare, and to Ita O'Brien for her help in steering the book through the production process.

We would like to sincerely thank the Chief Executive Officer of the MWHB, Mr Stiofán de Búrca, and his predecessor, Mr Denis Doherty, for their generous support in commissioning the research and supporting this book, and Mr Martin Duffy, Programme Manager, for his help and encouragement. It would be impossible for us to thank Ger Crowley, the Assistant Chief Executive Officer of the MWHB, enough for the enormous help and support he has given to this project from the outset and throughout the lengthy research process. We can only hope the research and this book repay his faith.

Finally, we wish to thank our families, and in particular Claire Mackinnon, Ellen, Susie, Ben, Katie and Madge Ferguson; and Joe McCrohan for their love and support.

Harry Ferguson
Máire O'Reilly

List of Abbreviations

A&E accident and emergency

AMO area medical officer

CARI Children at Risk in Ireland

CPN Child Protection Notification

CSA child sexual abuse

CWO community welfare officer

DCC director of community care

DoH Department of Health

DPP Director of Public Prosecutions

EHO environmental health officer

GP general practitioner

HHO home help organiser

ISPCC Irish Society for the Prevention of Cruelty to Children

JLO juvenile liaison officer

MOH medical officer of health

MWHB Mid-Western Health Board

NAI non-accidental injury

NSPCC National Society for the Prevention of Cruelty to Children

PHN public health nurse

1 Child Abuse, Protection and 'Safe' Practice

Introduction

At the beginning of a new millennium, public interest in the problem of child abuse in Ireland has reached extraordinary levels. From the early 1990s a series of disclosures of serious cases of child abuse focused unprecedented public and political attention on the 'failures' of the system to protect children known to be at risk (Department of Health (DoH), 1996a; Keenan, 1996; McGuinness, 1993; Moore, 1995; North Western Health Board, 1998).

Until recently the level of public interest in child welfare in Ireland was very limited. This is exemplified by the fact that until the 1990s child care was administered under the 1908 Children Act, legislation enacted under British rule. The voluntary sector, principally through the work of the Irish Society for the Prevention of Cruelty to Children (ISPCC), carried administrative responsibility for child protection for much of the 20th century. It was only in the late 1970s that the Irish State took on primary responsibility for child care policies and began to implement distinct child protection procedures and practices (Ferguson, 1996a). With the full implementation of a new Child Care Act (1991) by 1996 and the laying down of new Church and State child protection guidelines in the 1990s (DoH, 1987; 1995; 1999; Irish Catholic Bishops' Advisory Committee, 1996) more developments have occurred in child care and protection law, policy, and practice over the past decade than in the previous eighty years (Ferguson, 2001a, Ferguson and Kenny, 1995; Richardson, 1999).

Legal changes and greater use of child protection procedures have increased the level of accountability of those responsible for the welfare of children. Somewhat paradoxically, this increase has been accompanied by decreased confidence in the ability of the State to protect children and in a weakening of the power and moral authority traditionally held by the Catholic Church. This is primarily because the Church failed either to bring many known clerical child abuse perpetrators to justice or to prevent the systematic abuse of children cared for in residential institutions run by religious orders (Ferguson, 1995a; Raftery and O'Sullivan, 1999).

Adult survivors of child abuse who spoke out about their abuse and the failure of the system to protect them played a remarkable role in this change as did television documentaries which have become extraordinary cultural phenomena (Buckley, C., 1996; Fahy, 1999; McKay, 1998; Raftery and O'Sullivan, 1999). For example, the *States of Fear* series (broadcast April–May 1999) about the abuse of children in care institutions in 20th-century Ireland led to the Government's formal apology to survivors of institutional abuse and the establishment of the Commission on Childhood Abuse to examine the problem and to hear publicly the testimony of survivors (Ferguson, 2000). Yet, despite this extraordinary level of public interest and professional concern, there is still little published work on the nature of child abuse in Ireland and the operation of the child protection system. While we have come to learn more about how the system *fails*, we still know little of a systematic nature about how it *works*, both in the sense of what is done well, and of how professionals actually operate on a routine, day-to-day basis to protect children. This book aims to help fill that gap.

Keeping Children Safe documents the findings from a major three-year study of child care and protection practices in the Mid-Western Health Board (MWHB) area. It is the largest research project yet undertaken into child protection and welfare services in Ireland and provides the first systematic analysis of how the fully implemented Child Care Act (1991), with the new obligations placed on health boards to promote the welfare of children not receiving adequate care and protection, is working in practice. The MWHB region includes approximately 10 per cent of the population of Ireland. Its population profile, range of urban, town and rural locales and range of social problems are typical of those found across the country. Although each health board region—and even, as this book shows, each community care team within a health board—has its own character, we are satisfied that our findings are generalisable to the country as a whole in that the ways in which the work is done, and the key policy and practice issues grappled with, are typical of child care and protection work throughout Ireland. We believe that the findings have major implications for our understandings of child abuse and the direction of child care policy and practice in Ireland and even beyond.

This opening chapter sets out the context within which the research was conducted, the research methods employed and a brief overview of the findings.

The development of child 'protection' in Ireland

'Modern' child protection in Ireland began with the formation of a Dublin branch of the National Society for the Prevention of Cruelty to Children (NSPCC) in 1889, whose headquarters were in London. Irish branches remained under the administrative control of the London office until 1956 and the founding of a self-governing Irish society (Allen and Morton, 1961). Between 1889 and 1956 'no fewer than 478,865 children were helped by the NSPCC in the Republic of Ireland' (Mayo and District Branch NSPCC, 1955, p. 2). From the outset, 'neglect' predominated in agency classifications so that, by the 1930s, it was stated that 'cruelty is little known in Ireland' (Mayo and District Branch NSPCC, 1938). Recognition of physical abuse was comparatively rare, while child neglect cases accounted for almost 90 per cent of casework until the 1950s and 1960s (see ISPCC, 1957, p. 11). Recognition of sexual offences against children barely existed at well under 1 per cent of cases (Ferguson, 1996b).

During the 1970s, due to the professionalization of welfare services and a series of national and international developments, the problem of child 'cruelty' underwent a process of (re)definition and 'diagnostic inflation' into child 'abuse' (Dingwall, 1989). This led to the development of coherent Irish child protection policies. The 1970 Health Act established eight health boards, with community care teams, through which the State took over primary responsibility for child care and protection from the ISPCC (McGinley, 1995). In addition, policy was shaped by the reports of government-sponsored committees, in particular the *Kennedy Report* (1970) and the *Final Report of the Task Force on Child Care Services* (1981). The creation of health boards greatly expanded the expert system to include such pivotal positions in community care teams as social workers—who were given the primary responsibility for investigating child welfare cases—public health nurses (PHN), area medical officers (AMO), and the senior management positions of director of community care/medical officer of health (DCC/MHO) (Kelly, 1995).

Developments in Ireland to some extent mirrored those in the USA and the UK where more sophisticated models of programme coordination between various agencies were established from the early 1970s (Hallett and Stevenson, 1980; Nelson, 1984), arising out of the work of Henry Kempe and his medical colleagues and their construction of the 'battered child syndrome' (Kempe et al., 1962). The ISPCC took the lead in publicising in Ireland the battered child syndrome and high-profile system failures in the UK (Colwell Report, 1974) and engaged with the Department of Health on the development of appropriate policies (ISPCC, 1974, p.18). A new emphasis was placed on the child protection system as the crucial variable in the effective management of what were now known as non-accidental injury (NAI) cases. The first formal guidelines for professionals on handling child abuse cases were issued in March 1977 (DoH, 1977) and were revised in 1980 and 1983 (Ferguson 1996a). These guidelines dealt only with physical abuse and neglect, but a further revision in 1987 included emotional abuse and also gave systematic recognition to child sexual abuse on the basis that it 'has particular features which require special attention' (DoH, 1987, p. 23). Specialised child sexual abuse assessment units were established around the country (McGrath, 1996). These units deal almost exclusively with assessment reflecting how the Irish system has, until recently at least, favoured investigative responses to child (sexual) abuse, to the neglect of a broader definition of child welfare (McElwee, 1996; Murphy, 1996).

In the 1990s, the administrative structures for dealing with cases were tightened up through new official guidelines that require health board staff and gardaí to 'notify' one another of all suspected cases of child abuse (DoH, 1995; 1999). This followed inquiries into system failures where the absence of communication between the police and social workers played a crucial role (McGuinness, 1993). The series of clerical scandals and child abuse inquiries have involved every aspect of the child care and protection system. This process began with the Kilkenny incest investigation that examined why action was not taken sooner by the health services to halt the physical and sexual abuse of a girl/woman by her father over a sixteen-year period from 1976 to 1992 (Ferguson, 1994; McGuinness, 1993). Virtually every aspect of policy, particularly inter-agency and inter-professional co-ordination, became the subject of critical analysis and recommendations for change, leading to more comprehensive revised Child Abuse Guidelines in 1999 (DoH, 1999). Proposals have also been made for Constitutional reform to specify more clearly the rights of children (McGuinness, 1993) and there has been vigorous debate about how best to identify abused children. After a lengthy consultation process and much prevarication, in 1998 the Government finally committed itself to introducing mandatory reporting of child abuse, which—at the time of writing—has yet to happen (DoH 1996b).

Significant legal reform has also occurred. The role of the State in child welfare and protection has been clearly specified through the full implementation by late 1996 of the Child Care Act (1991). Under the 1908 Children Act, intervention was framed in reactive terms as a requirement merely to respond to possible criminal offences against children. Under the 1991 legislation, for the first time since its foundation, the Irish State has

been given the power and the responsibility to be proactive in promoting the welfare of children at risk. In placing a duty on health boards to promote the welfare of children in their areas the Child Care Act (Section 3) requires a health board to:

> take such steps as it considers requisite to identify children who are not receiving adequate care and protection and co-ordinate information from all relevant sources relating to children in its area.

A number of types of service are now being delivered under the rubric of the Child Care Act. An analysis of the Section 8 reports the MWHB and the other seven health boards are required to produce under the Act on the adequacy of the child care and family support services in their areas shows that in addition to the child protection duties carried out by community care social work departments, family support services typically include pre-school services, community mothers, psychiatric services, family centres and neighbourhood youth projects. Some also include family therapy under the family support label. The types of practical linkages between child protection and family support include:

—family support and community child care workers who work with children and families as part of community care teams

—family support services in the community, provided by voluntary and State agencies, through referrals from community care

—family support services in the community which accept referrals from the wider community as well as (or even instead of) from community care.

In addition, as this book will show, the developments of therapeutic child psychology and psychiatry services in health boards are making significant contributions to promoting the welfare of children. From the mid-1990s, children at risk of not receiving adequate care and protection have been interfacing with the services through a variety of routes. Thus, an evaluation of child care and protection services cannot be reduced simply to the activities of community care teams. Although the focus in this book is on the community care teams' work with children and families and limited attention is given to the services reaching children and families outside that system, the analysis does reveal the extent to which families referred to community care with child abuse/care problems are being offered social work, family support and other clinical/therapeutic services. This tells us a lot about the types of services that are, or are not, being delivered to the most vulnerable families and high risk children identified under the Act as not receiving adequate care and protection.

The dominance of child 'abuse'/protection

The striking feature of the Irish child care system over the past decade has been the dominance of child abuse and protection in its design and operation. Even before the Kilkenny Inquiry, and implementation of the Child Care Act, the system had developed firmly in the direction of child protection. The emergence of Child Abuse Guidelines in the late-1970s and their increasing importance led to social workers losing their traditional discretion to work with families in whatever ways they felt were best (Walsh, 1999).

During the 1980s the numbers of child abuse referrals made to health boards increased almost tenfold: from 406 cases in 1982 to 3,859 in 1991. Crucially, these referrals were investigated by a more or less static number of social workers. The result was that a less generic child care service was provided and time and resources were saved by cutting back in preventive child welfare areas. Such organisational pressures meant that the onus increasingly fell on referral agents to convince social workers of the 'high risk' nature of cases. Concerns framed in terms of 'abuse' were more likely to get a response and (scarce) services allocated to them. Formal 'entry' to the child care system and the threshold for provision of social work and support services was set lower for children at risk of child abuse than for

Table 1.1 Reported and confirmed cases of child abuse in Ireland, 1984–97

Year	Total reports received	Cases confirmed
1984	479	182 (38%)
1985	767	304 (40%)
1986	1,015	495 (49%)
1987	1,646	763 (46%)
1988	2,673	1,243 (47%)
1989	3,252	1,658 (51%)
1991*	3,856	1,465 (38%)
1992	3,812	1,701 (45%)
1993	4,110	1,609 (39%)
1994	5,152	1,868 (36%)
1995	6,415	2,276 (35%)
1996**	7,732	2,270 (29%)
1997**	7,312	2,659 (36%)

*No figures available for 1990

**Southern Health Board not included in these figures

Source: Department of Health *Child Abuse Statistics*

other children in need. In the process, child *care* was largely re-framed as child *protection* (see Ferguson, 1995b, pp 26–7).

Reports of child abuse grew relentlessly in the 1990s as public awareness increased and inter-agency co-operation was strengthened in the light of the Kilkenny and other child abuse inquiries (see Table 1.1). There was a sharp national rise in notified cases from 3,856 cases in 1991 to 7,312 in 1997, an increase of almost 90 per cent. However, as the number of reports increased the rate of confirmation of abuse declined from a high of 51 per cent in 1989 to a low of 29 per cent in 1996. This may reflect a raising by practitioners of the threshold for 'confirmed' abuse as the system strains to respond to the increased number of cases (Thorpe, 1997). However, it is well known within the system that there are problems with these figures, which makes it difficult to draw a definite conclusion.[1]

Unfortunately, the Department of Health's data is not reliable; for example notifiable child abuse is not defined in a rigorous manner, so that there are wide variations in how abuse is defined and responded to by community care teams even within the same health board (Kenny, 1995). The figures do not even refer to all *reported* cases, but only to those cases *notified* to the director of community care under the 1987 Child Abuse Guidelines. As this book shows, only a proportion of referred and investigated cases are notified as child abuse. A real measure of the work being done, and of the workload increases in recent years, is found in the number of reported cases, on which this study provides important original data, as part of a model for evaluation and information management of a kind which urgently needs to be developed on a routine basis by the Department of Health and health boards.

Table 1.2 Reported and confirmed cases MWHB 1989–97

Year	Total reports received	Cases confirmed
1989	178	56 (31%)
1990	407	183 (45%)
1991	515	254 (49%)
1992	655	388 (59%)
1993	525	179 (34%)
1994	695	212 (31%)
1995	826	237 (29%)
1996	904	275 (30%)
1997	936	225 (24%)

Source: Mid-Western Health Board *Review of Child Care and Family Support Services 1997*

The number of cases officially processed by the MWHB community care teams increased by 426 per cent between 1989 and 1997 (see Table 1.2). Trends in confirmation of cases in this health board mirror very closely national patterns, with a decline from a high point of 59 per cent in 1992 to 24 per cent in 1997. As our research shows, a more meaningful indicator of the assessed levels of risk to children and the work that goes on is 'substantiation' of abuse/problems. 'Confirmation' has a much stronger, legalistic meaning and a higher threshold in terms of the evidence needed than 'substantiation' which speaks more to whether in the professional's *opinion* the problem in the referral was borne out or not. While substantiation is undoubtedly more subjective, the key point is that substantiated cases provide the truest measure of the extent and nature of the problems being worked with by health boards. These increases in reported child abuse cases also reflect the availability of greater resources. Over £40 million has been injected into the system since 1993 to implement the Child Care Act and the numbers of staff and services available to report suspected cases and to respond to them has grown considerably. According to the Department of Health, by 1997 some 900 additional posts had been created nationally in professional and administrative areas (personal communication). These include child care development officers in each of the health boards, social work team leaders and additional posts in frontline social work, community child care work, psychology, child psychiatry and family support work. Between 1987 and 1995, nationally the numbers of social workers employed within health board child care services increased from 309 to 821 (Skehill, 1999).

Had it not been for the Kilkenny incest investigation and subsequent inquiries we would probably still be trying to excite political action to the point where resources would be freed up and the Act actually implemented (Ferguson, 1994). It is this increased awareness of child abuse since the 1980s and the emergence of child welfare as a political issue in the 1990s, together with the demand for greater accountability and awareness of risks, that have led to the consolidation of the dominance of child protection. Since around 1993 and the impact of the Kilkenny inquiry, the definition and structure of the service provided by community care has become more *explicitly* child protection. The administrative structures for dealing with cases have been tightened up through new official health board–gardaí guidelines for the notification and management of cases (DoH, 1995). In the MWHB, as in most health board areas, more formalised Child Protection Notification (CPN) systems have also been introduced under the terms of the 1987 and 1999 Child Abuse Guidelines. Inter-disciplinary management groups now meet regularly to process 'notified' referrals and cases, an initiative which represents perhaps the most significant organisational change as community care shifted its primary concern to child abuse. As one social worker interviewed for this study put it: 'We're not meant to take referrals that aren't a type, that don't have a child protection element'. In effect, the system has become much more influenced by (new) managers, bureaucracy and accountability (Lavan, 1998).

This book explores the extent to which this process has led to the bureaucratisation of social work and other child care disciplines, causing a loss of discretion for front-line practitioners and a policy and practice more concerned to protect the agency than to meet the needs of vulnerable children and families, as has occurred in other jurisdictions (Howe, 1992; Parton, 1991). Buckley (1996, 1999) provides evidence of generic social work service narrowing to child protection as manifested in the work of one Eastern Health Board community care social work team in the early 1990s. Out of 166 non-child abuse referrals made to the team over six months, 'only ten received any follow-up, as opposed to child abuse referrals, where most were investigated to some degree. . . . Even within the total number of referrals designated as child abuse in the study, only 25 per cent survived the investigative filters which decide whether or not they will receive a service' (Buckley, 1996, p. 49). Significantly, however, Buckley's research took place before the full impact of child abuse inquiries and before any of the main sections of the Child Care Act had been implemented. It was unable, therefore, to take account of the system development and changes in awareness that have occurred since the early 1990s. The present study was designed to do this by gathering data on the period 1996–7, by which time some of the seismic shifts brought about by the changed climate, Child Care Act and increased resources were well embedded in practice. The findings challenge many conventional wisdoms as we argue that, while 'child protection' does dominate child care systems in Ireland, the notion has been socially (re)constructed in this cultural context so as to include a concept of family support. The very notion of 'child protection' needs to be carefully deconstructed in terms of the policies and practices which go on in its name and its meanings in particular times and places.

There has been a lively debate in the international literature about the nature of child care systems, the meanings of 'safety' and 'risk', and the issues that arise in balancing child protection and family support services (DoH, 1995; Parton, 1997; Thorpe, 1997; Parton, Thorpe and Wattam, 1997; Ferguson, 1997a). What is happening in Ireland is part of a global

phenomenon. In Western Australia, for instance, rates of child protection referrals rose from 2,594 in 1989 to 6,982 in 1994, an increase of 169 per cent. Researchers in the Department of Family and Children's Services in Western Australia calculated that if those rates of increase were maintained, then every child in the State could become a subject of a child protection investigation by the year 2010 (Thorpe, 1997, p. 70). Local and international research in the early 1990s showed that a relatively small proportion of children reported to child welfare agencies received a service of any kind, as cases were screened out at every stage through the system (Gibbons et al, 1995). Many who did not fit the child abuse categories set by the agency concerned were screened out without the offer of other services, despite the fact that they were children in need, being reared in families in difficult circumstances (Ferguson, 1995b, p. 30). Here we get to the core of the concerns which have pervaded child care systems since the early 1990s: the narrowing of child care to child protection, so that many of those drawn into the child protection 'net' get little more than an investigation into child abuse while their child care problems, often severe as they are, remain under-resourced and children in need receive little or no service. It is against this background that the safety of the Irish child protection system is examined in this book, in the context of the impact of the full implementation of the Child Care Act and increased public concern about the ability of professional systems to keep children safe.

The research design and process

The brief of the research was

> to provide a fundamental review of the Mid-Western Health Board's child protection policies and practices and to evaluate the extent to which the elements of a safe, good-quality child protection service are in place in the region.

As we have seen, the research took place in the context of new legislative obligations for the State to promote the protection and welfare of children, and specifically in Ireland the new duty of health boards under Sections 8 and 11 of the Child Care Act (1991) to monitor the 'adequacy' of services. In response to public disclosures of system failures in high-profile child protection cases, the increased demand for accountability in child care, and the attempt to provide data which will assist in designing 'safer' systems, State agencies have become more strongly committed to evaluating services. The trend for public understandings and expectations of child protection to be dominated by the findings of child abuse inquiries and individual cases of system failures has intensified even during the period of this research (North Western Health Board, 1998). However understandable, this focus on inquiries into exceptional cases has been to the neglect of a deeper understanding of routine child care and protection work. In trying to illuminate that work, this book does not in any simple sense set out to establish what professionals do 'badly' but rather to identify the kinds of best practice that provide the foundations on which good child care and protection can be built (Ferguson, 2001b).

Evaluative research in the area of child abuse/protection takes two main forms. The first focuses on the nature of child abuse itself and typically includes clinical studies of samples of cases, examining the causes of different types of abuse, the 'abusive' behaviour of offenders, and the long-term effects of abuse on children (for examples of important studies, see Corby 1993; Egeland, 1988). The second focuses on child care practice and the processes and outcomes of child protection interventions—broadly the organisational routines and decision-making processes which produce a universe of 'cases' and an official phenomenon known as 'child abuse'. Attention is concentrated on the *meanings* and *outcomes* of intervention for parents and children, as well as for the professionals who operate the expert system itself. It was in this direction—the analysis of child care and protection services (see, especially, Farmer and Owen, 1995; Gibbons et al, 1995)—that the focus of research shifted in the 1990s, and it is in this area that the current study is framed (for reviews of some recent studies, see DoH, 1995; Kenny, 1996).

The politics of method and social construction of child abuse

Perceptions of and responses to this kind of research tend to differ according to where one is located in the system. For managers and administrators *effectiveness* questions loom large: 'Do child protection activities actually protect children?' 'Will the system fail?' 'How "safe" is it?' This approach invariably involves very direct evaluations of welfare 'performance'. It tends to frame research in terms of how the job is being done within notions of 'best practice' established by managers, and the agency/bureaucracy. Data produced primarily on the agency's terms tends to be descriptive and focuses on what is visible and evident in terms of 'what practice is'. The phenomena under investigation—'abuse', 'protection'—are broadly taken as given, as existing independently of how the agency itself has 'produced' them. The world is viewed as essentially knowable and measurable and it is assumed that sufficiently rigorous design and measurement will produce the truth. Once discovered, the truth—'proven facts'—can be used to guide or determine policy and practice (Trinder, 1996, p. 234). Within this positivist paradigm, more critical, non-technical matters—such as deconstructing notions of 'abuse' and 'protection'—are left out.

Evaluating *performance* is thus a profoundly political activity which cannot be separated from its social context. It can be seen as part of a shift which began in the 1990s towards managerialism, quality assurance, consumerism and the associated critique of professionalism. Increased emphasis on accountability and practices such as audit are moving in to fill the gap left by system failures in child care, unreliable professional knowledge and discretion (Parton, 1996). Frontline practitioners, while sharing a concern with effectiveness, want to include other issues that impose limits to best practice, such as (scarce) resources, on the evaluation agenda. In a context of increased accountability they may even wish to avoid such research altogether if it is viewed as a tool for management to increase performance expectations in an unfair way. Indeed, the social workers in this study sought a great deal of reassurance that the research was not intended as an 'inspection' of their work. It is, rather, an attempt to evaluate the system and consider what gets done well in addition to identifying apparent gaps.

This book argues that interventions cannot simply be framed as technical matters. The research design took full account of the importance of *process*, recognising that the practical complexities of 'following the guidelines', assessing risk, dealing with resistant clients and so on cannot be reduced in any simple way to certainties and bureaucratic procedures. Such an approach draws from *constructivist* social science and is generally concerned with evaluating 'what is going on here?'; how agency staff 'confront, identify, investigate and report instances of suspected maltreatment of children' (Dingwall, et al 1995). In a social constructionist approach the very definitions of 'protection', 'welfare', 'safety', 'risk', 'need', 'care' are the objects of analysis rather than taken as self-evident phenomena. Research questions ask, for example, 'what is it that children should be protected from?'. This, in turn, requires that the question 'what is child abuse?' be explored.

Answers to such questions are to be found within *the moral reasoning* of front-line workers and the *bureaucratic frames* of the expert system (Thorpe, 1994). Thorpe's research into child protection, for instance, shows that the seriousness of the presenting condition of the child—clinical evidence—is quite often not the best guide to determining official action. Other variables, such as judgements about the moral character of parents, their level of co-operation, and levels of family support are highly influential in shaping case definitions and outcomes. Such considerations underlie the kind of moral reasoning that constructs events and 'cases' and determines agency actions. Conceptions about risk and its management appear to have become central to this, as have the perspectives of lay people and service users in shaping the form that child welfare and protection take and their meanings (Ferguson, 1997a). From a social constructionist perspective, 'protection' can only properly be understood *in relation to* child 'care' and 'welfare'. For this study the notion of 'safety' was, in effect, recast so that the extent to which services not only provide immediate protection, but also promote child welfare and healing could be examined.

Within this conceptual framework, to fulfill the research brief, a long-term study was required not only of the inputs into cases but also of the outcomes of intervention over time. Rather than a retrospective approach based on analysis of data from case files on known outcomes—a method which dominates research on child protection in Ireland (Buckley, Skehill and O'Sullivan, 1997; McKeown and Gilligan, 1992)—it was decided to take a prospective approach and to evaluate the work of the child care and protection system as it actually processed cases in the here and now over a specified period. Crucially, the study was not confined to abuse/protection cases but included *all* referrals of children *at risk of not receiving adequate care and protection,* as defined by the Child Care Act (1991). The aim was to document all the work done by the MWHB under the label of child welfare/ protection so that the child protection work could be analysed in that broad context.

The research took place in three main stages:

Phase 1 The survey A survey identified all the cases referred over a three-month period to the MWHB. Data was gathered on all the referrals from the social workers involved by means of a questionnaire.

Phase 2 Tracking of case careers/outcome analysis The cases identified were tracked over the following twelve months and their outcomes analysed. This was done through direct interviews with all the social workers involved.

Phase 3 Case study—qualitative analysis A representative sample of the cases was identified and interviews were carried out with key actors—parents, children and professionals.

A number of factors influenced the research design and the decision to use both a survey and a qualitative analysis. It was apparent that important primary sources, such as agency case records, and official sources, such as Department of Health child abuse statistics, do not capture certain crucial information, for example, on the decision-making process. Although the quality of existing statistics and documentary evidence on child care and protection was no worse in the MWHB, and perhaps even better than in some other places, case files contain references to but not systematically clear information on the nature of the concern which initiated contact with the agency. This is a significant finding. The systematic detailed information on the referrals entering the system, and responses to them, gathered through the survey method, provided the data needed to analyse outcomes and proved crucial in the examination of the process of construction of cases, from the point of referral to definitions, responses and outcomes.

It also seemed likely that data such as case files and official child abuse statistics did not tell the full story of *what* was done and *how*. For example, 28 per cent of the referrals made to social workers in the study were 'pure' child welfare referrals, containing no child protection concerns as defined in the 'abuse' categories in the Child Abuse Guidelines (DoH, 1987; 1995). Yet these cases—which routinely involve seriously distressed children exhibiting behaviour and control problems, and very vulnerable parents in need of support—have little or no official organisational identity. They do not appear in official statistics as there is no requirement for them to be notified to the CPN system established to respond to child abuse. No comparable system for codifying and monitoring child welfare cases or family support work exists. A prospective approach made visible the meanings of child abuse and child care problems as currently defined and analysed how, in practice, child protection and welfare are constructed.

Domestic violence, which the research found looms large in child protection and welfare work, constitutes another example of the disparity between the actual work of the system and what is officially recorded. It is a neglected issue, only recently beginning to be recognised as having a crucial bearing on child welfare. (Ferguson 1997b; Humphrey, 1999). Brief mention is made of domestic violence in the 1995 Child Abuse Guidelines with respect to notifying suspected emotional abuse and the issue has begun to be taken up at policy level (Department of the Tánaiste, 1997). Beyond this, domestic violence has little reality so far as the 'official' discourse of the health boards and the Department of Health is concerned, as no statistics are produced on the numbers of cases coming to light and little procedural guidance is offered on best practice.

Previous research on child protection practices in Ireland further compounds this gap by ignoring domestic violence as it does not fit predetermined categories. The methodology of gathering primary data on child abuse cases from social workers' case files means accepting the categories of 'abuse' already defined by professionals and working within the parameters of the 'official' discourse established by the agency and government departments. It becomes methodologically very difficult to excavate this 'hidden' work retrospectively. Relying on case notes means these issues never surface. A prospective approach avoids this problem.

Phase 1 The survey

The research began in 1996 with the gathering of extensive data on all child care and abuse cases referred to the MWHB over a three-month sampling period, 1 April–30 June 1996. This produced a core sample of 319 cases. The health board contains three community care teams and the social workers in each were asked to complete a questionnaire form for every child care and protection referral entering the system. Some 32 social workers were directly involved in collecting the data. In addition, senior social workers and team leaders in each of the three teams provided invaluable backup support. To the best of our knowledge, all referrals during the period were identified, except perhaps for a few low-key, once-off telephone queries, which barely constitute the designation 'referral'. From discussions with seasoned practitioners we are satisfied that the referrals included in this study constitute a fair representation of the kinds of cases typically reported and of current health board child care and protection practices.

The survey gathered information on various aspects of the referrals, the decisions made and work done by the professionals involved including:

—source(s) of referral
—nature of referral/concern for the child/family
—suspected abuser/person with the child care problem
—designation of the 'case'
—definition of 'abuse'/child care problem involved
—response to the referral—whether investigated, passed on
—timing of interventions, between referral and investigation
—amount and nature of inter-agency work/collaboration
—operation of the 1987 and 1995 Department of Health Child Abuse Guidelines, the CPN system, gardaí notifications and case conferences
—uses of the criminal and civil law
—types of 'abuse' in substantiated cases
—family forms and types of households affected
—history of health board involvement
—outcomes in terms of children entering care, cases closed
—services offered to substantiated cases.[2]

The survey provided quantification and measurement in an attempt to give *scale* to the work. It provided an overview of all the referrals entering the system during the specified period and an analysis of how they were processed into either child welfare or child protection cases. It also allowed for an interactionist perspective which illuminated aspects of the moral reasoning underpinning practice (cf. Thorpe, 1994, pp. 30), the identification of key variables and processes and the way they interacted in the construction of events and cases. A good example is the finding on the importance of a history of health board involvement to 'case careers', or outcomes. This also produced significant data on the forms of abuse and other child care problems being processed by official agencies, and the kinds of adversities experienced by children, parents and families.

Phase 2 Tracking case careers/outcome analysis

The case careers of referrals entering the child care system can be mapped in terms of differing pathways and outcomes (Thorpe, 1994, pp. 30–33). This involves identifying factors in interventions which generate particular outcomes, and the key decision-making points and other influences on case careers. One is looking for the contingencies—in combination and in sequence—which create particular official identities in terms of clients/cases. In our study, the 319 identified cases in the three-month sample were tracked over the following twelve months to 30 June 1997. The outcome, or 'case career', of each referral was analysed in terms of the types of 'abuse' and child care problems involved, the services provided, and the attempts made to promote the safety and welfare of the children.

This follow-up phase took place from July 1997 and involved gathering data on standardised survey forms from all 35 social workers who took part in the research[3] on the outcome of each of the 319 cases one year on. It was decided to collect this follow-up data through direct contact with social workers to guarantee a 100 per cent response rate and also to create an opportunity for general discussion about the issues arising. This was an extremely time-consuming process which took until February 1998 to complete. A 100 per cent follow-up was eventually achieved which means that we are able to document the outcomes for all 319 referrals.

Phase 3 Case study/qualitative analysis

In this phase, which aimed to deepen understanding of the harder quantitative data, a case-study approach was adopted. It was beyond the scope and the priorities of the research to provide a qualitative evaluation of the processing of all 319 cases so a representative sample of the typical concerns was chosen and the main actors were interviewed. Central to sound sampling is the avoidance of a methodological process whereby complex data is rendered manageable by being over-simplified. Choosing our sample required careful and comprehensive analysis of the data, generating categories and building up the analysis from the bottom. Without such an effort at understanding there is a temptation to under-analyse and 'cherry-pick' data, by selecting dramatic and interesting cases and capturing only superficial understandings (Trinder, 1996). 'Case profiles' for every referral in the study were created, and all 319 were carefully analysed to generate key categories for inclusion in the qualitative sample.[4] In the interest of a balanced evaluation across the region sensitive to local practices, cases were included from all three community care teams, covering the different types of child abuse and child care problems. All the referrals/cases involved were analysed and 32 (10 per cent) were chosen for in-depth analysis. As many as possible of the key actors—children and parents, and professionals who worked with them (involving, on average, three professionals per case)—in the selected cases were interviewed, and the case files were read. A total of 131 interviews were carried out during this phase which began in July 1997, at the same time as the follow-up phase. (For a detailed breakdown of the sample, see Appendix 1.)

A total of twelve mothers, four fathers and thirteen children were interviewed about their experiences of the child care and protection system. Eighteen of the 35 social workers were interviewed about their particular involvement in cases and their experiences of working within the system. Fifty professionals other than social workers were interviewed: thirteen gardaí, eleven public health nurses, four family support workers, one child care worker, three teachers, six school principals, one school inspector, one counsellor, two hospital consultants, three GPs, one nurse, one director of nursing, one area medical officer, one foster mother and one member of a voluntary organisation. All the interviews were tape-recorded and transcribed, generating a huge amount of data. The case studies were written up; as many as possible are presented here in a manner which documents the numerous lay and professional perspectives on the system and how it actually operated in those cases. This kind of case-study approach breaks new ground in accounts of child care and protection work by showing all the work done in its totality and the various perspectives and behaviours that constituted the case. There is a remarkable absence of detailed case study material in the international child welfare literature. Most other research presents the views of professionals, parents and children in isolation from the totality of the case. The nature of the child abuse problem itself and the work done with it from beginning to end do not then emerge with the clarity that is required if we are to further deepen our understanding of child protection and welfare practices and processes. The case studies here are intended to represent practice in a way that provides for an extensive analysis of the meanings of safety and welfare in relation to different types of child abuse and child care problems.[5] In addition, the data provided for a general analysis of different lay and professional perspectives in their own right; the book includes an assessment of how social workers and the other professional disciplines represented view the system, as well as the consumer perspective of parents and children.

As noted, this phase began in July 1997, at least one year after the referrals entered the system between April and June 1996. It was not possible to carry out the interviews at the early stage of the child protection process as priority had to be given to the gathering and analysing of baseline data on all of the cases entering the system and the initial responses to them. As most of the 32 cases included in the qualitative sample were still open at the time of interview, the research does capture how professionals and family members make sense of intervention in the here and now, as well as including reflections on the earlier stages of the child care and protection process. This also means that the analysis of the longer-term meanings of risk, safety, protection and welfare is particularly strong and that parents and children were afforded the opportunity to reflect on substantial periods of intervention work.

The key research questions

Of the 319 cases referred to the MWHB between 1 April and 30 June 1996, 286 were referred directly to the three MWHB community care teams in Clare, Tipperary/East Limerick and Limerick, while 33 referrals were made to MWHB social workers based in a women's refuge in the region. For the purposes of analysis, the refuge cases have been kept separate as they constitute a distinct sub-sample and, unless otherwise stated, what follows refers to the 286 community care sample. We adopt the notion of filters to show the various ways in which referral information is processed, passing through a number of decision-making stages which filter cases out of the system. As Figure 1.1 shows, 41 per cent of referrals were still open one year after they came in, having survived all the decision-making filters. This means that 59 per cent of referrals were filtered out at various stages in the system over the period (April 1996–June 1997).

The key research questions are:

—What cases remain in the system, and why?

—What services are made available to, and what are the implications for, those children and families who do and who do not receive services?

—How 'safe' are the practices that go on and how effective are they at promoting the welfare of children?

The findings

In this book, we examine in what ways and to what extent efforts were made to promote the welfare of children suspected of not receiving adequate care and protection, if indeed efforts were made at all. We have noted already that case files do not contain clear, systematic, information on the concerns prompting referrals. In Chapter 2 we document how information relating not just to child abuse but to a broad range of problems concerning children suspected of not receiving adequate care and protection flows into social workers in the health boards. We examine the processes through which referrals were defined as child 'abuse' in 53 per cent of cases, or child 'welfare' in 47 per cent, that is how social workers categorised the referrals in terms of the main presenting problem. Most referrals included a range of child care concerns: 48 per cent (138 cases) both protection and welfare concerns, 23 per cent (67 cases) protection concerns only without reference to welfare, while 28 per cent were 'pure' welfare referrals (81 cases) with no child protection concerns. Thus, a mixture of 'welfare' and 'protection' concerns can be taken as the norm in health board child care cases; we examine the implications of this in detail.

A key issue in the light of the new duties placed on health boards to identify children who are not receiving adequate care and protection is who is reporting these children. As Chapter 2 shows, 64 per cent of cases came to light through professional sources, while 36 per cent were referred by the lay public. Mothers were the single biggest referral category, which reflects well on the perceived trustworthiness of the health board's practices. The chapter also provides the first systematic data in Ireland with which to (re) examine the merits of mandatory reporting of child abuse and the effectiveness of professionals in identifying child care and protection problems.

Figure 1.1 shows that 92 per cent of referrals were directly investigated, and in Chapter 3 we argue that this is a very high investigation rate as screening cases out at the referral stage is clearly the exception. Its significance

Figure 1.1 Funnel and filter diagram of referral outcomes, 1996–7

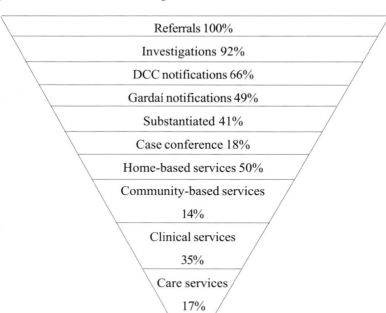

Referrals 100%

Investigations 92%

DCC notifications 66%

Gardaí notifications 49%

Substantiated 41%

Case conference 18%

Home-based services 50%

Community-based services

14%

Clinical services

35%

Care services

17%

Note: 41per cent (n=116) of cases were still open after one year.

is greater still when viewed in the context of research in other jurisdictions, such as England and Wales, where as many as 26 per cent of referrals are screened out without an investigation (Gibbons, et al, 1995). A proportion of these referrals become officially defined as child abuse through the Child Protection Notification (CPN) system. Sixty-six per cent of referrals in the community care sample were notified to the DCC under the Child Abuse Guidelines (1987), and Chapter 4 analyses the strengths and weaknesses of this management structure for safe practice. It also identifies the ambiguity surrounding the 34 per cent of non-notified cases which were not in fact screened out of the system. High proportions of them are worked with, albeit outside the official child protection procedure, and we raise important questions about the status of these cases. The notion of 'a child protection concern' has come to dominate what is seen as the legitimate work of the health board and we show that this notion is operationalised in an elastic way. For instance, the health board is doing an enormous amount of work with domestic violence, much of which is not notified, and also with more general child welfare problems which do not easily fit into conventional 'abuse' categories notifiable under the Child Abuse Guidelines.

Chapter 5 examines the relationship between the law and safe practice, and the 49 per cent of referrals notified to the gardaí under the 1995 Child Abuse Guidelines. A number of advantages and disadvantages of this system are identified. Neglect cases are dealt with inconsistently, with practitioners clearly confused about what constitutes 'wilful' neglect for the purposes of garda notification. Twenty-six per cent of these notified cases were actually investigated by the gardaí, but only a small fraction, six cases to be precise, ended in criminal proceedings. These cases were mainly concerned with child sexual abuse and we identify the way responses to them were dominated by the rigours of the criminal law and a forensic, legalistic approach. Opportunities for meaningful therapeutic work with children were sacrificed in the process. Interventions in terms of the civil law are the subject of less criticism. In total, 17 per cent of referrals received a care-based service during the study period (see Figure 1.1), the vast majority of which were voluntary receptions into care, some carrying the threat of statutory intervention should the family not co-operate. Parenting difficulties, control and behaviour problems in children, neglect and addiction problems dominated these cases, accounting together for 67 per cent of the referrals ending in children entering care.

Of the 262 investigated cases, abuse was substantiated, that is to say the referral was found to have some substance to it, in 61 per cent, of which 83 per cent were concerned with child protection. The remaining 17 per cent involved child welfare only. Most referrals were concerned with a number of problems (see Chapter 3 in particular). A crucial finding is the relatively low number of cases with actual physical or sexual injuries to children and the preponderance of neglect and multi-problem families. This does not mean that these children are not viewed as at high risk. Some 70 per cent of substantiated child protection cases were previously known to the social work department, most involving problems of neglect, poor parenting and resources, domestic violence, and the emotional and developmental problems such adversities bring for children. These problems were severe for children precisely because they took multiple forms and were so longstanding.

Case conferences occurred at around the time of the referral in 18 per cent of referrals. The number of conferences taking place has increased in both relative and absolute terms, reflecting the greater inter-agency co-ordination under the Child Care Act and post-'Kilkenny'. Chapter 6 examines the factors which influence whether or not case conferences take place and the implications of these processes, for instance for the allocation of scarce resources and long-term service provision. A huge amount of formal (and informal) inter-agency work goes into cases. In assessing safe practice, it is the direction of that work that is at issue rather than the sincerity with which it is carried out. The case studies documented in this book show the importance not only of a co-ordinated strategy for intervention, which regularly reaches impressive levels, but also of a clearly articulated and shared view of the correct way to work with abusers and their victims, one based on a deep understanding of the requirements of effective child protection. Problems arise when agencies and individual professionals have different perspectives on what is needed in the case. Individuals may have different values and theoretical perspectives and practices not fully understood by others in the professional network.

Long-term services were initiated for 64 per cent of *all* the referrals in the community care sample. As Figure 1.1 shows, these can be broken down into four main types of services: home-based (50 per cent), community-based (14 per cent), clinical (35 per cent) and care-based (17 per cent). The remaining 36 per cent of referrals were not engaged with by either a social worker or a specialist child care service on a long-term basis. Chapter 7 examines the legitimacy of these decisions, their implications for promoting child safety and welfare and the gap between identified need and the provision of services. For example, in some instances, because the referral was not substantiated, the absence of post-investigative services was appropriate, while in other, substantiated, cases, it was not appropriate and the reasons for the 'service gap' are explored. Significant services are being offered and we analyse the variety of ways in which they are provided by different disciplines, either alone or in combination with others. This makes it possible to present a profile of how the child protection and family support aspects of the Child Care Act are working in practice. The analysis is developed further in Chapter 8 which examines specifically the response in child welfare cases and the degree to which the service response is striking a balance between child protection and family support. The analysis in Chapter 9 of the interviews with parents and children reveals a range of perceptions about their experiences of the child care and protection system, some complimentary, others very critical.

We emphasise again and again that neglect is the most common form of abuse, and the biggest single deficit in meeting identified need lies in the area of parenting skills. In evaluating the effectiveness of the system to protect children and promote their welfare, we argue that an analysis of re-referrals strikes to the core of the 'safety' question. Chapter 10 analyses the key issue of the re-emergence of known at-risk children for whom protective action had been taken during the twelve-month follow-up period. We identify a relatively high number of multi-referred, high-risk cases which just keep coming back to the attention of the system. These invariably involve neglect and/or child behaviour/control problems, with hostile and uncooperative parents, often lone mothers with an addiction problem, and a violent partner present or in the background, a finding that represents perhaps the single most significant theme in this book. These are the cases that absorb the bulk of resources and energy and promote anxiety within the system. We show how acutely aware social workers and other professionals are of the ambiguities involved in providing safety for children, but there is huge pressure, in the context of public concern arising from child abuse inquiries, to aspire to some abstract or idealised notion of safe practice, or avoidance of 'dangerous' practice. Professionals are having to respond to these pressures in a context of high caseloads involving extremely complex, often intractable problems for children and families, over-stretched resources, poor working conditions, and routine threats to their personal safety from hostile clients. Any definition of system safety which can provide a realistic baseline for policy and practice needs to take all of these conditions into account. Chapters 10 and 11 consider the different types of 'safety problem' revealed and the implications of a meaningful definition of 'safety' and the promotion of child welfare and healing.

While each chapter has general relevance to child care and protection work, within each efforts are made to analyse the specific issues that arise with respect to intervention into particular forms of child abuse and child care problems. In this way, the book gives detailed attention to how the child care and protection system actually 'works' and to the forms of child abuse and other adversities which are the reason why we must develop our capacities to keep children safe.

Conclusion

In essence, then, this book analyses the effectiveness of the child protection and welfare system in Ireland in terms of the functioning of each key decision-making stage/process: identification of children at risk, referral taking and case definition; investigative practices; the management of abuse and risk through the CPN systems and case conferences; and the effectiveness of the law (prosecuting abusers, the use of care and supervision orders, barring orders). It provides detailed analysis of the nature of child abuse and other identified childhood adversities and the degree to which children, their families and other caretakers are enabled to resolve those problems. This book also seeks to identify and illuminate the kinds of parenting and childhood adversities that *don't* become 'cases' in any meaningful sense. Of central importance to this search was the following up of every referral in the sample one year on from the initial referral. This method makes it possible to explore why some cases are defined within an 'abuse' frame and others are not, and to map out the different kinds of services and outcomes for particular case definitions/official identities. The aim is to track the 'case careers' and outcomes of different categories of referrals once they have entered the system and been defined, to produce an analysis of the factors influencing this 'work' and their various implications. Thus we can analyse not only how 'safe' the system is in some limited sense of 'performance' but also the very meaning of 'safety', 'protection' and 'welfare' for children and significant others can be established in the context of illuminating the priorities and constructions of reality driving the system.

Of crucial importance to such analysis is a prospective methodology which gathers data on the construction of referrals/cases from the moment information about them enters the system. The primary task and concern of deconstructing child protection and welfare practice in this manner is not to decide whether social workers and other professionals made the right or wrong judgement but to try to make transparent the criteria they used for carrying out the central tasks of child protection work (cf. Parton, Thorpe and Wattam, 1997, p. 126). This applies to practices at every stage of the child care/protection process, from decisions about whether or not to investigate, about what it is one is deciding about in the first place—the very nature of the referral/case in question—to substantiation, non-substantiation, risk assessment and on-going case management and decision-making. In the light of this 'sense-making' of practice, the 'safety' or otherwise of the practice and the child protection system can be analysed, debated and established in the full light of the complexities involved in constructing 'cases' and practice to begin with. Following simple 'performance'-led approaches to evaluation tends to provide simplistic solutions to complex phenomena. It is likely to result in further bewilderment and disillusion for professionals as the complexity of the system in practice belies the simplicity of the performance-led research recommendations. The sociological approach sketched out here is more challenging for agencies, and indeed for researchers. Ultimately, however, it allows us to make visible the complex way in which realities are constructed and leads to more realistic, meaningful findings and conclusions.

Definitions of 'protection/welfare', 'abuse/need' can be critically examined in their social, political and institutional contexts in terms of their consequences for all the professional and lay actors involved in keeping children safe.

Notes

[1] Indeed, at the time of writing, no national figures were available for the period after 1997.

[2] The questionnaire contained 112 questions; it runs to 51 pages and is too long to append.

[3] This includes a refuge social worker, a hospital social worker and a child sexual abuse assessment social worker, as well as the 32 area social workers.

[4] On this method of 'theoretical sampling', see also Arber (1993), and on evaluation processes see McKeown (1999) and Winston (1999).

[5] While the case study materials used in this book record actual events some details have been changed to protect the anonymity of the families/individuals involved.

2 Identifying Children 'At Risk' and Defining Child Abuse

The first stage in the process of child care and protection is the identification of children 'at risk' by referring them to the health board community care social work teams. Professional obligations and the parameters for identification and referral are set out in the Child Abuse Guidelines (1987, 1995, 1999)[1] and Section 3 of the Child Care Act (1991). In this chapter we examine the identification of children at risk and the referral processes as they occurred in the MWHB between 1 April and 30 June 1996. We consider the steps that are, or should be, taken by health boards under the Child Care Act to *identify* children who are 'not receiving adequate care and protection', especially those who are 'at risk of being neglected or ill-treated'.

The nature of child abuse and child care problems worked with

Between 1 April and 30 June 1996, 319 referrals of children at risk were made to the three MWHB community care social work teams, of which 33 were made to refuge social workers (see Table 2.1).

Table 2.1 Referrals to MWHB community care teams, 1 April–30 June 1996

Community care team	No. of referrals
Clare	86
Tipperary (NR)/East Limerick	104
Limerick	96
Refuge	33
Total	*319*

The pattern of referrals across the region corresponds broadly with the size of the social work teams and the nature of the locales covered. Hereafter, reference to 'the community care' teams or 'the sample' refers to the 286 sample, while cases reported through the refuge social workers will be referred to as 'the refuge cases'. Referrals go through a number of stages in the process of case construction, not necessarily in the sequence listed:

Stage 1 network check
Stage 2 consultation with line manager

[26]

Stage 3 social work team meeting

Stage 4 child protection notification (CPN) meeting

Stage 5 case conference.

The referral may be investigated, that is looked into by one or more professionals, before any of these phases take place. Most referrals in the study went through Stages 1–3. Whether a case went through Stages 4 and 5 depended on assessments of the problem and the degree of risk. Sixty-six per cent were processed through the CPN system, and 18 per cent were case conferenced (see Figure 1.1). A 'network check' is the social work practice of gathering relevant information about the child and family from other professionals at the referral stage. Some network checks have to wait until after the investigation if the level of concern is so high that gathering information has to wait. A referral may be discussed at the CPN meeting after it has been investigated and the kind of action recommended by the CPN process may, in some cases, already have been taken. Conversely, some referrals may not be investigated until after the CPN meeting has made a recommendation. It was beyond the scope of this research to gather qualitative data on each referral as it went through the various stages. We did, however, map out this 'construction' process through the representative sample of the case studies. In this chapter we aim to establish the bigger picture, including the patterns of problems being referred to the health board and the nature of the response to them.

Information on a broad range of child care 'problems' concerning children suspected of being at risk flows into the health board. For the study, social workers who dealt with individual referrals were requested to determine what, in their professional opinion, constituted the most important presenting problem, that is the primary definition of referrals at the point when network checks (Stage 1) and CPN meetings (Stage 2) had occurred. This allowed for the initial response to the referral, the networking stage and CPNs to be taken fully into account in the construction of 'cases'. The methodology employed meant that in our research social workers were not presented with definitions of abuse as a means of categorising referrals. They were asked for their *own* definition of the problems, in tandem with how the professional system constructed cases. Not all referrals were directly investigated and became cases and it is the post referral actions—investigation, assessment, intervention and outcomes—which ultimately constitute a 'case'.

Neglect was the biggest 'abuse' category, accounting for 21 per cent of referrals, with 13 per cent defined as sexual abuse, 8 per cent physical abuse, 4 per cent emotional abuse and 7 per cent domestic violence. Child behaviour/

control problems accounted for 21 per cent;[2] 16 per cent were parental difficulties[3]; and 3 per cent were parental addiction[4] A miscellaneous category accounted for another 3 per cent and included underage pregnancy, no presenting problem/child in care and adoption queries (see Table 2.2).

Table 2.2 Main problem in the 286 referrals to community care teams

Main problem	%	No. of referrals
Physical abuse	8	23
Neglect	21	60
Emotional abuse	4	11
Sexual abuse	13	36
Domestic violence	7	19
Behaviour/control	21	61
Financial/housing	4	11
Parental difficulties	16	45
Parental addiction	3	10
Miscellaneous	3	10
Total	*100*	*286*

Adopting the categories used by the Department of Health and health boards for CPNs (DoH, 1987; 1995; 1999), referrals categorised by social workers primarily as neglect, sexual abuse, physical abuse, emotional abuse or domestic violence (which can be notified under emotional abuse) fit the generic classification of 'child protection/abuse' and account for 53 per cent of all referrals. The remaining 47 per cent can be defined as primarily concerned with problems of child 'welfare'. To some extent, the protection/ welfare categories over-simplify a more complex reality insofar as many cases involving, for example, child behaviour/control problems were situations of real danger and risk to the children, yet they could not be placed in 'abuse' categories as the parenting in the case did not fit such a category. Most referrals had a range of child care concerns and the above figures show how they were categorised by social workers in terms of the *main* presenting problem. Thus, although welfare problems were viewed as the main presenting problem in 47 per cent of referrals, 28 per cent were 'pure' welfare referrals (81 cases) with no child protection concerns. Abuse was raised as a concern in 72 per cent of all referrals, 23 per cent of referrals (67 cases) raised protection concerns only, without reference to welfare problems, while 48 per cent (138 cases) of the sample raised a combination of protection and welfare concerns.

The true complexity of the process of definition is apparent in the multifaceted nature of most referrals. It is the exception rather than the rule for just one problem/issue to be identified, occurring in only 25 per cent of referrals. Thus in 75 per cent of referrals social workers were faced with a choice when deciding on a single most important category. This applies both to choices between 'abuse' and 'welfare' type problems, where both were named in the same referral, and to choices within those categories where more than one abuse concern was referred, with no welfare concerns, or more than one welfare problem was identified, with no protection concerns. In 24 per cent of referrals two problems were identified as causing concern, in 18 per cent three were cited. Eleven per cent (31 referrals) had four problems, 8 per cent had five, 3 per cent six, 3 per cent seven, while one referral had as many as eleven suspected problems (see Table 2.3). The choice of definition was imposed to some extent by the research project, which aimed to make analytical distinctions. The notion of main presenting problem is not meant to imply that other problems were necessarily subordinate, although in some cases they were.

We shall return to this theme as we examine the relationship between the ways in which cases are officially and unofficially constructed and the kinds of interventions and outcomes which follow. Examination of such practices allows a critical analysis of the way in which official statistics are gathered:

Table 2.3 Number of child care problems cited in community care referrals

No. of problems cited	%	No. of referrals
1	26	74
2	24	68
3	18	51
4	11	31
5	8	24
6	3	8
7	3	9
8	1	3
9	1	3
10	–	–
11	–	1
No presenting problem*	5	14
Total	*100*	*286*

*No presenting problem—child in care, access/custody disputes, adoption

Table 2.4 Type of child care problem in single problem referrals to
         community care

Child care problem	%	No. of referrals
Sexual abuse	28	21
Neglect	22	16
Emotional abuse	1	1
Domestic violence	7	5
Parents under stress	12	9
Behaviour	8	6
Physical abuse	8	6
Parent/child relationship problems	5	4
Parent/mental health problems	3	2
Child out of control	3	2
Juvenile crime	1	1
Alcohol abuse/mother	1	1
Total	*100**	*74*

*Total does not add to 100 per cent due to rounding.

health boards submit annual child abuse statistics to the Department of Health
in terms of single categories in each case—as physical, sexual, or emotional
abuse, or as neglect. As we can already see, such official classifications over-
simplify a more complex reality of case definition and response.

The contingencies of case definition are further apparent in significant
regional variations in the proportions of single problem referrals. Fourteen
per cent (n=11) of all single problem referrals were from Clare, 22 per cent
(n=16) from Tipperary, while 64 per cent (n=47) were from Limerick. This
is more likely to reflect differences in categorisation practices between teams
than a difference in the nature of the presenting problems. The construction
of cases and the reaching of a definition must therefore be understood in the
context of the wide range of child care problems evident in the referral/
information-gathering stage. Child sexual abuse was the most cited single
problem, accounting for 28 per cent of such referrals (see Table 2.4). Twenty-
two per cent were concerned with neglect. In 52 referrals sexual abuse was
cited, in 36 of which it was defined as the main presenting problem, and in
21 of which it alone was cited. This means that in 40 per cent (n=21) of
referrals where sexual abuse was cited it was the sole concern and that 60 per
cent of sexual abuse referrals were also concerned with other problems. Neglect
was cited in 97 referrals, in 16 per cent of which it was the sole problem,
while 84 per cent also raised other concerns. Domestic violence was cited in

55 referrals, of which five (9 per cent) were concerned with it alone. Thus a massive 91 per cent of referrals involving domestic violence also cited a range of other presenting concerns. Physical abuse was cited in 37 referrals of which six (16 per cent) were concerned with it alone, while emotional abuse was cited in 56 referrals, in one (2 per cent) of which it was presented alone.

Considered in more detail, in 16 referrals sexual abuse was cited as a child care concern but was not considered to be the most important presenting problem. In eight of these the child's behavioural/control problems were deemed to be more important, in four it was emotional abuse, in two neglect, in one parental addiction, and in one parental difficulties. Case 12 was concerned with the sexualised behaviour of an eleven-year-old boy towards other children and, although sexual abuse was cited as a problem, the behaviour of the child was defined as the main problem. The case was referred by a child psychologist at a CPN meeting following contact from a school principal after a sexual incident in the school playground. The social worker completed a network check with the psychologist, school principal, PHN and community welfare officer and this heightened concerns about the child's behaviour. Case 29 involved a sixteen year-old girl and alleged underage sex; the referral was primarily defined in terms of a child behavioural problem, having been referred by gardaí as the girl had run away from home. The child was previously known to child psychiatry services due to incidents of self harm. The social worker networked with child psychiatry, the GP and the gardaí, and in light of the child's history with child psychiatry, the referral was defined as child behaviour. The referral for Case 41 stated that 'child emotionally abused by father, is being kept in and father refuses to let her attend [youth service]'. Suspected sexual abuse was cited as a concern, while emotional abuse was regarded as the main problem. Case 49 again involved a sixteen-year-old girl and alleged underage sex. The case was referred by a mother who was concerned that her daughter was living with a thirty-five-year-old man. Suspected sexual abuse and parent-child relationship problems were noted. Following a network check with a community welfare officer the social worker discovered that the girl and her boyfriend had applied for rent allowance and given their ages as seventeen and twenty-four. The referral was seen as possibly an attempt by the mother to 'break up this relationship'. Case 60 involved alleged sexualised behaviour by a twelve-year-old boy towards his ten-year-old stepbrother and emotional abuse was cited as the most important presenting problem. The alleged behaviour took place in another jurisdiction. At the time of the referral the child was resident with a relative in the MWHB region after his father had removed him from voluntary foster care outside

Ireland. Social services referred the case in light of their concerns. In the 36 referrals where sexual abuse was the main presenting problem, other child care problems suspected included parental difficulties in 26 per cent (n=9), behaviour/control problems in 22 per cent and domestic violence in 11 per cent.

Physical abuse was identified as a problem in 13 per cent (n=37) of referrals, in 62 per cent (n=23) of which it was defined as the most important presenting problem. Hence, in fourteen referrals physical abuse was considered to be an ancillary problem. In five of these neglect was deemed to be more important, in four it was emotional abuse, in two domestic violence, in two behaviour/control, in one parents' addiction/difficulties. In Case 266, referred by a teacher, physical abuse, domestic violence and financial problems were known or suspected problems. The social worker contacted the women's refuge as part of the network check and was informed of an incident of physical violence. The main presenting problem was considered to be domestic violence. In Case 320, a sixteen-year-old male disclosed to a social worker and family support worker that he was subjected to sexual, physical and emotional abuse in a residential setting outside the MWHB. The child was resident in the region at the time of the referral. The social worker noted that emotional abuse was the main presenting problem as '[child] finds it extremely difficult to trust people and form relationships, blames himself to a certain degree and very angry at gross misuse of power'. Parental difficulties also featured quite strongly, cited in 51 per cent (n=12) of physical abuse referrals. Emotional abuse was also evident in 39 per cent of referrals defined as physical abuse. Domestic violence, behaviour/control problems and financial/housing issues featured equally, at six referrals.

In 34 per cent (n=97) of referrals neglect was identified as a problem, in 62 per cent (n=60) of which it was considered to be the most important problem. Of the 37 remaining referrals, in eight parental addiction was considered to be the most important problem, in three physical abuse, in eleven parental difficulties, in two domestic violence and in three sexual abuse. In a further three financial/housing difficulties were the most important problem, in two it was emotional abuse and in five the child's behavioural/ control problems. In Case 155 the gardaí made the referral after an anonymous caller alleged that she found a five-year-old boy wandering the streets looking for his mother and that the mother was 'mistreating' her children by continually leaving them unattended. A network check with a PHN established that the mother was separated, attending a course and leaving her eight- and five-year-old children with 'young girls babysitting'. The referral was defined in child welfare terms as 'loss of parent through family breakdown'. In Case 306 concern was expressed by a home help that a five-year-old boy and ten-year-old girl were 'being neglected and hit at home'. Suspected problems included physical abuse, neglect, emotional abuse, child out of parental control, behaviour problem, loss of parent through family breakdown and parent's mental health problems, with physical abuse considered to be the main presenting problem. In the 60 cases where neglect was cited as the main presenting problem, parental addiction featured in over half, in 35. Parental difficulties were also cited in 50 per cent of referrals primarily concerned with neglect, with financial/housing problems being present in 33 per cent of neglect referrals.

Twenty per cent (n=56) of referrals cited emotional abuse as a problem. The main problems were: emotional abuse in eleven (or 20 per cent); domestic violence in eight; physical abuse in nine; neglect in nine; behaviour/control in eight; parental difficulties in eight; sexual abuse in two; and financial/housing in one. In the eleven referrals where emotional abuse was cited as the main problem physical abuse was also suspected. Physical abuse was also suspected in four cases, sexual abuse in four and domestic violence in another four. Parental difficulties were evident in ten of the eleven emotional abuse referrals. In 14 per cent (n=8) domestic violence was the primary problem. In 19 per cent (n=55) of community care referrals domestic violence was a child care problem, in nineteen of which it was categorised as the main problem. The main presenting problems were: domestic violence nineteen; neglect eight; physical abuse six; parental difficulties six; sexual abuse four; emotional abuse four; financial/housing problems two; parental addiction three; behaviour/control two; miscellaneous one. In 7 per cent of cases dealt with by front-line community care social workers domestic violence was considered the most important problem. Parental difficulties were suspected in 85 per cent. Parental addiction also featured strongly, being present in over half, while emotional abuse was suspected in eight, or 42 per cent.

Although these combinations of concerns in referrals are the norm, hereafter we shall refer to referrals/cases as defined by the main presenting problem. At the risk of oversimplifying, it is necessary to have an organising variable for further analysis. Thus, when reference is made, for instance, to 'a physical abuse referral', it must be remembered that this was usually not the only concern present and investigated. While health boards may have (re)constituted their community care child care services as child protection, the lay public and many professionals still insist on reporting child care problems that are wider than child abuse as defined within the guidelines. A crucial issue is what the notion of 'child protection' actually means in practice and the evidence here suggests that its meaning is in fact quite broad, in that it includes a range of child-focused and carer behaviour problems. Social workers are making active efforts to accept and categorise referrals that do not simply fit into a limited 'protection' frame and to meet a broader definition of need and child welfare. The fact that over a quarter (28 per cent) of the referrals processed by social workers in this study were concerned solely with child welfare rather than protection issues (in terms of the official 'abuse' categories) exemplifies this and raises important questions about the status of non-child abuse referrals. They are not processed through the CPN system and do not have an organisational identity since the child care system is now primarily framed as a child protection service. The short and long-term consequences of these classification practices are considered throughout the book, with particular attention given in Chapter 8 to outcomes in 'pure' child welfare cases. What can be concluded at this point is that information management systems need to be capable of recording all the cases referred in both 'welfare' and 'protection' categories. Policies on the response to non-child abuse cases need to be esablished. Responses should be driven by the level of childhood adversity and need rather than the category of case within which the referral falls.

Referral sources and reporting processes

We turn now to consider the processes through which referrals are made and are constructed as 'cases'. In recent years there has been renewed interest in how child abuse is discovered, disclosed and reported to the authorities. This was prompted in large part by the recommendation of the Kilkenny *Report* that mandatory reporting of child abuse be introduced (McGuinness, 1993). The Kelly Fitzgerald Report (Keenan, 1997) made a similar recommendation and the system failures in clerical abuse cases have added further to public and professional interest in identification and referral practices (Moore, 1995). Despite this, little or no primary data has been available on who actually reports child abuse in Ireland.

In the past, most reporting of child abuse cases in Ireland was by the general public which, prior to the 1970s, was responsible for reporting some 80 per cent of ISPCC cases (see, for instance, ISPCC *Annual Report*, 1956). Since the 1970s, when health boards took over primary responsibility for child welfare and protection, although lay people have continued to be a significant source of referrals, the trend has been towards a greater involvement of professionals in instigating concern in child abuse cases. This reflects the

Table 2.5 Source of referrals received by MWHB community care teams, 1 April–30 June 1996

Source	%	No. of referrals
Anonymous	5	13
PHN	10	28
GP	2	7
Hospitals	6	16
Other medical professionals	3	10
Schools	12	34
Social workers	9	26
Other professionals	12	34
Gardaí	8	24
Parents	20	56
Child him/herself	1	4
General public	10	29
Voluntary organisations	2	5
Total	*100*	*286*

growing role that the professions in general, and medicine in particular, have played in the recognition and identification of child abuse since the 1970s (Ferguson, 1996a). Unfortunately, the Department of Health ceased gathering information on sources of referrals in child abuse cases in 1987. This book provides the first detailed data on who reports child care/protection cases in Ireland with new insights into the meanings and definitions of 'child abuse' and the processes through which child care problems are constructed and agency responses organised.

Lay people as referral sources

Of the 286 referrals made to the three community care teams, 20 per cent (n=56) were reported by parents, of which 73 per cent (n=41) were by mothers (see Table 2.5). Twenty per cent of 'parental' referrals were reported by fathers, while both the mother and father together referred 7 per cent[5]. Mothers were the biggest single source of referrals in the entire sample. Other general public sources[6] accounted for 10 per cent (n=29) of the referrals. The child her/himself made the report in just four cases, 1 per cent of referrals, although the child brought the concern reported by someone else to light by telling/

disclosing to the referral agent in another 11 per cent (see below). Meanwhile, 5 per cent of referrals were reported anonymously.

The expert system as referral sources

Agents categorised under the heading of 'medical sources' reported 21 per cent of referrals, totalling 61 reports.[7] PHNs were the largest single category of professional source, referring 46 per cent (n=28), 10 per cent of all community care referrals. GPs referred 11 per cent, a hospital referred 6 per cent. Of these, accident and emergency departments (A&E) made three referrals, paediatric departments seven, an ante-natal department referred one and maternity hospitals five. The gardaí were almost as active as PHNs, making 24 reports. Schools referred 12 per cent of the sample, which included reports direct from teachers as well as school principals. 'Other professionals' accounted for 12 per cent of all referrals.[8] Social workers from a range of agencies reported 9 per cent (n=26), while voluntary organisations—the St Vincent de Paul, Childline/ISPCC, and CARI (Children At Risk in Ireland)—referred under 2 per cent (n=5).

The identification and referral process

Identification and referral of children at risk can be seen as a process depending on a series of links between different persons and organisations which bring cases to public—i.e. professional—attention. The 'referral chain' can comprise both individuals acting as private citizens, here called lay persons, and/or professionals operating on behalf of agencies (Waterhouse and Carnie, 1991, p.373) here called the expert system. The statistics presented in Table 2.5 represent the completion of the referral chain in the sense of recording the agent who reported the case to the community care social work teams. The adequacy of this process is influenced by at least three factors: levels of awareness of child abuse/child care problems; willingness to recognise abuse and act on it; the existence of guidelines and the quality of communication within the child welfare and protection system. While it is extremely difficult to establish if cases go unreported, it is possible to consider how the various links in the referral chain operate and the effectiveness of the way information about children at risk flows into and through the system.

In 59 per cent (n=169) of referrals, the agent directly experienced the concern, saw the child/incident in question and took the initiative of reporting it to the social work team. Therefore, no referral chain was involved in such cases. Almost 11 per cent (n=30) of reports involved referrals where the child disclosed the problem to the agent who reported it. Children were more likely to be a direct part of the referral chain in the sense of disclosing to the agent in physical abuse and sexual abuse referrals. In 30 per cent (n=7) of all physical abuse referrals and in 25 per cent (n=9) of sexual abuse referrals the child disclosed to the referrer. In Case 83, for instance, a five-year-old girl disclosed to her mother that a neighbour had allegedly sexually abused her. The mother referred the case to the social work department and the gardaí, who also referred the case.

Referrals in cases defined primarily as neglect and emotional abuse were less likely to come to light through children saying things to the agent, the children disclosing in 8 per cent and 9 per cent of such referrals respectively. Children did not disclose to the agent in any of the referrals defined as domestic violence. This is probably because these problems require professionals and lay people to be more proactive on children's behalf and involve identification through clinical evidence and visible signs of distress/risk, or the testimony of abusing parents and/or carers. In 2 per cent (n=6) of referrals the information passed to the social work team was third-hand as the child disclosed information to someone else who then told the referral agent.

The mother of the children told the agent in 13 per cent (n=37) of referrals and the person told was usually a professional—this was the pattern in 35 of these 37 referrals. In 30 per cent (n=11) of these cases, child welfare/parental difficulties were defined as the main problem. In 22 per cent (n=8) of referrals where the mother informed the agent, domestic violence was defined as the main presenting problem. The significance of mothers in the identification process proves even greater, then, when their involvement in the referral chain is considered. Fathers informed the referrer in 4 per cent of referrals. In 16 per cent a range of other sources, including members of the extended family, neighbours and other professionals, informed the agent. Taken together, mothers raised initial concern in 27 per cent of *all* referrals to community care teams (totalling 78: 41 as the initial referral source and 37 to other referrers). In addition, 70 per cent (n=23) of the 33 reports made to the refuge social worker (considered separately) were also from mothers.

The expert system remains highly significant in identifying cases. Sixty-four per cent of reports (n=184) were made by experts on completion of the referral chain (see Table 2.5). Some 43 per cent of these 184 referrals were brought to the attention of the professional by a lay source. For example, in 18 per cent of professional referrals the problem came to attention as a result of a disclosure from a mother, in 12 per cent the child first disclosed. Hence, 57 per cent of the sub-sample of professional referrals were directly referred to the social work teams. This means that just 36 per cent (n=104) of all the referrals to community care were authentically brought to light by professionals identifying concern for children' without the intervention of mothers or others. Of these 90 directly observed the child in question and in the remaining 14 another professional alerted the referring professional. These figures provide an important baseline for measuring trends in identification and reporting of child care and abuse under the Child Care Act and for considering a crucial aspect of the relationship between State services and the lay public.

Sources in reports of different forms of abuse/child care problems

As we have seen, child care problems come to light in a variety of ways. Some 30 per cent of physical abuse referrals were referred by lay sources (parents, anonymous, general public) while professional sources reported almost 70 per cent. Schools reported 22 per cent of physical abuse referrals (see Appendix 2). The number of non-accidental injury referrals made by medical sources, especially hospitals, is disturbingly low in the light of the large numbers of children who pass through these services, with only two physical abuse referrals coming through the hospital route. Some 32 per cent of neglect referrals were referred by lay persons, with extended family members making seven and neighbours three. Four parental referrals were all made by fathers. It is interesting that mothers were not involved in the making of any neglect referrals. Of the professional sources, schools are again relatively well represented reporting 15 per cent (nine cases), while PHNs referred eight, and hospital paediatric departments three (see Appendix 2).

The numbers of emotional abuse referrals are much smaller, 27 per cent of which were referred by lay sources. As with physical abuse, neglect and emotional abuse, approximately one-third of sexual abuse referrals were made by non-professional sources (see Appendix 2). Three referrals were made by the mother involved and one was made by both parents together. Two were referred by GPs, two by PHNs, two by hospital paediatric departments, one by a learning disability service and one by a maternity hospital. 'Other professionals', who referred four sexual abuse cases, were staff in a children's home, a youth worker, a project leader, and a priest. In 64 per cent of domestic violence referrals the referral agent was a professional (see Appendix 2). By contrast, 73 per cent of the refuge referrals on domestic violence were reported by lay sources, 70 per cent of which were mothers. The gardaí (26 per cent) are the most significant professional referrers of domestic violence cases. Taking the 319 case sample in total, lay people are much more highly represented at 62 per cent of referrals where domestic violence was the main presenting problem than in child abuse cases. Twenty-six (55 per cent) of these referrals were made by parents, of whom 24 were mothers. In the remaining two, the fathers were non-resident and reporting the suspected abuse of their ex-partners by new cohabitees/boyfriends. The corollary of this pattern is that domestic violence is under-reported by the expert system, especially medical sources. Only one domestic violence referral was made by a hospital A&E department and one by a hospital paediatric department. Hospitals appear to be failing to be proactive in identifying and reporting domestic violence, the responsibility for which is essentially left to the abused women themselves (see also Stark and Flitcraft, 1996).

Parents were by far the most significant referral agent where child-centred difficulties behaviour/control was the main presenting problem, reporting 30 per cent (n=18) of such referrals (see Appendix 2). Mothers referred fifteen of these, a father one, while both parents made the referral in two cases. Children themselves reported 3 per cent. Schools are the most significant single professional referrers in this category, reporting 18 per cent, which reflects the way they identify concerns about children's behaviour and control issues at school. Other professionals are also highly represented here at 20 per cent and they include staff in children's homes, youth workers and child psychologists. Parents were also by far the largest single source of parental difficulties referrals, accounting for 36 per cent (n=16) of reports, thirteen of which were made by mothers and three by fathers. PHNs were the next highest source, making seven reports. Parents (a mother) (self-) referred just one of the ten referrals where addiction was defined as the main presenting problem. A GP, community psychiatric nurse and speech therapist, made three referrals, extended family members two while other professionals, including UK social services, made two.

Reporting of child care/abuse problems constitutes an important and too often ignored aspect of 'partnership' between expert systems and the lay public. Partnership tends to be thought of and measured by the degree of inclusion of parents or carers in case conferences and decision-making. The extent to which lay people, and especially children and parents themselves, are prepared to take risks by making referrals is a crucial marker of the degree of trust that exists in services. The data shows the importance of lay people, and mothers in particular, both in making reports and in alerting professionals to child abuse/care problems. Moreover, cases reported through these sources tend to be defined more within welfare categories, suggesting that the moral character of parents is not called into question to the same extent as when cases are referred by third-party sources, a higher incidence of which are categorised under 'abuse'. Public information about the help-seeking behaviour of mothers needs to be provided. The aim should be to boost trust and public confidence in child care and protection services so that as many vulnerable carers and children as possible are encouraged to seek help with their difficulties.

Network checks and 'case building'

How, then are the phenomena documented here—'abuse', child care problems—defined? In the literature the definition of child abuse/care problems is represented as being under the control of social workers, but this minimises the influence of professional networks at the referral stage. While the health board discharges its obligation under the Child Care Act to respond to referrals and promote the welfare of children through community care social workers, what professionals have to negotiate between themselves and with lay people is the nature of the risk to the child and the construction of the case. Once a report is made, the focus shifts to social workers and case definition. The dominant view of child abuse reporting represents the process as straightforward where a report alleging known or suspected abusive behaviour is made to social workers who either investigate it directly or do not, substantiate it or not. This assumes that the phenomenon reported is recognisable as (possible) abuse; and that 'abuse' has a simple ontological reality distinct from the professional 'work' that constructs 'protection' cases (Wattam, 1997). This does not mean that some forms of behaviour are not obviously child abuse. Quite clearly, some allegations are unambiguously concerned with child protection matters. Significantly, however, no form of alleged 'abuse' or child care problem falls outside the process of definition and construction by social workers and other professionals. As Parton, Thorpe and Wattam (1997) argue:

> Viewing social phenomena as socially constructed does not mean that they are subject to relative definition *per se*. It means that definitions must be *achieved* on each and every occasion of practical application, wherever it is necessary to consider what is, or whether it is, in this case, child abuse (p. 72, original emphasis).

At the core of this 'achievement' process of case definition and construction are consultations with other agencies and what are called locally 'network checks' to gather further information about the child and family. All referrals involve 'case-building', a process of attempted corroboration of the referral information/alleged concern, definition and the gathering of information to build up a picture of the child and family. In 88 per cent (n=251) of the referrals social workers consulted with other professionals to gather further information about the family. Thus in only 35 of the 286 community care referrals (12 per cent) did no such 'network checks' and consultations take place. A total of 59 professional groupings were consulted in these 251 cases. On a case-by-case basis, contacts ranged from one to seven professionals contacted. In total, 595 network contacts were made at the referral stage with the 59 professional groups (see Table 2.6).

Table 2.6 Professions consulted by social workers at referral stage

Profession	%	No. of contacts
Medical	97	243
School/educational	35	88
Other professionals	31	79
Gardaí	28	71
Social work	44	120
Vol. organisations	2	4

Note: The per cent total adds to more than 100 due to multiple responses.

In 97 per cent of referrals where a network check took place, consultation occurred with a member of the medical profession.[9] PHNs were the most actively consulted, at 50 per cent (n=125) of referrals. This ratio is higher still when only cases with children under five are considered. GPs were consulted in 30 per cent of referrals, the gardaí in 28 per cent while 88 (35 per cent) of the 251 referrals involved contact with school/educational professionals.[10] Again, this proportion is higher when only those cases with school-aged children are considered.

Four types of information/assessments are apparent in the information gathered through network checks (see Table 2.7). In 67 referrals (27 per cent), no other concern was expressed by the consulted professional beyond that recorded in the referral information. In 170 referrals (68 per cent) there was evidence of other concern. In just six referrals (2 per cent) were positive statements made about the child/family, lessening the level of concern expressed in the referral. In eight referrals (3 per cent) added concern was expressed by some of the other professionals but not by others. In total, over 70 per cent of those consulted expressed concern for the children named in the referral.

Table 2.7 Nature of information obtained from professional network checks

Information obtained	%	No. of referrals
No added concern	27	67
Other concern	68	170
Positive statement	2	6
Concern from some but not all	3	8
Total	*100*	*251*

The extensive network consultations with other professionals (both within the social work profession and outside it) indicate very good inter-agency communication at the referral stage of a social work response. It reflects the institutionalisation of network checks into the decision-making process, thus fulfilling obligations under Section 3 of the Child Care Act to co-ordinate information on children not receiving adequate care and protection. We consider the *quality* and *impact* of those communications and inter-agency relationships at various points in this book, and at this point in terms of the type of response that followed. What is striking is that social workers do not appear to use the lack of added concern as a reason not to investigate. In just five of the referrals where no added concern was expressed did no direct investigation take place. A similar level, 7 per cent, of referrals (although a higher number at twelve) were not directly investigated although other professionals did express added concern.

As one social worker described the importance of the network check, 'You can have your own little bird's eye view of a case so you need to get the big picture of a family'[11]. The majority of social workers carry out network checks on all new referrals to assess the level of concern. Some do this only with families they are not familiar with, as 'the first port of call'. It helps 'to find out what I'm going to be walking into'. Case 273, for example, was referred by a psychiatric social worker. A network check was not carried out by the community care social worker because 'we had very clear concerns coming from the psychiatrist based in the service so we felt that we had the information, so we didn't necessarily need to go for a network check on that particular occasion'. The content of the referral also influences the decision: 'If we find that our information is scant, we would always try and get something from the other professionals like the GP, or the PHN'. The less serious the referral the less need for network checks. They help 'to assess whether there's enough cause for concern'. They are extremely important with an anonymous referral because if the network check does not heighten concern it may be viewed as malicious.

Whether a network check takes place or not is usually discussed at the social work team meeting, although the decision is often made by the team leader: 'because a referral can come in and the urgency of it may dictate that you have to deal with it before the team meeting, so very often it will be in the best interest of everyone for a network check to be undertaken and that can be an individual decision'. Network checks explicitly assist social workers in case definition and orientation: 'A lot of referrals we'd get would be neglect but we wouldn't necessarily see them as child protection, I suppose it's to be clear for ourselves, the network check helps us to be very clear on whether it's child protection or support.' The nature of the referral also influences which professionals are contacted. As one social worker said: 'I mean in relation to child protection the very first one that I would contact would be the doctor, in relation to does he have any contact with the family . . . If the referral is more to do with behaviour [problems], you'd probably make contact with the school first.' Case 274 highlights how the network check can affect the level of concern and the social work response. The case was referred anonymously and the social worker noted that 'innuendo suggested in a letter referring to single man [child's uncle] as possibly a homosexual and child sex abuser'. The social worker made an 'informal network check' with the gardaí, who 'didn't know anything about this man so they didn't add to our concerns, they knew nothing really, they were concerned about the nature of the referral so the agreed action was at that time if this were to re-occur again we were to get the gardaí involved and they would fingerprint the anonymous letter. They viewed it as potentially malicious'. Because the gardaí had no information on the alleged abuser, the concern in the referral was minimised. The fact that a garda history would have increased concern was evident in another case of alleged sexual abuse referred by a member of a child's extended family. On checking with the gardaí, no sexual convictions were recorded. However, there were 'one or two convictions of a sexual type nature which could be viewed as minor so we've raised the question do we confront this man and let him know that we've heard some stuff about him.' Thus, as the social worker who dealt with both cases reflected:

> 'What's outstanding for me on this new referral which has relevance to this is the gardaí were saying they knew nothing about [the alleged perpetrator in Case 274] so we felt that there was no point in us approaching him at that time because this was an allegation, while we have convictions in terms of this other man but not child sexual abuse in orientation even though they are of a general sexual nature. We're just seeking legal advice on it at the moment . . . so these convictions would add to our concern, but when the gardaí hadn't any stuff on him we were happy to leave it. We were reassured in a sense by the gardaí to

whom we made an indirect enquiry and they weren't aware of him and secondly Mum seemed to be the very genuine type. The referral hasn't come back since.'

The network check directed a non-investigative approach in one case while in the other it added to social work concerns, and legal advice was sought to decide whether or not to make direct contact with the suspected abuser. Whether network checks are completed prior to direct contact with the family or following the initial contact appears to be up to individual social workers. Several feel that it is important to obtain the parents' permission before a network check, particularly in relation to GPs and schools. Out of 'common courtesy', they would not contact other professionals until the family had been seen, so as to 'get the family's side of the thing' before the network check. 'I would say surely people have rights as well and they need to be observed, I can delay any referral for 24 hours to give myself time to contact the people'. This social worker likes to be 'up front' with clients and tell them about the network check, 'but if you run around contacting three or four different people to make a check, where's the confidentiality there?' The timing of a network check is also dictated by the nature of the referral. If it is raising a serious allegation it will be completed before the home visit, but if it is less serious the parents will be interviewed before the check. The consensus view on the timing of network checks was nicely encapsulated by one social worker on a case where worker safety, as well as child safety, was on the agenda:

'In terms of the very serious referrals that come in, we try to do a network check before we actually go near the parents, now that's my perception of how we do network checks, that might be a very different answer from what management would give you, but certainly I would have conducted network checks on fairly serious referrals prior to meeting [the family]. If the safety of a person is called into question we certainly like to try and get a sense of how safe are we as professionals going into a person's home who is allegedly the perpetrator of whatever kind of injury, hurt or violence on another person. We try to get a sense of not only what information do other professionals have about this family but the level of risk that this person may pose to our safety, because if you're talking about a man who's physically beating his sixteen-year-old, I've been frightened by a father who physically threatened me in other referrals. And this is why we can't issue a blank statement as a worker because I have to be checked up on by my own management in terms of what they are saying . . . But in other cases then we'll say to families we have concerns, we're letting you know about them, is it okay if we do a network check with other professionals just to see that things are okay. So there's a two-pronged approach in some instances depending on the referral, but certainly if it's a referral that's very serious and could be going to court and if it's a referral where other professionals could have very serious worries or concerns the network check may not throw up extremely relevant things but it can give us a sense of how safe is it in a situation when we're dealing with people as professionals.'

Social workers' perspectives on identification and referral processes

The general perception of the social workers and most other professionals interviewed for this study is of a system heavily focused on responding to child abuse cases to the relative neglect of other categories. To some extent the research findings bear this out, while in others the picture is much more complex. How the referral agent initially became aware of the child care concern and the referral chain is very important in shaping the response. If the referral is second- or third-hand in that the referral agent did not directly see the child/incident in question, it is viewed as important to interview the person who brought the child care problem to the attention of the referrer: 'the original piece of information can be lost and through the second- or third-party there could be a different emphasis placed on the referral'. Although the referral chain does appear to affect how social workers respond to referrals it was not a factor in making the decision not to investigate. An attempt would often be made to contact the initial referral source.

In Case 305 a school principal made the referral to the social work department following concerns expressed by a project leader at a summer school, to whom the child, aged nine years, disclosed that her uncle had sexually abused her. The project leader informed the school principal who then made the referral. The social worker felt that it was important to meet with the project leader as well as the school principal as 'at least you are talking to a direct person that has heard the information, that's important in terms of evidence and clarity of what was said, so it would be important rather than using a third party with hearsay evidence'. The social worker met with both the school principal and the project leader on the day of the referral. In relation to self-referrals, one social worker commented that 'it can make work easier if they are the ones that are going to approach you. I think too clients would feel they're more in control if you like, if they're the ones who'll ask you for help or whatever. You're not barging in there'. This social worker was involved with Case 6 where a mother approached the social work department requesting respite foster care for her five children—she had recognised her inability to cope. Acknowledgement of the child care problem and request for support makes such referrals 'easier' to respond to—in this case the mother was open to intervention and social work support. In effect, the moral character of the mother is viewed in a much more positive light than when the health board initiates contact through a third party. As another social worker expressed it, self-referrals mean that 'you've something more to work with, the fact that she's actually coming forward and looking for this, it's much more to work with. When you get an anonymous referral, if you've never heard of it, if you don't have the information, you're very much working from a "what is this?" You're stepping into the unknown'.

In Case 33, a mother referred the case requesting respite care for her children while she went into hospital. She was previously involved with the health board because of child care concerns arising from alcohol abuse. The social worker noted that the mother had approached the health board and the case had never been referred by another source. She was of the opinion that had concerns been raised by either a professional or other lay source, the case would have been considered higher profile. The social worker opted to work with the mother and not submit a CPN and 'formalise' it as a child protection case. The moral character of the mother was placed in a more 'favourable light' as she herself had referred the case. It would have been treated more 'seriously', in the sense of leading to a CPN, if it had been referred by someone other than the mother. Thus, it is not simply the intrinsic nature of the concern in referrals, but the way they come to light that is important to case definition and type of response. While social workers emphasised that referrals are taken very seriously no matter who they come from, the dominant view was that the information in a professional referral is normally 'much more clear and concise compared to a lay person's referral'. It is not that a lay referral would be considered to be less 'serious', it just often needs further clarification. Professional referrals are 'easier because you've that much more information, you've a named person, you've much more substance'.

In Case 239 the gardaí made the referral having received a call from a neighbour that five children aged eleven, ten, nine, five and three were left unattended while the parents were in the pub. The gardaí called to the house and found the children alone. The fact that the gardaí had actually witnessed the child care problem had an impact on how the referral was responded to by the social worker, who commented 'it would impinge greatly, it was a fact, it makes it clear, it is extremely clear'. According to the social worker, if the gardaí had not found the children alone, the allegation would have been unfounded and they would not have made the referral to the social work department. The social worker made a home visit accompanied by the gardaí two days after the referral. According to the social worker the parents were 'cautioned re the consequences of their behaviour should there be a reoccurrence'.

Anonymous referrals are viewed as the most difficult and ambiguous of all to deal with. They cannot be verified by going to the person who saw the incident, they 'lessen our capacity to respond faster' and real difficulties arise if the parents deny the allegation or substance of the report. Such reports are not, however, responded to differently, a direct investigation does occur but they are 'just harder'. One social worker had the view that 'we're not strictly meant to deal with anonymous referrals, you're not meant to deal with them if they're crank calls'. But the dilemma is how to decide it's a crank call unless it's looked into? Some social workers do even more extensive network checks rather than going straight to see the family. Social workers were sensitive to the need to clarify the legitimacy of a referral because 'it is quite a shock for people to have social workers knocking on their door . . . most people are quite shocked at the end of an interview'. Where the referrer identifies her/himself it is much easier to approach the family and, better still, if it is a professional who has said it's all right to use their name: 'like it's more difficult when you can't actually say and you're just approaching out of the blue'.

In any event, regardless of the source, it is difficult to respond when only 'suspicions' are raised by the referrer. This is exemplified by Case 310 which was referred by a school. The child told a school friend that her father 'lifts her nightie and plays with her'. The social worker remarked that 'they were only suspicions because we could get nothing, you can't do anything until you are sure'. The father was interviewed by the social worker but denied the allegation and the case was not further investigated as 'it was only a suspicion'.

When is a referral (not) a referral? Case study 279

We shall conclude the chapter with a case study[12] which encapsulates many of the dilemmas surrounding the identification and referral processes discussed and brings into sharp relief the way unsafe child protection practice can occur at the referral stage. It is based on interviews with a social worker, two teachers, an area medical officer, and a garda. It is a compelling example of the ambiguities of the referral process, how the decision not to respond directly to a referral is reached and the reasoning behind the view that referrals are not 'enough to go on' and further clarification from the referral source is necessary. In essence, it raises the fundamental issue in child protection of what constitutes a referral and when is a referral (not) a referral?

The case was initially brought to the attention of the social work team by a teacher who expressed concern for a five-year-old boy. Referral information in the case file included:

> Teacher expressing concerns with child in class, child said that his father tried to smother him. . . . teacher wanted to discuss with principal. Informed teacher that we would hold until the school came back to us.

The teacher also made positive statements regarding the care of the child in relation to school attendance, his appearance and the quality of his school lunches. Both physical abuse and parent/child relationship problems were identified as suspected child care/abuse problems. The referral was made to the social work team four months after the child disclosed to the teacher. At this referral stage, information on the child's family background and siblings was not made available to the social work team. The social worker met with the school teacher three days after she referred the case. It was not considered to be a 'formal referral' in that the teacher was discussing concerns with the social worker without actually formally referring it. The referral was brought to the attention of the team leader seven working days after it came in and the social worker was advised to write to the teacher requesting her to make a formal referral. Following the meeting between the social worker and teacher, a letter was sent requesting the teacher to make a formal referral and provide further information. As this did not happen, it was noted in the case file that 'action could not be taken at this point'.

At this stage, the gardaí were not notified as there was 'not sufficient reason for concern as the case stands' and nor was the DCC. The social worker was unclear whether the family had been previously involved with the health board because a 'record check' had not yet been completed. The referral was not directly investigated by the social work team—the child, parents and/or suspect abuser were not interviewed: 'this teacher had difficulties in making the referral to me . . . she wasn't comfortable making this referral, she didn't want to be the named person. She was fearful of making a referral'. The social worker expressed difficulties in 'tying down' the referral, 'our problem was that there was not a referral being made in a formal way, I suppose people were unsure as to what to do with it at the time. The overriding opinion of people at the time was look, we can't act because a referral had not been made'. He had difficulties regarding risk assessment: 'I don't know what the measure of risk is, how you go about measuring is very difficult where it hasn't been followed up.' Referral procedures were outlined to the teacher by the social worker and 'advice was given as to how she would make the referral'. He felt that the teacher was informally notifying him of the child care concern. However, the child's name and address were given to the social worker, which raises the question of what constitutes a formal referral? Does the referral agent decide that he or she does not wish to make a formal referral but does wish to discuss concerns, or does the social worker/team make the decision that the information does indeed constitute a referral which warrants a direct social work response, regardless of the referrer's wish to remain anonymous?

Clearly, from a practice and management perspective, this referral was considered to be 'informal' and not enough to act on. However, the social worker felt that the referral was treated 'very formally. I brought it to the team meeting, I wasn't happy just to leave this go and say "Look, I heard nothing"'. It was noted in the case file that 'there is no referral on the case at present'. The social worker was awaiting clarification from the school before acting on the referral: 'I was waiting in hope really'. The teacher 'wasn't standing over information, even though she was stating it informally. I presume where I was caught was that we don't have an official referral.' The social worker reflected that perhaps it should have been treated as an anonymous referral and 'it probably should have been followed up'.

The school perspective

The child disclosed to the teacher four months before the referral to the social work team. The teacher claimed that she had called the health centre on five or six occasions 'and there was nobody available . . . it was actually my desperation at the end of the year, because it was June. I wanted to meet somebody while I was teaching the child'. The teacher felt that there was no facility to discuss concerns with a social worker without it being officially recorded and did not want her concerns recorded officially. 'He was taking my confidentiality into account but it meant that, by him taking my confidentiality into account, nothing was being done about it'. She expressed fear that parents would feel threatened by teachers if it became known that they referred cases to social workers and this would 'establish a barrier' between parents and teachers. She revealed acute uncertainty about teachers' responsibilities to be proactive in promoting child welfare and unless her confidentiality was protected feared possible recriminations for the child:

> 'I would have terrible fears that if the situation was not as I had suspected, that it would be impinging on the rights of a family to be a family. I suppose really it's a huge area, the thought: am I safeguarding the rights of the family? And I'm very aware of how I am prying. As a teacher we don't want to ask him questions, ask him the truth and things, that has to do with their lives, that has to do with

their parents, as I suppose you could call it private lives, it's not our role.'

When she approached a social worker she was informed that if she wished to make a complaint 'it would have to be official, if somebody approached them from the health board, or if anyone approached the house even to check it out I think that my name would have to be mentioned, that they would have the right to ask'. She would have made an 'official referral' if her anonymity had been guaranteed. After consultation with a line-manager, the case was closed three weeks after the referral with no social work intervention, 'pending further information from class teacher who made initial referral' (case file).

Further concerns for the child

After a school medical during the follow-up period of the research, concerns were expressed by the school to the AMO that 'child staying up late watching TV and often appearing tired' and about the child's 'family background' and 'marital disharmony' (case file). The child had mentioned to a teacher alcohol and possible drug abuse in the home. The child's mother was very young and, the AMO explained, the father was 'sort of a domineering man and they [teachers] wondered was there marital disharmony between them'. The AMO noted that positive statements regarding the child's appearance and school attendance were made. These concerns were not immediately notified to the social work team by either the AMO or the school. Although they were subsequently referred, the AMO explained this initial hesitation: 'I felt that there probably wasn't enough to go on, these concerns were about his social background and a lot of their concerns about the kids they were talking about were social and a lot of the concerns were terribly vague. . . . What they were telling me wasn't very meaty for referring to social workers, the concerns weren't really enough'. It appears that the school, in notifying the AMO of these concerns, was questioning the child's care, 'there seemed to be a suspicion about the level of care he was getting at home, because the child passed some comments about drinking and they picked up somewhere along the line that there might be drugs being taken in the house. There was nothing to suggest physical abuse had been remarked at that time'.

The AMO felt that the teachers were not actually making a referral to her in that they were not looking for specific action. She felt that teachers 'like having somebody that they feel they can talk to . . . sometimes you get the feeling that they're just kind of ventilating when you go into a school. They haven't got anyone to talk to, someone outside of themselves'. Although the

AMO considered the concerns of the school to be somewhat vague, she felt that they did warrant a report to the social work department. She had intended making a referral when further concerns were brought to her attention, again by the school, and a dual referral was made outlining the earlier and most recent concerns. The AMO emphasised that if new child protection concerns had not been raised by the school a referral relating to the earlier concerns would still have been made.

Re-referral information

Ten months after the initial referral another teacher expressed concern to the AMO regarding the child. This was a different teacher from the one involved in making the first referral in 1996. The AMO informed the social worker that the child had been 'drawn to my attention as being one of the children with whom there were concerns, these concerns were due to his background . . . [child] may be left a lot to his own devices, TV in bedroom, watches programmes late at night, often appears tired. Also teachers wondered about his level of care from comments he has passed about alcohol and drug taking at home'. The child also made a disclosure to a teacher during a Stay Safe programme which focused on bullying about which the AMO subsequently made a formal referral to the social work team. Referral information included the following:

> He said that his daddy beat him with a pencil, initially the teacher made little of it by saying that pencils were small, so [child] said no, that this was a big wooden pencil like you'd buy in the pound shop, so he became very tearful and upset that his daddy takes down his pants and shorts and hits him with this big pencil and keeps him until he calls water. [child] then asked [teacher] if she remembered his face being scratched some time previously and at the time he telling her he had fallen, he said in fact what had happened was that Dad had hit him with his pencil, but had threatened to kill him if he told anyone' (case file).

The child expressed concern to the teacher about his father being informed of the referral. It was also noted in the referral that '[teacher] has never noticed remarkable bruising or marks on [child]'. In referring these concerns to social work, the AMO noted in the referral that 'putting these latest more specific concerns together with the earlier less specific ones of this and last year I feel referral to yourself for follow-up is all the more important and urgent'. These concerns were notified to the director of community care by the AMO. The AMO made a network check with the PHN who had no contact with the child and the child's pre-school records were not available at that time.

In relation to the second referral, the (second) teacher expressed similar concerns to the first regarding confidentiality in making referrals. 'I wouldn't be prepared, I would like it to be followed up or whatever but is there any other way? I would not like getting involved, especially when I know the mother and father, no, no I would not, not at all, I am a professional teacher and I have been trained but we are not trained for that'. The teacher was fully in agreement that a social work investigation should take place, 'I mean I don't mind giving this, I felt so strongly about it that I rang, you know I rang the doctor'. She still had concerns about her identity as the referrer being revealed: 'I would have a problem with that, I think I would, why should they name the source, I feel that they are putting the onus back on us and that is not right, I reported the incident, what else can I do?' The teacher felt that the onus is on the social worker to investigate whilst maintaining confidentiality. On one occasion the teacher mentioned to the child that she would talk to his father and he replied, 'oh, please don't—he'll kill me, he'll kill me'. The teacher felt that the child was 'obviously terrified of his father'.

Response to re-referral

The social worker brought the new referral information to the attention of line management who directed him to speak with school staff in order to clarify the information about the family, to complete a network check with the family's GP and to review with management. As with the first referral, emphasis was placed on clarification from the referral source. A home visit was not recommended at this stage. However, further direction from the CPN meeting in response to the AMO notification included 'talk to relevant professionals and line manager and do a home visit'. At the time of the research interviews, four months after the second referral and three months after directions from the CPN meeting, neither a network check nor a home visit had been completed: 'no work has been undertaken' (social worker).

The delay in responding to the referral was due to the fact that the social worker was unable to 'clarify' referral information with school staff because the school was closed over the summer months. The social worker emphasised 'on the basis that the teacher hasn't been met yet, one of the first tasks was to clarify the information with the teacher, so due to not seeing the teacher, the rest hasn't taken place. I'll have to wait until September, I imagine'. And regarding the delay in investigating the case: 'I suppose a home visit perhaps should have taken place all right . . . because we had sufficient information, the teacher was quoted quite clearly by the AMO. I suppose we're trying to play it safe in that we want to try and get information first hand, then that almost gives us a sense of authority to say, look, we have heard from the person themselves, not hearing it third hand'. The rationale for clarifying the information is 'we're eliminating misinformation in the process, a third party could easily be misinformed, or have misunderstood, or heard something that actually wasn't said. We rarely go on third hand information'. For the social worker now, 'admittedly the referral should have been followed up [four months ago]'.

Again, as with the first referral, difficulties were expressed in relation to risk assessment. 'I have no measure of risk to this child, the child is at risk, there's no doubt about it, the child is at risk.' The second referral was notified to the gardaí under the 1995 guidelines and this was identified as 'possibly' minimising the level of risk as the gardaí were made aware of the child care concern. The child's age was also identified as a determining factor: 'The risk may be less . . . presumably [he's] a bit bigger, hopefully he'll be a bit more able to protect himself.' The social worker expressed fears for the child: 'We haven't heard anything else about this child, so my hope is that nothing else has happened, I just hope that nothing serious has happened to this child. I certainly have a fear for the child right here and right now.' He himself considered the lack of a social work investigation to constitute 'dangerous practice'.

The social worker met with the gardaí on one occasion to discuss the referral after it was formally notified. Garda involvement in the case was limited to this one formal meeting and two informal telephone discussions with the social worker. The outcome of the meeting was that they would meet again to discuss the case further and should a home visit take place, the guard would be available to accompany the social worker if requested. But as the garda commented in interview: 'Unfortunately, in things like this your time is not your own, number one. We'd arranged to meet all right, but it didn't work out, when I went for him he [the social worker] was gone and when he came to me I was gone as well'. The garda perception of the case was that the school had observed something and the 'child was being slapped by somebody'. Although attempts were made by the social worker and guard to liaise, it did not happen but the garda still felt that the inter-agency work 'went well' in this case. The garda did not discuss the case with any other professional and nor did he take unilateral action to investigate, a discretionary power the gardaí have under the 1995 guidelines. The guard considered it the responsibility of the social worker to contact him to discuss the case further.

In terms of post-referral multi-disciplinary work, the initial referrer was contacted and requested to make a formal referral. In the absence of this, the teacher was not contacted again by the social work department. This (first) teacher felt that there should be 'some setup whereabouts the teacher can talk to somebody about the problem a child has and guarantee confidentiality, and in some way, something can be done about it'. She felt that 'the link between the schools and the health board is very weak', and identified a lack of understanding amongst teachers and social work. In relation to the second referral by the AMO, there was no evidence of post-referral liaison. The AMO does not routinely receive feedback from the social work team unless it is specifically requested or the case reaches a case conference which the AMO will attend and hence receive an update. In this instance, the AMO was unaware of the outcome of the case and highlighted the need for formal communication from the social work team. Unless she asks for it, she doesn't get it.

In relation to the second teacher who notified the AMO of the child's disclosure, there was no evidence of post-referral liaison. This particular teacher did not meet with the social worker and was unclear as to what happened with this referral and expressed concern that she received no feedback from either the AMO or social worker: 'I went to the trouble of ringing and unless I get feedback there is no point in ringing just for the sake of it, I mean I don't know what the follow-up on it was.' The gardaí had no further involvement and noted that 'on most occasions, these matters are solely dealt with by the social workers'. At the time of the final research interview, four months after the second referral came in and a full fourteen months after the first referral, the social worker still had plans to contact the (second) teacher and the GP and then review the case with the line manager with a view to carrying out a home visit. The CPN system, meanwhile, was unaware of the fact that its directives had not (yet) been carried out.

Conclusion

By any standards, the response to the referrals in Case 279 was dangerous practice. Thankfully, as this chapter has shown, it was not the norm. Yet it has helped to reveal the kinds of difficulties that can lead to the breakdown of a child-centred response. The risk to the child clearly got lost amidst procedural concerns about the 'formality' of referrals and whether the referral *was* a referral. The degree of accountability and 'ownership' of referrals that other professionals are prepared to take is a legitimate concern for social workers. Yet it is difficult to understand precisely what difference it would have made to the health board's responsibility to investigate the welfare of the child had the teacher put the initial referral in writing and been seen to make a 'formal' referral. It is hard to avoid the conclusion that the social work team used the teacher's ambivalence about being identified as the referral source as an excuse for avoiding investigation of the case. While the long delay by the first teacher in making the initial referral caused real difficulties for the health board, no such doubts surround the fact that the response to the second referral was very poor where the degree of suspected risk to the child was greater and the rationale for not investigating straight away was particularly unsustainable. The fact that such a poor response was the exception in this study—the vast majority of referrals were directly investigated— underlines this conclusion. Yet, as the statistical and qualitative data have shown, the high numbers of cases referred through the referral chain mean that there is huge scope for systems to fail unless these issues are absolutely clear.

There were undoubtedly problems with the way the first teacher in particular handled the referral process, which appear to have their origins in her confusion about the distinction between anonymity and confidentiality and the absence of a corporate approach by the school to making referrals. Both teachers felt isolated and fearful in raising concerns about parenting. One of the teachers discussed the situation with the school principal and felt that she had the principal's support; however, there is no indication that the school, through the head teacher or management committee, had a proactive corporate policy of making referrals. This contrasts starkly with the approach taken by some other schools whose approach to making referrals can be seen to approximate to best practice. In Case 305, for instance, the school had no hesitation in making an immediate referral following a child's disclosure. As the school principal commented: 'We would have a policy of referring it as a school, making a school referral rather than naming any individual, that the staff have referred it as such and this kind of takes away some of the fears that people have around an individual referring'. In this school all referrals are made by the principal on the basis that individual teachers are not covered by school insurance in the event of a 'false allegation', whereas according to the principal 'the principal is covered for that kind of activity'. The principal further commented: 'Personally I believe schools should have no hesitation in making referrals and have a duty and responsibility to do so. I think if we're in the business of safety and protection and the management of children and their futures we have to take some risks . . . so our staff are very comfortable with that'.

Health boards need to clarify the precise status of, and the expected response to, referrals that come through the referral chain:

(1) where social workers are unable to verify the referral information with the person who passed the information to the referral agent;

(2) where the referral agent is contacted and wishes to remain anonymous and is ambivalent about making a 'formal' referral for fear that his or her identity will be revealed.

It is the content of the information, and the level of need or suspected risk to the child, that should guide the response rather than the complexities of the source of the information. Policy and practice also need to be clarified with respect to whether or not referral sources should be disclosed to parents and children who are the subjects of referrals. This will help to remove ambiguity about responses to cases where it has not been possible to verify the referral information with the person who passed the information to the referral agent. Schools (and other organisations making referrals) need to develop a corporate approach to making referrals, where it is the organisation rather than the individual employee which is accountable for raising concerns about children at risk. Multi-disciplinary training is required to enable staff and organisations to recognise and adopt best practice. The precise responsibilities of social workers in responding to anonymous referrals, taking account of the ambiguities experienced, also need to be clarified.

A common criticism of inter-agency work in this study is the failure of key agencies, especially social work, to provide feedback to professional referrers or those who are heavily involved with families with whom network checks have been made. PHNs complained of routinely having to follow-up referrals and request feedback. One commented that when she does receive feedback following a request for it, it is often provided in an informal manner in the form of snatched conversations in corridors or at the end of the working day in the car park. A formalised system to routinely provide feedback to referral agents should be instituted as a matter of urgency. A hospital social worker had similar concerns and felt that this poor communication has created a 'barrier' between the hospital and community care. Difficulties arise when a referred child is discharged from hospital and then re-admitted without the hospital being made aware of the outcome of the initial referral.

This chapter tells us a great deal about the investigative and administrative workloads of various agencies, how disciplines are—or are not—working together to identify and investigate child abuse, and how the general public are working together with professionals in the protection of children (see also Birchall, 1989). Health boards are obliged under the Child Care Act to identify children at risk of abuse and neglect and it is evident from our data that the overall trend is for health board staff to play a major role in identifying the increasing numbers of children at risk of child abuse that have come to attention since the mid-1990s. The number of cases reported by the lay public, and by mothers in particular, also reflects well on the perceived trustworthiness of professionals and overall standards of the board's child protection work. The data shows the multi-faceted nature of the referrals, which in 75 per cent of cases contain more than one suspected child care problem. Classification practices indicate that social workers are making efforts to define cases in term of welfare needs and are not simply rushing to contain everything within a narrow lens of child abuse.

A striking pattern that emerges is the placing in non-abuse categories of cases that were referred by parents, most of whom were mothers. As we have seen, this should not be taken simply to reflect the concern expressed in the reports, but reveals the moral reasoning at work in the categorisation of referrals. It suggests that the moral character of parents, especially mothers, is generally viewed more positively in situations where they, as opposed to professionals, bring the concern to light. The latter referrals are more likely to generate an 'abuse' definition. Given that a high proportion of the reports categorised as non-abuse included child protection issues in the referrals, the option was there to define them as abuse.

The data raise important questions as to whether current identification practices are adequate to meet the board's obligations under the Child Care Act to actively identify children at risk. Is child abuse in fact under-reported by professionals? While we found no actual evidence of non-reporting by professionals, the number of cases coming to light through hospitals in particular seems very small relative to the numbers of children passing through those services. We cannot echo strongly enough the conclusion of the *Report of the Kilkenny Incest Investigation*, where the operational values of some disciplines are cited as acting as

> constraints on the flow of information within the health care system, within hospitals and between hospitals, GPs and community care [and] which derive from a deeply held tradition of respect for the privacy of family related information, coupled with professional practices in relation to confidentiality especially where adults are concerned. (McGuinness, 1993, p. 87)

There is a need for community care and hospital programmes to set out clearly the roles and responsibilities of the different professionals in identifying children at risk and ensuring that child abuse guidelines are adequately drawn up (and followed). This process should be facilitated through multidisciplinary training which promotes mutual understandings of professional identities and roles and of the structural dynamics of professional systems, particularly the corrosive impact of the use of stereotypes and perceptions of power and status.

Once abuse is suspected, information has to be communicated effectively to community care social workers and the CPN system. We have seen that a huge amount of work goes into processing referrals and 'case-building' through network checks, which have become firmly institutionalised through Section 3 of the Child Care Act. However, a good deal of potential exists for this good work to be compromised because of an inadequate structure for co-ordinating information flow in the health board system. A more co-ordinated and systematic approach is needed, with a simple administrative procedure based on regional and national referral forms. In analysing social workers' case files, it proved difficult to extract referral information, including its source. The information tended to be included in the narrative of case records rather than standing alone and being recorded as a distinct practice and phase in the child care and protection process. The introduction of such an administrative procedure would help place decision-making processes and the categorisation of referrals on a much more systematic and transparent basis. It would make the types of responses and services required to meet the protection and welfare needs of children much more apparent and deliverable, and would also assist in the design of information management systems and the collection of reliable local and national case data.

Notes

[1] The 1999 Child Abuse Guidelines (DoH, 1999) appeared after the fieldwork for this study was completed and do not form part of this evaluation.

[2] This includes: behaviour problems in the child; child(ren) out of parental control; juvenile crime; parent/child relationship problems; behaviour problems while child in care; self destructive behaviour/eating disorder-mutilation; self-destructive behaviour/ suicide attempt; substance abuse; sexual behaviour by child.

[3] This includes: loss of parent through family breakdown/imprisonment/death; parent(s) under stress, general coping difficulties; parent(s) experiencing mental health problems; communication problems between parents; access and custody disputes; financial/ housing problems; child(ren) homeless; financial problems; housing problems.

[4] This includes: alcohol abuse by mother, father or other carer; substance abuse; alcohol abuse by both parents.

[5] In four parental referrals a professional subsequently referred the concern.

[6] Including neighbours, grandmothers, cousins, uncles, great aunts, aunts, mothers of abuser, grand stepfathers, publican, neighbour and foster parents.

[7] This includes: GP, PHN, other psychiatric service, mental handicap service, hospital accident and emergency, hospital paediatric, health board psychological service, hospital ante-natal, hospital maternity, child psychologist, community psychiatric nurse, speech therapist and child psychiatric team.

[8] This includes: community welfare officers, staff in children's homes, youth workers, child and family centres, child care workers, counsellors, home help organisers (HHO), project leader, priest, manager of homeless unit, family support worker, Rape Crisis Centre, housing office, refuge, CIC, foster parents, former foster parents, staff in a social services centre, court and the probation service.

[9] This includes: PHN, GP, psychologist, EHO, child psychiatric service, paediatrician, mental health service, speech therapist, adult psychiatry, AMO, children's hospital, community psychiatric nurse, psychiatric services, local health centre.

[10] This includes: school/principal, teacher, liaison officer, education department, educational psychologist, school guidance counsellor, and school chaplain.

[11] Unless otherwise stated all quotations come from interviews with professionals.

[12] As already stated, while the case study materials are used to detail actual events, some details have been changed to protect the anonymity of the families/individuals involved.

3 Investigating Child Abuse and Child Care Problems

Once cases are referred and a child is identified as 'at risk', the next task is to investigate or enquire into the expressed concern for the child and family. In this chapter we analyse how the MWHB investigates child abuse and child care cases. The key themes are the filtering out of referrals without an investigation and the 'safety' of such practices; the investigative process, including speed and the role of medical examinations in child protection; the degree of contact with parents/suspected abusers and the extent to which children are seen and engaged with as part of the investigation. We also present a profile of the children and families referred to the community care teams for child care and abuse problems and the nature of the problems substantiated on investigation.

Other key themes discussed are how decisions are made about investigation, case definition and the allocation of services to children and families. As we have seen, the notion of 'filtering' has become central to the analysis of child care systems, as research from other jurisdictions has shown that surprisingly high numbers of referrals are filtered out of the systems without so much as an investigation, never mind provision of services. Many investigated cases are also left without services despite the fact that there are children in need in such families (Gibbons et al, 1995). The central task, then, is to 'refocus' child care systems to take account of welfare cases, children in need and family support, as well as child protection (Department of Health and Social Security (DHSS), 1995). In this chapter we compare and contrast such international experience with the new evidence from the Irish situation.

The following analysis shows that notions of 'child protection' have come to dominate Irish definitions of legitimate work and that this threatens to exclude childhood adversities which cannot be so defined. Much depends, however, on how, in practice, a 'child protection concern' is defined and we have found considerable elasticity in this. A striking finding is the relatively low number of referrals to the MWHB community care social work teams that are screened out of the system without an investigation and the relatively high numbers of (substantiated) cases offered long-term services, many of which are supportive and/or therapeutic. As Figure 1.1 shows, 92 per cent of referrals were directly investigated, over 50 per cent of which were provided with long-term services (see Chapters 7 and 8 for an extended discussion). The high investigation rate of referrals demonstrates the high level of account-ability operating in the system at the investigative stage, and this reflects a good level of 'safe' practice. However, evidence was found of unsafe practice in terms of children not being seen or adequately engaged with. A crucial finding is the relatively low numbers of cases with actual injuries to children and the dominance of cases of neglect and multi-problem families. This does not mean that these children are not viewed as at high risk and in need. A high proportion of cases have multiple and longstanding child care problems and it is in this context that the meanings of risk and need and the challenges of intervention need to be seen.

Referrals not investigated

Ninety-two per cent of all referrals to the community care social work teams during the sampling period were directly investigated by social workers. By *direct* investigation is meant that a member of the social work team inter-viewed one or a combination of the child(ren), parent(s) or suspected abuser(s)/person with the problem. In 8 per cent of the referrals, 24 cases, no such interview took place. On a team by team basis, there is a remarkable con-sistency—at around 91–92 per cent—in the investigation rate within the three MWHB teams. Three of the 24 referrals not directly investigated were defined as sexual abuse and another three as neglect; physical abuse was the primary concern in two, and domestic violence in another two. Five were primarily concerned with child behavioural problems and four with parental difficulties. It is important to distinguish between referrals not directly in-vestigated by community care social workers but looked into by someone else, and those that were not investigated at all. Sixteen of the 24 non-inves-tigated referrals were checked out by a professional other than the front-line social worker.[1] Just seven referrals, therefore, were not directly checked by another professional and were literally not investigated. This is a remarkably low filtering-out and high direct investigation rate, which is all the more impressive when compared to the high numbers of filtered-out cases in other jurisdictions (Gibbons, et al, 1995; DHSS, 1995).

Of the non-investigated referrals, the three defined as neglect, the three as sexual abuse, the one as physical abuse, one of the two as domestic vio-lence, four of the five child behaviour, and three of the four parental diffi-culty, were checked out by another professional. The professionals commu-nicated their findings to the social work team through a telephone conversation for eight referrals; written report for one; informal face-to-face communication for four, and formal communication at case conference for one (more than one form of communication was used in some referrals). For 11 non-investigated referrals the decision not to investigate was reached after consultation with a line manager; for seven it followed consultation with other disciplines; for four the front-line social worker made the decision alone, while for five the decision was made through consultation with more than one source. In ten of the non-investigated referrals the children and family had been involved with the health board prior to the research referral and this prior knowledge had a bearing on decision-making. Eight of the 24 non-investigated referrals were notified to the gardaí, while 15 were not (information was missing in one case). In 11 cases the parents were informed that a referral had been made concerning their children, while in eight the parents were not informed; in one case the parents had not yet been informed but were about to be.

Health boards need to establish a clear policy on informing parents about referrals in situations where social workers do not directly investigate the referral, or where another professional investigates. It needs to be clearly stated on case records who made the decision not to investigate directly and on what grounds. In the interests of accountability and clear communication, the outcome of all referrals not investigated by the social work team but looked into by another professional should be communicated in writing to the social work team. The implications for the assessed level of risk to the children should be noted by the social work and/or child care manager. Where referrals are not investigated at all the person making the decision, and the grounds for it, need to be clearly stated.

Why referrals were not directly investigated

We now consider the reasons why referrals were not directly investigated by social workers, or were not investigated at all, and the legitimacy of those decisions. In Chapter 2 the ambiguities of when a referral is (not) a referral were illustrated through Case 279 which was not investigated by any one. The most benign reasons for non-investigation included families moving from the area (Case 14), and unsuccessful attempts by social workers to see the family (Case 256) (see Figure 3.1). A common reason for non-investigation was that the referral did not fit the brief of community care social work: adoption queries were referred on to the appropriate agencies (Cases 19, 81, 137, 139), and custody issues were also regarded as inappropriate (Case 277). Case 81 was referred by a school counsellor who had 'met with fourteen-year-old girl . . . [who] explained that she was adopted and felt that she needed to talk with someone outside of her own family' (research forms). The social worker referred the case to an adoption society and the family was to be met by an adoption counsellor. Case 139 was referred by a social

Figure 3.1 Reasons for non-investigation of referrals

Physical abuse

Case 130 Parents making effort, no concern

Case 279 Case closed pending further information from teacher

Neglect

Case 136 Letter from parents alleging social work harassment, seeking legal advice, requested no further social work involvement

Case 14 All parties moved from area

Case 80 Social worker from other agency followed up case

Sexual abuse

Case 197 Child unwilling to discuss matter with health board

Case 202 Gardai to conduct interview

Case 47 Child married, no abuse

Domestic violence

Case 26 Case referred by gardai, notification purposes only

Case 288 Contacted women's refuge, informed gardai

Behaviour/control problems

Case 24 PHN maintained contact with parents

Case 119 Will make a home visit

Case 152 Referred to psychological services

Case 221 Child psychiatry involved, social work deemed unnecessary

Case 277 No child protection concerns/custody issue

Parental difficulties

Case 160 Met with children's teacher

Case 236 Parents purchased home of their own

Case 256 Attempted unsuccessful home visit

Case 276 No child protection concerns

Miscellaneous

Case 19 Case transferred to adoption society

Case 81 Case referred to adoption society

Case 137 Case transferred to adoption society

Case 139 Referred for report regarding adoption of child

Case 285 No child protection concerns

worker from the Adoption Board with 'a request for a report regarding adoption of a child' and the frontline social worker correctly decided she had no investigative role.

The health board could not investigate some referrals due to lack of co-operation from the child or family. In Case 197 a sixteen-year-old informed a teacher that she had been 'abused as a child for a two-week period only at the age of seven years . . . the alleged abuser is an extended family member' (research forms). The child was unwilling to discuss the disclosure with social workers or gardaí. Case 136 was referred by an uncle expressing concern for sixteen-, fourteen-, twelve-, eight-, seven-, six- and five-year-old children, alleging that they were constantly unsupervised and 'parents not taking on responsibility . . . children throwing stones at neighbours' windows . . . parents laugh . . . one child stealing regularly and not attending school' (research forms). The case could not be investigated because the parents, who were well known to the health board, alleged harassment from social workers and wouldn't let them in. The case was re-referred in June 1996 and was subsequently investigated. A case conference was held which the parents attended. However, it was noted by the social worker that both parents 'withdrew co-operation' and the case was monitored 'from a distance'.

Referrals explicitly judged to contain 'no child protection concerns' (Cases 276, 277, 285) illustrate the way community care social work prioritises 'protection' cases. Case 285 was referred by a regional maternity hospital because a 'nurse in hospital knew that a mother leaving [the hospital] with her baby was seventeen years old and did not get on well with her boyfriend (sixteen years)'. The referral was not directly investigated as 'no child protection concerns presented, mother had good support from family' (research forms). It was also deemed inappropriate for community care social workers to take up the concern with the family in some referrals where other agencies were already involved (Cases 24, 80, 221). Case 24 was referred by a PHN: 'PHN involved with family following enuresis plan with a nine-year-old boy in looking at reasons for bedwetting, only stress factor was an alcoholic uncle who had been staying in the house . . .' No child protection concerns were identified by the social worker, and it was noted that there were 'no concrete concerns, queried reason behind bedwetting, PHN concerned about level of stress in the home and level of emotional abuse which resulted from uncle's drinking'. The referral was not directly investigated as 'communication remained between parents and PHN involved'. The decision was made in consultation with a line manager as the 'concerns were insufficient to warrant a social work investigation. It was felt more appropriate that PHN remain involved' (research forms). The referral was defined within child welfare and is a good example of the kind of scenario that raises questions about the direction of community care social work and the dominance of protection within service provision. The social worker clearly did not feel it appropriate to follow the PHN's concerns and define the case as possible emotional abuse. This justified leaving the PHN to deal with the boy's welfare difficulties herself. There is no evidence that this was inappropriate to the child's needs, but the question is whether the social worker would have provided a supportive service to the family had there been fewer pressures to do child protection work.

Thus the perceived absence of child protection concerns can be misleading and the decision-making questionable in cases where the referred behaviour is not deemed serious enough to warrant a response within the 'abuse' categories of the agency. A further important example of this from the sample of non-investigated cases is Case 26 which was referred by the gardaí directly to the DCC in April, 1996 and then assigned to a social worker. The referral concerned 'domestic violence in house following alleged assault incident at Christmas' with respect to children under twelve, whose 'emotional welfare may be affected' by virtue of the domestic violence in the home. The mother and children were residing with a man who had served time in prison for violence-related offences. The gardaí had reason to believe that this woman had been hospitalised when she was pregnant because of alleged domestic violence. While the woman in question accepted that she had been hospitalised, she vehemently denied that this was due to domestic violence. The social worker did not check with the hospital to clarify this.

The case was notified to the DCC and a decision made not to directly investigate and it was 'closed'. This decision rested on the view that 'the case as presented by gardaí was for notification only, not a request for specific action. Thus the case was noted for future information in light of any future referral and is noted for statistical purposes' (research forms). The social worker's view was that the child protection meeting governed the decision not to investigate the referral, construing that the gardaí were notifying it, but not requesting 'specific action'. The case was re-opened six months later when the gardaí re-referred it, having been called to the house due to further suspected domestic violence. The social worker carried out a joint investigation with the PHN, and the mother insisted the referrals were malicious. She did admit that her partner had arguments with his own family and the social worker was still unsure about whether the domestic violence was substantiated because of the mother's denial. The social worker asked the mother to meet her with a garda at the social work department and the woman denied that the gardaí had ever called to her home, while the garda gave a detailed account of the home visit made about domestic violence. The mother stressed that no physical or emotional abuse occurred, feeling that she and her partner had the same arguments as other couples. The social worker did not make face to face contact with the alleged batterer or the children. The case was closed because of 'none or insufficient evidence of child care/abuse problem'. The PHN had developed a good relationship with the mother and was to continue to monitor the case, as were the schools.

The case is a good example of how the child protection system at the most official level decides to filter out a referral and of a theme that looms large in the findings of this research: the ambiguous position of domestic violence as a child protection and welfare issue. Domestic violence can be notified as suspected emotional abuse under the 1995 Health Board/Gardaí Child Abuse Guidelines (DoH, 1995; 1999). A distinction needs to be made between information passed by the gardaí to the health board 'for notification only' under the guidelines, and referrals which are 'a request for specific action'. Policy should be established on the status of domestic violence cases in child protection and welfare work and the need to respond to them consistently in a child-centred way with the same degree of seriousness as any other form of 'abuse'.

Profiles of the children and families

Before moving on to analyse the response to the cases that were investigated, a profile of the children and families involved provides vital background information against which to interpret the findings of the study. A total of 845 children were involved in the 286 community care referrals, either as a direct cause of concern or as a sibling of a child who was a direct cause of concern; 49 per cent were males and 51 per cent females. The most frequent family size was two children (26 per cent of the families), single child families constituted 24 per cent of the sample, while 18 per cent consisted of five or more children. One family had 13 children, and three had 11. The average family size was three children.

The children: Four per cent (n=31) of the children were under one year of age, 14 per cent between one and three years, 19 per cent between four and six, 16 per cent between seven and nine, 18 per cent between ten and twelve and 17 per cent between thirteen and fifteen years. Fifty-three per cent (n=425) of all the children were under ten years of age, and 11 per cent between sixteen and eighteen years of age. This 11 per cent represents a crude measure of the increase in service demand arising from the extension of the age of the 'child' to eighteen years under the Child Care Act.

The parents and family types: Forty-four per cent (n=118) of the biological parents of the child(ren) were married at the time of the referral, including three cases where, although the parents were married, the father was not the biological father of all the children in the family. In 21 per cent (n=56) the biological parents were unmarried, including four cases where the father was not the biological father of all the children in the family. In 29 per cent (n=77) of families the biological parents were separated/divorced and in 7 per cent (n=18) the parent was widowed. However, in itself the marital status of parents tells us little about the 'type' of families children referred for child care/ abuse problems actually live in.

Table 3.1 Family types in community care sample

Family type	%	No.
Both parents	37	100
Lone parents	41	111
Reconstituted families	11	30
Relatives/others	6	16
Not applicable	5	14
Total	*100*	*271**

*Information missing in 4 cases and unknown in 7.

Just 37 per cent of cases involved children living with both biological parents, while 41 per cent were living in a lone parent family, the majority headed by women (see Table 3.1). Another 11 per cent lived in reconstituted families in that both parents were not the biological parents of all the children, and 6 per cent lived with extended family members and not with their parent(s). In eleven cases child(ren) were residing in care at the time of the referral, in one case a child lived part-time in an adolescent unit and part-time in a rented flat; in another the child lived alone with no parent resident.

Socio-economic status: In 74 per cent (n=187) of the families the main source of household income was social welfare, while in 26 per cent (n=66) it came from employment. Where information was available (in only 90 cases), 22 per cent (n=20) had a net weekly income of under £100, 32 per cent (n=29) earned between £100 and £140 and 17 per cent earned between £150 and £180. Almost 80 per cent of the families have a net weekly income of under £180, with the remaining 20 per cent earning more than £180 per week.

Housing status: In 77 per cent of referrals the children were living in the family home, with the remainder living with relatives, in foster care, residential care, a flat, trailer or homeless. The majority —62 per cent—were living in rented local authority housing, 11 per cent in the private rented sector and 27 per cent owned their own homes. Of the cases where the family was resident in the family home 92 per cent lived in a house, 6 per cent in a flat, and 2 per cent in a caravan/mobile home/trailer. Ninety-three per cent of the families were from the settled community, 5 per cent from the travelling community, 2 per cent were settled travellers, 1 per cent from a mixed community background and 1 per cent were described as 'new age/alternative community'. Thirty-four per cent were city-based, 30 per cent resided in a town, 19 per cent in a village and 17 per cent in a rural locality. Twenty-three per cent of the families lived within one mile of the social work office, 34 per cent between one and three miles, and 9 per cent over twenty miles from the social work office.

The striking pattern is that only 48 per cent of children were living with two parent figures: 11 per cent in reconstituted families and 37 per cent in conventional families being reared by both their biological parents. Some 41 per cent of children in referrals were being reared by lone parents (mostly mothers), most of whom were living on social welfare or low wage incomes, in corporation housing. As will be seen, this social and demographic profile has a major bearing on the types of problems substantiated and worked with.

Responses to investigated referrals by the social work teams

We will now consider the overall response to the 92 per cent of referrals directly investigated. Effective child protection and welfare work involves engaging with children, parents and/or suspected abusers. The Child Abuse Guidelines are very clear that children must be seen immediately concern arises for them. In a significant proportion of cases, however, this does not happen. Seventy-two per cent of the children included in the referrals were seen or interviewed by a social worker (see Table 3.2). In 40 per cent at least one parent, if not the suspected abuser, was interviewed. The suspect abuser or the person with the child care problem was interviewed in 50 per cent of all referrals. In total, 91 per cent of adults were interviewed by a member of the social work team, hence in 9 per cent of referrals an adult member of the family concerned was not directly interviewed. When only investigated cases are taken into account the percentage of children being directly seen or interviewed increases to 78. Thus 22 per cent of the children in investigated cases were not seen or interviewed. The percentage of suspect abusers or

Table 3.2 Responses of community care social work teams to investigated referrals

Response	%	No.
Suspect/person with problem interviewed	50	144
Child(ren) seen/interviewed	72	205
Parent(s) (if not suspect) interviewed	40	113
Grandmother interviewed	3	8
Father spoken to by phone	0.3	1
Carer of child interviewed	0.7	2
No interview with child, parent(s) and/or suspect abuser(s)	8	24

Note: The per cent total adds to more than 100 due to multiple responses.

carers interviewed increases by 5 per cent to 55 per cent when only investigated cases are taken into account.

Examining the cases investigated and notified to the DCC allows for a more meaningful analysis of the investigative response in 'official' child protection cases. The absence of notification does not necessarily mean that the need or risk to the children was always substantially lower, but rather that it was not deemed appropriate to the 'child protection' framework. The act of notifying does, however, draw the case into the official child protection system with the enhanced sense of management responsibility and accountability implied. In 80 per cent of the 169 referrals notified to the DCC and investigated, the children were seen or interviewed, so that 20 per cent were not seen. If the referral was initially defined by the social worker as child protection as opposed to child welfare the children had a greater chance of being interviewed, 80 per cent as opposed to 77 per cent. Notification of a referral to the CPN system, then, increases minimally the chance of a child being interviewed by a social worker.

When it comes to interviewing suspected abusers, social workers clearly experience doubt as to what constitutes abusive behaviour. A suspect 'abuser' or a person responsible for the child care/protection problem was not cited in every case. In some cases the child was in care at the time of the referral and a suspect abuser was not cited by the social worker, in other instances the child him/herself was noted to be the 'abuser'. Furthermore, particularly where neglect was notified, the social worker did not view the parents as abusive and a suspect 'abuser' was not identified. Consequently, when analysing the extent to which suspect abusers were interviewed it is important to include only those cases where the social worker identified a suspect abuser. Of the 169 investigated cases notified to the CPN system, a suspect abuser was identified in 146. Of these, parent(s) were cited as the suspect abuser in 118 cases, other family in 11, and non-family in 17 cases, in 73 per cent of which the suspect abuser was interviewed. The 27 per cent not interviewed were primarily extended family and non-family members. Of the 118 suspect abuser parents, only 16 were not interviewed, 14 of whom were fathers, and 2 mothers. Of the 17 non-family suspect abusers, 16 were not interviewed and of the 11 'other family' suspect abusers 3 were interviewed, all of whom were female. It is significant that of the 8 'male other family' suspect abusers none were interviewed. This shows the importance of gender to an analysis of how child care and protection systems work (Buckley, 1998; Milner, 1993; 1996). Men/fathers were screened out of the system much more readily than women/mothers.

The suspect abuser was interviewed by the social worker in 55 per cent of all investigated cases, compared with 73 per cent in investigated and notified cases, showing that notification clearly increases the likelihood of a suspect abuser being interviewed. To deepen our understanding of the investigative response it is necessary to consider the types of concern raised about the children, whether they were previously involved with the health board and the level of need or risk suggested in the referral. This raises the key question of whether professionals should see and interview all children in all referrals. What, if any, are the conditions where this may be deemed unnecessary? Do child protection cases have priority, i.e. they should always be seen, while child welfare referrals rank lower because of the apparent lack of immediate danger? Can the letter and/or spirit of the Child Care Act be followed and the welfare of children promoted without direct involvement with, and sight of, the children concerned? What can be said is that once a referral/case is placed in an abuse/protection category this implies a level of risk to the children which requires direct investigation. Thus in evaluating standards of 'safe'/best practice it is crucial to determine the circumstances in which children were not seen/interviewed. The same issues arise in domestic violence situations where risk and danger to adult victims is a primary concern in the referral.

In 90 per cent (n=19) of investigated physical abuse cases the children were seen or interviewed by the social worker and in two cases they were not. Case 200 involved an allegation by a sixteen-year-old girl that her brother physically assaulted her. She was living in another, distant, health board area at the time of investigation and could not be seen by the MWHB social worker, but was met by a social worker from the other health board. Case 11 involved an allegation by the ISPCC that two children were physically abused by their mother's boyfriend, and allegedly had bruises on their faces. The children were not initially seen as appointments were offered but broken. But a subsequent joint home visit with the gardaí led to an interview with the children who denied being hit.

The children were seen or interviewed in 84 per cent (n=48) of investigated neglect cases, while in twelve they were not. Case 122 involved neglect, physical abuse and alcohol abuse by both parents of three children aged eight, seven, and six. The parents were interviewed but not the children. Case 145 involved alcohol abuse, physical abuse, emotional abuse, family breakdown, parents under stress and financial problems as well as neglect. The children, aged sixteen, eleven, eight, three and one, were not seen or interviewed. Significantly, however, the case was open at the time of this referral and the family had been involved with the health board for two years. Nor were the children, aged eleven, eight and five, seen in Case 146 which involved alleged neglect, emotional abuse and children out of parental control, parents under stress and financial problems. In Case 230 the suspect abuser (mother) was interviewed, although the children named in the referral, aged fourteen and ten, were not seen. This referral was made by an anonymous source alleging that the mother had 'ignored her children for the past five days'. In 93 per cent of investigated neglect cases, the suspect abuser was interviewed; in 4 per cent of cases a parent, if not the suspect abuser, was interviewed; in a further 4 per cent the child's grandmother was interviewed.

In 64 per cent of investigated emotional abuse cases the suspect abusers were interviewed, while the children were seen in 82 per cent. Some 27 per cent of parents, if not the suspect abusers, were interviewed. The children referred were not seen or interviewed in three cases. Case 144 was referred because of the mother's alleged abuse of alcohol, inappropriate punishment, domestic violence, physical abuse, financial problems, parent/child relationship problems and parents under stress. The children, aged fifteen, thirteen, eleven, ten, seven and six were not interviewed or seen. In Case 261 an allegation was made by a father living in England that his children who were living here with their mother were exposed to an 'environment of drugs and adult behaviour'. The children, aged fifteen, thirteen and eleven, were not interviewed. Case 303 involved an access dispute between separated parents, the mother was interviewed but the children were not.

In 35 per cent of domestic violence referrals the suspect abuser was interviewed, while the children were seen/interviewed in 59 per cent. Sev-

enty-six per cent of parents who were not the suspect abuser were interviewed, virtually all of whom were women, clearly mothers who were themselves being abused. In only 9 per cent (n=3) of investigated sexual abuse
referrals was the suspect abuser interviewed by social workers, while 85 per
cent (n=28) of parents, if not the suspected abusers, were interviewed. In 6
per cent the grandmother was interviewed; in 82 per cent (n=27) the children were seen or interviewed. This clearly reflects the primary role of the
gardaí in investigating possible criminal offences in sexual abuse cases, while
social workers dealt predominantly with non-abusing parents. In six referrals
the children were not initially seen or interviewed. In one of these cases a
CSA assessment took place, in one the parents were offered an assessment
but declined and in two the children were seen by the social worker during
the follow-up period of the research but not in the initial sampling period.
The father of the child in Case 201 alleged that he witnessed a four-year-old
behaving sexually with his eight-year-old 'mentally retarded' son. The eight-
year-old was cited as the suspect abuser and his parents were interviewed but
not the parents of the four-year-old. Sexual abuse was substantiated although
neither child was seen/interviewed. Case 245 involved an allegation by a six-
year-old child's mother that her former partner may have sexually abused the
child. The child was not seen or interviewed. In Case 247 a fifteen-year-old
allegedly sexually abused a four-year-old neighbour and his ten-year-old sister. The parents of the fifteen-year-old were interviewed, but neither of the
children named were seen or interviewed by the investigating social worker.
In Case 54 a twelve-year-old alleged that her uncle sexually abused her and
the child was seen by a private counsellor but not by any health board staff.
The case was closed as the suspect abuser moved from the area. Case 114
involved a vague allegation of sexual abuse—no specific incident was cited.
Concern arose over a previous incident of child sexual abuse within this
family which resulted in the perpetrator leaving the family home. The referrer,
a cousin, was concerned about the access visits between the perpetrator and
two children. The mother was interviewed but the children were not. Nor
were the children seen in Case 20 which involved children 'behaving sexually' in terms of 'inappropriate' sexualised conversation.

Effective child protection and welfare practice requires that children be
seen and interviewed but of crucial importance is what they are interviewed
about: the very definition of the problem being investigated. This issue is
discussed in detail in Chapter 4. What can be concluded at this point is that
children were seen or interviewed in the vast majority of investigated physical abuse, sexual abuse, neglect and emotional abuse cases. In domestic

violence cases, however, the number seen or interviewed is relatively low. As far as accountability is concerned, the level of contact with children in child protection investigations is good. However, in some cases where the children are not seen or interviewed, the reasons why, and the degree of child-centredness involved, need to be carefully monitored by frontline workers and management and recorded on case files. The suspected abuser was most likely to be interviewed by community care social workers in neglect, and least likely in sexual abuse cases. This reflects the division of professional labour in sexual abuse cases where a lot of work is done by the gardaí and specialist health board child sexual abuse assessment units (see also the extended discussion of this issue in Chapter 5). The interview rate of suspected abusers in domestic violence cases is very low by comparison. This particularly reflects the 'gendered' nature of child protection practice and the relative avoidance of suspected male perpetrators of domestic violence and child abuse and the avoidance of men in child welfare more generally.

Length of time between referral and investigation

There are few better indicators of risk, safety and sense of danger to children than the speed of response to expressions of concern. At its most basic, unless children suspected of being at risk of abuse are reached in time, they cannot hope to be protected (Ferguson, 1996b, 1997). Responding to children in time does not always mean quickly. There are situations where a more 'timely', that is to say a safer investigative response, involves taking time to plan and strategise intervention, thereby slowing down the actual process of making direct contact with suspected abusers and victims (see, for instance, Case 234, Chapter 4). Some 40 per cent of the 262 directly investigated referrals were investigated within one day of receiving the initial referral, while 74 per cent

Table 3.3 Length of time between referrals and investigation

Number of days	%	No.
Same day	20	49
1 day	20	49
2 days	12	30
3 days	8	20
4–5 days	14	35
1–2 weeks	15	36
Over 2 weeks	12	30
Total	*100*	*249**

*13 missing cases

were investigated within five working days. In 10 referrals an investigation did not take place until after twenty working days (see Table 3.3). One such referral (Case 60), which was primarily concerned with parental addiction, took sixteen weeks (80 days) to be investigated. Of the 249 cases where information was available, 20 per cent were investigated on the day of the referral. Sexual abuse and domestic violence received the quickest investigation (see Table 3.4).

Table 3.4 Main presenting problem in referrals investigated on the day referral received

Main problem	%	No.
Physical abuse	8	4
Neglect	10	5
Emotional abuse	8	4
Sexual abuse	16	8
Domestic violence	14	7
Child out of control	2	1
Parent/child rel. problems	8	4
Family breakdown	2	1
Alcohol abuse by mother	4	2
Parents under stress	10	5
Mental health/parents	4	2
Housing problems	4	2
Access/custody disputes	2	1
Substance abuse	6	3
Total	*100**	*49*

*Total does not add to 100 due to rounding.

Of the 49 referrals investigated on the day the referral was received, 57 per cent were primarily defined as child protection, and 43 per cent as child welfare. In the 21 child welfare referrals investigated on the day of reporting, child protection concerns also featured in 13, while the remaining 8 referrals were solely concerned with child welfare. This means that 94 per cent of child welfare only referrals were not investigated on the same day. Hence 84 per cent of referrals investigated on the same day involved some concern with child protection. Another 49 referrals were investigated one day after the referral, 35 per cent of which were defined as child protection and 65 per cent as child welfare. Again, in 10 of these 32 child welfare referrals protection concerns were also identified, although not regarded as the main problem. Therefore, in 55 per cent of referrals investigated after one day a child protection concern was evident. This suggests that it is the perception of levels of danger/harm/risk to children, whether from suspected direct injuries (abuse) or from child behaviour problems or parents struggling to cope (child care problems) that structures intervention and underlies definitions of child welfare and protection. Thus, children can be seen as in grave danger from problems in what are child welfare cases. This can be illustrated by Case 186 concerning 'a twelve-year-old disruptive in school . . . becoming increasingly violent to other pupils' (research forms)and was investigated within one day. The child's behaviour was considered to be the main problem, although neglect was also noted. While child welfare problems were the primary cause of concern, the quick response to this referral can be explained by the concerns regarding the child's violent behaviour and its consequences for other children.

It might reasonably be expected that referrals notified to the CPN system, and thus officially defined as child protection cases, would contain a degree of risk resulting in a swifter response than non-notified referrals. Ironically, however, the cases notified got a *slower* response. Some 17 per cent of these investigated referrals were responded to on the same day, compared with 27 per cent of non-notified cases. Seventy-two per cent of all notified cases were responded to within one working week compared with 83 per cent of non-notified cases, while 14 per cent of notified cases waited over two weeks compared with only 7 per cent of the non-notified cases.

Table 3.5 Form of investigative interview into types of referrals

Main presenting problem	*Interview with other*		*Interview alone*	
	%	No.	%	No.
Physical abuse	55	11	45	9*
Neglect	53	30	47	27
Emotional abuse	55	6	45	5
Sexual abuse	36	12	64	21
Domestic violence	24	4	76	13
Behaviour/control	24	13	76	42
Financial/housing	27	3	73	8
Parental difficulties	26	10	74	28
Parental addiction	40	4	60	6
Miscellaneous	20	1	80	4

*Information unknown in 1 case

While other factors may also be influencing these outcomes, this can be explained, in part, by the time taken waiting for the CPN meeting to take place and to process the referral through the notification system.

The investigative process

In 63 per cent of the investigated referrals, social workers conducted the interview alone, while in 37 per cent they were accompanied by another professional. Social workers in both the Clare and East Limerick/Tipperary teams were more likely than the Limerick team to conduct the investigative interview alone. Of the investigated cases, 72 per cent were conducted alone in East Limerick/Tipperary, 70 per cent in Clare and 45 per cent in Limerick. In 55 per cent of physical abuse referrals the social worker was accompanied by another professional, while in 45 per cent the social worker conducted the interview alone (see Table 3.5). Joint visits were most often made in cases of neglect, occurring in 30 cases (53 per cent). In the child protection category, 'lone' investigation occurred in 64 per cent of sexual abuse cases. Significantly, cases defined as protection are more likely to elicit a joint investigative response than those defined as welfare. Thus, interviews in 24 per cent of behaviour/control referrals were held 'jointly'. Interviews were jointly held in 26 per cent of parental difficulty referrals (74 per cent).

Surprisingly perhaps, given what one would expect about workers' fears for their safety, only 24 per cent of investigations into domestic violence referrals (4 cases) were conducted with another professional. This may be because rates of engagement with the suspected abusers in such cases are low, the perpetrator being excluded from the investigative process with the main focus the abused woman. In the 94 cases where a professional accompanied the social worker, 44 per cent involved a front-line social work colleague. A child care worker accompanied the social worker in 19 per cent, while in 5 per cent the social worker's line manager attended the interview.[2] Gender has an important influence on this aspect of the investigative process. In 12 per cent (n=32) of the cases the investigating social workers were male, 88 per cent (n=230) were female. The majority of professionals who accompanied the social worker were also female—74 per cent. This still constitutes an over-representation of 'male accompaniers' given their much smaller number. The ratio of male/female investigating social workers is 1:7, and of male/female accompanying professionals is 1:3. This clearly shows the importance of male staff to staff protection.

Table 3.6 Main presenting problem in referrals that were substantiated by community care

Main problem	%	No.
Physical abuse	6	9
Neglect	21	33
Emotional abuse	6	9
Sexual abuse	11	18
Domestic violence	9	15
Behaviour/control	24	39
Financial housing	6	9
Parental difficulties	14	22
Parental addiction	3	5
Miscellaneous	1	1
Total	*100**	*160*

*Note: The % total does not add to 100 because of rounding.

The role of medical examinations

The majority of investigated cases, 81 per cent, did not involve a medical examination of the children. GPs were the most active in the 54 cases (19 per cent) where examinations occurred, carrying out 42 per cent, followed by paediatricians, in 27 per cent. Accident and emergency departments conducted four examinations (8 per cent) and area medical officers six (12 per cent). In the 233 investigated cases where a medical examination did not take place, the most frequent reason was that the 'referral did not justify it', followed by 'degrees of suspected injuries did not justify it'. In two cases the parents of the child refused to allow a medical examination and in two others the child refused.   A medical examination took place in 33 per cent of the physical abuse referrals, in 28 per cent of sexual abuse referrals, and in 18 per cent of neglect referrals. Emotional abuse (8 per cent) and domestic violence (12 per cent) were the least likely types of suspected abuse to result in a medical examination. Seventy-four per cent of medical examinations resulted in a substantiated case.

Substantiated cases: the nature of child abuse and child care problems

Of the 262 investigated cases, 61 per cent (n=160) were substantiated. Protection concerns were evident in 133 of these. This is not to say that these were the only concerns, or the primary definitions of the case. As we show in Chapter 8, for instance, the significant numbers of cases containing child protection concerns were primarily concerned with often serious child welfare issues, such as child behaviour and control problems, parents under stress and so on. Because the research brief was to evaluate the protection system, the research was designed to gather data primarily on the nature of abuse in substantiated cases. The research still provides many insights into the nature of the problems in non-abuse/child welfare cases, but this is not as comprehensive as the data on what were defined as protection concerns. Thus, for example, 24 per cent of referrals where the problem was defined as child behaviour or control problems were substantiated on investigation as were 14 per cent of cases where parental difficulties were the main problem (see Table 3.6). Because so many of these welfare referrals also contained protection concerns, detailed data has been gathered on many forms of substantiated abuse, but less systematic information is available on the non-abuse problems, although in many of the case studies in this book these do become apparent. For similar reasons, the data undoubtedly fails to record the true scale of child welfare problems that may have been present in child protection cases, although again this does come out in case studies and other analysis (see Chapter 8).

Turning, then, to the nature of abuse in substantiated cases, the most prevalent was neglect, present in 44 per cent of substantiated cases, followed by

Table 3.7 Nature of abuse in substantiated cases

Nature of substantiated abuse	%	No.
Sexual abuse	12	19
Neglect	44	71
Behaviour problems	6	9
Parent/child relationship prob.	1	2
Emotional abuse	32	51
Parents under stress	4	6
Physical abuse	10	16
Domestic violence	26	42
Self abuse	1	2
Child perpetrator of sexual abuse	1	2
Homelessness	3	4
Substance abuse	6	9
Child suffering from effects of sexual abuse	0.6	1
Underage pregnancy	0.6	1

Note: The % total adds to more than 100 due to multiple responses.

emotional abuse (32 per cent) and domestic violence (26 per cent) (see Table 3.7). When the welfare cases are excluded, neglect was present in over half—53 per cent—of the substantiated protection cases. This does not mean that abuse problems such as neglect and domestic violence were always treated as the main problem in all these cases as they were often substantiated in combination with other problems. The figures show the prevalence of these problems in the sample.

Neglect was substantiated for 164 children, 48 per cent male, 52 per cent female. Thirty-six per cent were under five years of age, 31 per cent were between six and ten, 33 per cent were eleven or over. Poor parenting skills was the most prevalent form of neglect, occurring in 70 per cent of substantiated neglect cases. Being left unattended, so-called 'home alone' cases, was the next most common form of substantiated neglect at 45 per cent. Very poor home standards as a result of poor parenting capacity, accounted for another 27 per cent. Ninety-six per cent (n=155) of the responsible carers in substantiated neglect cases were parents. Thus the greatest single need for services in all current child protection and welfare work is for children suffering adversities due to the poor parenting competencies of mothers and fathers. Children being left alone or with underage babysitters is also a very significant problem and suggests a more active, wilful form of neglect needing an authoritative response from the services (see Table 3.8). Some children experienced combinations of 'neglectful' parenting (of the kinds set out in Table 3.8) as well as other forms of abuse.

Physical abuse was evident in 12 per cent (n=16) of substantiated cases, involving 25 children, 57 per cent of whom were male. Thirty-four per cent were under five years of age, 24 per cent between six and ten years, and 43 per cent over eleven. The most common symptom of known or suspected physical abuse was current bruises to victim's body, in 6 cases, followed by the child being hit, but no visible evidence or marks (see Table. 3.9). Seventy-six per cent of children in substantiated physical abuse cases were abused by a parent. Sexual abuse was evident in 14 per cent (n=19) of substantiated protection cases, and increases to 17 per cent when one case of 'child suffering from effects of sexual abuse' and two cases of 'child was perpetrator of sexual abuse' are included. Sexual abuse was substantiated for 25 children, 32 per cent of whom were male. Twenty-four per cent were under five years of age, 24 per cent between six and ten and 52 per cent were over eleven. Contact non-penetrative sex was the most prevalent form of substantiated sexual abuse, occurring in six cases or 24 per cent of this very small sub-sample, followed by suspected contact non-penetrative sex. Penetrative sex featured in 16 per

Table 3.8 The nature of neglect in substantiated cases

Nature of abuse	%	No. (children)
Poor parenting skills/capacity	70	116
Children left unattended/ underage babysitter	45	74
Very poor home standards due to poor parenting capacity	27	44
Children unkempt/poor hygiene	18	30
Children poorly fed and hungry	12	20
Non-attendance/problems at school	9	14
Failure to get medical treatment for child	8	13
Wilful withdrawal of care	9	14
Children underweight/ failing to thrive	7	12
Children inadequately clothed	6	11
Failure to control behaviour	2	3
Miscellaneous (3)	6	11

Note: The % total adds to more than 100 due to multiple responses.

cent of substantiated sexual abuse cases (see Table 3.10). Twenty-nine per cent of children in substantiated sexual abuse cases were abused by a neighbour, 13 per cent by an uncle, while 'children on the estate' were cited as the abusers in 13 per cent of cases. Other abusers included a cousin, school friends, staff at a crèche, ex-employee, brother, adult male—underage sex, child is abuser.

Domestic violence was substantiated in 32 per cent of the 133 substantiated child protection cases, involving 105 children, 58 per cent of whom were male, 42 per cent female. Seven cases were substantiated as domestic violence only, which means that in the vast majority, 83 per cent, another child protection concern was also substantiated. This represents a huge and hitherto undisclosed amount of domestic violence in child protection work. Five per cent of children in substantiated domestic violence cases were under one year of age, 55 per cent under ten years and 40 per cent ten or over. The most common form of domestic violence was verbal/psychological violence by the male against the female partner, affecting 58 per cent of the children concerned (see Table 3.11). Physical violence by the male partner towards the female partner was the next most common form of domestic violence,

Table 3.9 The nature of physical abuse in substantiated cases

Nature of abuse	%	No. (children)
Current bruises	24	6
Child hit, no evidence of marks	16	4
Child fears father	5	1
Suspect child hit, no marks	10	2
Self-inflicted injuries	5	1
Healed scars from previous incident	5	1
Occasional physical correction by father	5	1
Father assaulted mother with child in arms	5	1
Accidental cigarette burn	5	1
Burns on foot	5	1
Burns on abdomen	5	1
Child kicked/punched by father	10	2
Child reported being hit by staff in residential unit	5	1

Note: The % total adds to more than 100 due to multiple responses.

evident in 55 per cent of the cases. The findings show the range of abusive behaviours perpetrated on victims, including isolation/control of movements, and abuse through the control of money. The vast majority of the victims were women, of whom some experienced some or a range of these problems, while others experienced all of the problems. This picture represents

Table 3.10 Nature of substantiated sexual abuse cases

Nature of abuse	%	No. (children)
Non-contact sexual abuse	16	4
Contact non-penetrative sex	24	6
Penetrative sex	16	4
Suspect non-contact sexual abuse	4	1
Penetrative/possible finger or object	4	1
Suspect non-penetrative sex	20	5
Child perpetrator of sexual abuse	12	3
Child suffering from previous sexual abuse	4	1
Penetrative sex with a minor	4	1
Suspect penetrative sex	4	1

Note: The % total adds to more than 100 due to multiple responses.

Table 3.11 Nature of domestic violence in substantiated cases

Nature of violence	%	No. (children)
Physical by male to female	55	58
Injuries by male to female	27	28
Verbal/psychological by male to female	58	61
Physical by female to male	3	3
Verbal/psychological by female to male	11	12
Control of money and female's movements by male	31	32
Depression/mental ill-health of female caused by violence by male	23	24
Depression/mental ill-health of male caused by violence by female	3	3
Evidence children's adversity/distress caused by domestic violence	32	34
Suspect verbal/psychological violence by female to male	2	2
Suspect physical violence by female to male	11	11
Suspect adversity/distress for children caused by domestic violence	24	25
Suspect physical violence by male towards female	22	23
Suspect verbal/psychological violence by male towards female	12	13
Previous domestic violence	3	3
Suspect violence by male towards female through control of money and her movements	3	3
Suspect depression/mental ill-health of female caused by violence by male	7	7
Suspect physical injuries on female caused by violence by male	9	9
Evidence of domestic violence/ unspecified	3	3

Note: The % total adds up to more than 100 due to multiple responses.

the totality of 'coercive control' which characterises domestic violence (Stark and Flitcraft, 1996). Ninety-four per cent of children in substantiated domestic violence cases were a daughter or a son of the abuser. A neighbour, grandparent and uncle were also cited as the suspect abuser in domestic violence cases.

Emotional abuse was substantiated for 110 children, 57 per cent of whom were male. Twenty-six per cent were under five years of age, 33 per cent between six and ten and 41 per cent were over eleven. Emotional abuse was cited in 51 of the substantiated protection cases, 10 of which involved emotional abuse alone. This again means that emotional abuse typically occurred in combination with other problems. In 61 per cent of cases where emotional abuse was substantiated, domestic violence was also substantiated. The correlation is evident in that witness to domestic violence was the most prevalent form of emotional abuse, experienced by 26 per cent of children for whom emotional abuse was substantiated (see Table 3.12). Nine per cent of children witnessed alcohol abuse. The mother and/or father of children were responsible for the child care problem in 90 per cent of substantiated emotional abuse cases. A wide range of other behaviours emerged under the heading emotional abuse in social workers' accounts, such as inappropriate discipline, child not allowed to have friends or outside interests, and inconsistent parenting.

Risk assessment, history of health board involvement and prevalence of multi-problem substantiated cases

A clear profile emerges of the nature of substantiated abuse being worked with in Irish child protection. While detailing the nature of abuse has much to contribute to our understanding of the issues, the true nature of the experiences of these children and families and the complexity of intervention work only becomes apparent when it is realised that in almost half of the cases (44 per cent) more than one form of abuse was substantiated. In 56 per cent of substantiated child protection cases only one form of abuse was substantiated. Neglect dominated this category with 41 cases (see Figure 3.2), where more than one form of abuse was present. Domestic violence and emotional abuse was the most common dual combination, with neglect, emotional abuse and domestic violence also prominent (see Figure 3.2).

The evidence of multiple child care and abuse problems in a wide range of combinations in almost half of substantiated protection cases has many implications for the provision of an effective short and long-term response. In addition, a great deal of protection work is focused on children and families who are well known to the system as well as experiencing multiple problems. In

Table 3.12 The nature of emotional abuse in substantiated cases

Nature of abuse	%	No. (children)
Witness to violence	26	29
Witness to alcohol abuse	9	10
Parent(s) verbally abusive	8	9
Impact of marital breakdown/separation	8	9
Child not knowing mother's plan	5	6
Caught between parents' access dispute	6	7
Conflict between mother and boyfriend	4	4
Parent(s) mental health	4	4
Witness to arguing between parents	2	3
Children used by father to get at mother	2	3
Child exposed to drugs and adult behaviour	2	3
Mother rejecting child	2	3
Very poor emotional environment	12	3

Note: The % total adds up to more than 100 due to multiple responses.

Buckley, Skehill and O'Sullivan's study of a sample of South-Eastern Health Board cases, 'almost half' of the families had previous contact with social work services (Buckley et al., 1997). In the current study, a massive 70 per cent (n=91) of substantiated child protection cases were previously known to the MWHB.[4] It is probable that a history of health board involvement increases the likelihood of cases being substantiated in the first place. Children and families who are well known to the services and experiencing multiple problems receive a great deal of attention from the child protection services; 62 per cent of the 286 referrals in the community care sample were previously known to the social work teams and 56 per cent (105) of these cases were actually open at the time of the referral included in this study. Health board involvement prior to the referral varied from less than one week (two cases) to over six years. The most frequent length of involvement was between two and six years, occurring in 28 per cent, while 16 per cent were known for over six years.

A crucial finding is that only a relatively small number of cases investigated involve actual harms to the bodies of children in the form of sexual and physical abuse. Of the 845 children in the community care sample, actual physical injuries were substantiated for just eleven children aged between one month and fifteen years, in the form of visible bruises/burns/other evidence of physical abuse. In relation to sexual abuse, actual injuries were

Figure 3.2 Combinations of substantiated abuse

Nature of abuse	No. of cases
Neglect only	41
Sexual abuse only	15
Emotional abuse only	10
Domestic violence only	8
Physical abuse only	3
Domestic violence & emotional abuse	14
Neglect & emotional abuse	9
Neglect, emotional abuse & domestic violence	8
Neglect & domestic violence	6
Physical abuse & neglect	3
Physical abuse, emotional abuse & domestic violence	2
Physical abuse, neglect & emotional abuse	2
Physical abuse & domestic violence	2
Physical abuse, emotional abuse & sexual abuse	2
Physical abuse & emotional abuse	1
Physical abuse & sexual abuse	1
Physical abuse, neglect & domestic violence	1
Neglect & child suffering from effect of previous sexual abuse	1
Emotional abuse & self abuse	1
Emotional abuse & child was perpetrator of sexual abuse	1
Sexual abuse & domestic violence	1
Child was perpetrator of sexual abuse	1

substantiated for nineteen children aged between three and seventeen. This does not include the impact of other significant traumas on those children who suffered abuse which was not *directly* injurious to their bodies. The bulk of the work involves neglect, poor parenting and resources, domestic violence, and the legacy of emotional trauma these failings and other developmental, behavioural and relationship problems bring for children. This finding is similar to those of research carried out in other jurisdictions (especially Australia and the UK) and has been used to argue that child care systems are dominated by protection approaches which essentially 'police' families on the margins of society (lone mothers, ethnic minorities, the very poor) without supporting vulnerable parents (Thorpe, 1994; Parton, Thorpe and Wattam, 1997). Yet this interpretation is flawed because the emphasis is on the relatively small numbers of cases involving actual direct harms to children in a way that de-contextualises those forms of 'lone' abuse from their histories and milieus. The present study illustrates how abuse viewed on its own tells only part of the story. The combinations of problems in substantiated cases and the context within which they are known—such as the very high level of previous involvement—are crucial to understanding the nature of risk and child protection work.

This is further borne out by the fact that, despite the relatively low numbers of actual injuries to children, when asked to assess the level of risk, social workers placed 54 per cent of children in substantiated child protection cases at very high risk or high risk. Some 46 per cent were identified as low, very low, or no risk.[5] Extensive analysis of high risk cases and the response of the child protection system to them is provided throughout this book. At this point it is sufficient to conclude the chapter with a few brief illustrations of the typical kinds of high-risk scenarios involved, as a way of contextualising the key argument. Case 62 involved five children (seven-, six-, and five-year-old girls and four- and two-year-old boys) at 'very high risk' who were in care for a year, and returned home six months previously on a supervision order. Domestic violence and neglect were substantiated in the referral made by both a PHN and a speech therapist raising concern over the parent's failure to bring children to appointments. As a result the supervision order was deemed ineffective and a care order was recommended. In Case 273 a psychiatric social worker referred a three-day old female baby who was considered to be at very high risk of neglect as 'mother was unable to cope', the referral being made prior to the birth of the child. The child was placed in voluntary foster care at birth due to the mother's psychiatric condition: 'delusions, schizophrenia and psychosis'. Case 173 involved a thirteen-year-old girl who was living at home with her mother under a care order. Neglect was substantiated as the child went to the UK without the knowledge or consent of the health board, and she was considered to be at very high risk.

Neglect and domestic violence were substantiated in Case 249; the sixteen-year-old male concerned had been previously in care and some siblings were still in care. The referral was made by a social worker who was informed by the youth service that the boy 'has caused thousands of pounds worth of damage to youth service property during angry outbursts'. The boy was viewed 'as one of those for whom there are no resources in the area', although deemed at 'very high risk' as he was living in a derelict flat with an alcoholic father who had been physically and psychologically violent to the boy's mother. Neglect was substantiated in Case 172, referred by the gardaí, concerning a twelve-year-old male 'out of control—26 charges were against him'. Exhibiting severe behavioural outbursts he was considered to be at very high risk; residential care was offered as an alternative to detention. Emotional abuse of two boys, aged twelve and six, was substantiated in Case 242, which was referred by a social worker. There was a long history of social work involvement due to domestic violence and alcohol abuse. The investigating social worker witnessed 'consistent frenzied roaring in communication between mother/children' and the 'twelve-year-old slapped his mother when taunted by her' during a home visit.

Conclusion

This chapter has shown that the MWHB is taking its responsibilities to investigate child care and abuse cases very seriously. Relatively few referrals are filtered out of the system without an investigation of some kind. While some concerns have been expressed about the manner and legitimacy of all these decisions, a high level of accountability is evident. This extends in most cases to an acceptably swift and timely response to referrals, although the propensity of the CPN process to slow responses requires attention. Important gaps in practice have been shown in that a significant proportion of children in investigated cases are not being seen or interviewed. Gaps in engaging parents/abusers need to be addressed, particularly professionals' avoidance of men/fathers.

A clear profile has been presented of the children, parents and types of families/households coming to the attention of health boards and of the nature of child abuse and other problems being substantiated and worked with. The striking pattern is of families of lone parents—mostly women— living on social welfare in disadvantaged circumstances. Relatively small numbers of abused children suffer actual injuries and harms, although the nature of the physical and sexual abuse and serious neglect (including failure to thrive) experienced by some children is of grave concern. The vast majority of 'abused' children are living in households with parents and other carers who appear to lack the skills and resources to parent well enough and are struggling to cope, often in the context of domestic violence, poverty, alcohol and relationship problems. Some are more wilfully neglectful than others, most commonly through leaving the children unattended or inadequately cared for. A core population of high risk cases has been identified, characterised by multiple child care problems and extensive histories of health board involvement, which absorb the bulk of the system's energy in responding to children at risk. These are cases with a broad range of problems, many of which are not classic 'abuse' in the sense of direct injuries and harms to children, including control and relationship problems and a high presence of domestic violence which significantly weakens mothers' capacities to provide good enough parenting. The response of the health board and child care system to these cases will be examined in Chapter 4.

Notes

[1] The professionals involved in checking out the 16 cases were: PHN, money advisor, teacher, gardaí, speech therapist, psychologist, school principal, CWO, worker in women's refuge.

[2] Family support workers, the gardaí and PHNs also accompanied the social worker in nine, six and six cases respectively. Other professionals who also accompanied social workers were residential staff member, health board counsellor, school chaplain, psychiatric nurse, county council social worker, social worker for the homeless, youth service and a psychiatric social worker.

[3] The miscellaneous category includes: children taken to pub late at night, child brought to UK without health board consent, overcrowding, child not allowed to develop emotionally, child bullied, poor speech, mother a suspected prostitute, child brought to cliffs and shown where people commit suicide.

[4] The most common reasons for previous health board involvement were: child abuse/child protection concerns in 36 per cent (n=32) of cases, and family support type intervention in 33 per cent (n=30). Domestic violence featured in 29 per cent.

[5] In Case 34, for example, although domestic violence was substantiated the child was considered to be at 'no risk' as the parents were now separated and 'child is out of situation'.

4 Managing Child Abuse Cases and Defining Child Protection and Welfare Work

We have seen that health boards typically put a huge amount of effort into processing and responding to referrals. To explore how appropriate this work is we focus in this chapter on management structures and their relationship to child care and protection practices. The Child Protection Notificatiion (CPN) system is the key mechanism through which child abuse cases are formally managed and we examine how it operates in practice and assess the degree to which it helps to promote safe practice. This leads us to question the entire function of the CPN system and, more generally, the role of management in child protection and welfare.

Constructing the child protection system

The underdevelopment of management roles (McGuinness, 1993) has been identified by child abuse inquiries as a key dimension of system failure in child protection. As a result, child protection is becoming much more managed and bureaucratised. At the time of this study, a senior administrative post of director of child care services had been established in the MWHB. Team leaders had been appointed to social work teams to supplement senior social workers and the new posts of child care managers were about to be filled. Since 1999 child care managers have formally replaced the director of community care (DCC) and carry key managerial responsibility for child care and protection (DoH, 1999). From around 1993, the health board had tightened the administration of cases through the creation of the CPN system. Until then the system was managed—in theory—by the directors of community care (DCC) under the 1987 Child Abuse Guidelines. However, interviews with senior staff show that in practice senior social workers managed the system on a day-to-day basis. As one senior social worker put it:

'Well, anxiety was around social workers carrying the can for everything and in particular I was carrying it and I was the only one with an overview of what was going on, or didn't have an overview as the case may be. A lot of times I didn't have it because it depended entirely on my memory. And if I remembered there were issues around and brought them up they were brought up but if I didn't they weren't. There was no system of looking on a regular basis at what was there and it was the luck of God that we didn't have a sort of Kilkenny Incest Inquiry because we had many good people on the ground, I mean people on the ground who had been there a long time.'

In this senior's experience, prior to the 1990s, the absence of a formal system for processing and reviewing cases extended to a lack of case conferences. The CPN system introduced discipline as well as shared responsibility in a context of heightened awareness of risks to children and professionals from system failures:

'The anxiety was there and the social workers were carrying total responsibility for everything and that if it blew up we'd all be in trouble. So there was a motivation there to be seen to spread the responsibility a bit. When I came here the nurses were stopping their social workers on the corridor and saying you know I am worried about so and so and are you dealing with it and the social workers were going around carrying all responsibilities.'

This situation began to change in 1993 when CPN committees composed of multi-disciplinary teams of managers from social work, psychology, public health nursing, AMOs and DCCs were set up. They meet weekly. Referrals in prescribed categories only—physical abuse, sexual abuse, emotional abuse and neglect—should be notified to the committees through the completion of a CPN form immediately a case enters the system (DoH, 1987). Cases falling outside the prescribed categories are not meant to be notified, although we have found that the definition of 'abuse' is far from clear, and is routinely negotiated and socially constructed. Our findings suggest that child protection and disciplines such as social work have become more managed and bureaucratised (see Howe, 1992). This is perceived by managers such as senior social workers as a necessary and positive step:

'It's the only multi-disciplinary meeting we have on a regular basis. And because we have . . . a senior clinical psychologist, she sits there and she will volunteer to take on cases, she will volunteer to provide therapy. It has broadened out the responsibility for child protection enormously. We now have a multi-disciplinary group taking responsibility.'

At its best, the system helps workers to feel secure in the knowledge that managers are accountable and share responsibility. Yet considerable flexibility is evident in the way management and the CPN system operate. At the time of the study, a CPN committee followed up and monitored cases in only one of the three community care teams after the initial guidance when referrals had been entered into the system. The real managerial power to shape intervention and responsibility lies at the front line with team leaders and senior social workers. At its worst, the CPN system has little real impact on how work is done and simply creates an illusion of accountability. On the other hand, even as an administrative procedure it has a lot of symbolic power in helping workers to feel safe. It does have some influence on *what* gets done by deciding whether referrals fall inside the prescribed categories of abuse, and in allocating services to families. But even this is often debatable or negotiable because there is little operational guidance for social workers or CPN committees, or consensus, on what constitutes a 'child protection concern'. This is especially true with respect to neglect cases. There is considerable confusion about what the CPN system is actually for, about the correct timing of notifications, whether all referrals are meant to be notified, irrespective of the content, or only 'child protection concerns' and, in that event, what is a 'child protection concern'? The importance of the latter question cannot be overemphasised: as we have seen, a wide range of child care concerns are referred to the health board for which the definition of 'child protection' has to be achieved through case-building and the investigative process. A critical analysis of management issues and the CPN system are inseparable, then, from the construction of cases and the work done; of constructing what child protection and welfare *are*.

Thus, in looking at management procedures, we need to ask, what is it that is being managed? The findings suggest that, in terms of promoting safe practice, what an investigation is deemed to be about, and the direction of the intervention, are as important as the fact that investigation and notification take place at all. In the majority of cases, as Chapters 2 and 3 have shown, referrals contain more than one presenting problem. To put it simply, if sexual abuse is suspected, for example, to what extent are those specific concerns taken up, or is the case defined in another way and approached differently? There are two inter-related issues here, identified and discussed earlier: the definition of the referral/case as 'abuse' or 'child care problem' and the type of 'protection' or 'welfare' practice response. In essence, 'abuse' cases are typically thought to require a 'protection' response, implying an authoritative, 'forensic' concern with gathering evidence of parental or extra-familial deviance. Child care 'problems', meanwhile, are said to require a more 'gentle touch' (DHSS, 1995), a 'welfare' response where the emphasis is on family support and a less intrusive, partnership approach.

However, there are at least two potential problems with this approach: 'abuse' cases may receive a welfare response and 'problem' cases a protection response. Most of the research and literature have emphasised the latter, arguing that child protection has come to dominate child care systems in a manner which prematurely defines children 'in need' as children 'in danger', leaving families with little more than an investigation into child abuse and their needs for support unmet. However, little attention has been given to the dangers involved in 'abuse' cases receiving a welfare-type response. This is probably due to the impact of inquiries on child care systems and the relentless criticisms of child protection systems over the past twenty-five years in the UK, and in Ireland over the past decade. As this book shows, notions of 'child protection' now dominate Irish discourse on what is regarded as legitimate work but the legitimacy of this depends on what can be carried out within the child abuse frame and what happens to those child welfare cases which cannot be accommodated within a classic protection framework.

Patterns of CPNs

Sixty-six per cent (n=177) of all referrals to the community care teams were notified to the DCCs under the Child Abuse Guidelines (1987). These are the referrals that become officially defined as child 'abuse' through the CPN system. This does not mean, however, that non-notified cases (34 per cent) were screened out of the system. High proportions of them were in fact worked with, albeit outside the official child protection procedure. The status of these cases is, to put it mildly, ambiguous and the need to clarify this is a key recommendation of this book.

Table 4.1 Main presenting problem in referrals notified to the DCC

Main presenting problem	%	No.
Physical abuse	11	19
Neglect	27	48
Emotional abuse	5	8
Sexual abuse	16	29
Domestic violence	4	7
Behaviour/control	18	32
Financial/housing	3	5
Parental difficulties	11	19
Parental addiction	4	7
Miscellaneous	2	3
Total	*100**	*177*

*Note: The % total does not add exactly to 100 due to rounding.

Neglect was the problem most commonly notified, accounting for 27 per cent of notifications, followed by child behaviour/control at 18 per cent and sexual abuse at 16 per cent, while 11 per cent were physical abuse (see Table 4.1). Sixty-three per cent of referrals notified to the CPN system were primarily defined as protection, while 37 per cent were defined as welfare. Of the 66 referrals defined as welfare and notified to the CPN system, 53 per cent (n=35) also cited a protection concern. Hence 82 per cent of referrals notified to the CPN system had a concern with child protection and were technically legitimate notifications. The 18 per cent with child welfare problems only were—from a management perspective—technically inappropriate because they did not fit the 'abuse' categories. They reflect the practice, discussed below, of those social workers who notify everything, irrespective of what the referral is. Forty per cent (n=69) of notified referrals were notified before the social work investigation took place—which is technically the correct procedure as laid down by the 1987 Guidelines (DoH, 1987)—while 56 per cent (n=99) were notified after the social work investigation. The logic and consequences of these decisions are analysed below. The Guidelines allow for referrals to be notified by any community care professional, not just social work, and 4 per cent (n=7) were notified by a professional other than community care social workers.

Table 4.2 Main presenting problem in referrals not notified to the DCC

Main presenting problem	%	No.
Physical abuse	3	3
Neglect	8	7
Emotional abuse	2	2
Sexual abuse	4	4
Domestic violence	13	12
Behaviour/control	27	25
Financial/housing	4	4
Parental difficulties	27	25
Parental addiction	3	3
Miscellaneous	8	7
Total	*100**	*92*

*Note: The % total does not add exactly to 100% due to rounding.

Twenty-seven per cent of cases not notified to the DCC were defined as behaviour/control, another 27 per cent as parental difficulties, sexual abuse 4 per cent and physical abuse 3 per cent. Domestic violence (12 cases) was the most significant category of non-notified case involving potential abuse (see Table 4.2). Some 33 per cent (n=30) of non-notified referrals were primarily concerned with protection. The consequences can be seen in the way cases processed through the CPN system are more likely to get long-term treatment/support services, although the variation is quite small: 53 per cent of notified cases were provided with a home-based treatment/support service compared with 46 per cent of non-notified cases; 16 per cent (n=28) of notified cases with a community treatment/support service compared with 10 per cent of non-notified; 38 per cent (n=67) of notified cases with a clinically based service, compared with 35 per cent of non-notified; while 20 per cent (n=35) of notified cases received a care based treatment/support services compared with 12 per cent (n=11) of non-notified cases. This trend is due in part to the very practical reason that senior professionals who attend these meetings often agree to ensure that frontline staff take on referred cases for longer-term work. As a senior social worker put it, using psychology as an example, 'the senior clinical psychologist [will say] look give me that case, I'll get one of my people to look at that'. Thus, the CPN system is more than a simple administrative procedure which can make the system safer for frontline workers. It is a key 'framing device' in case construction, service provision and intervention outcomes.

A more meaningful examination of the figures shows that 86 per cent (n=19) of all physical abuse referrals were notified. Those not notified included non-investigated referrals (Cases 130, 279) and Case 194 which involved an allegation by a seventeen-year-old girl that her foster parents had 'beaten' her, but the abuse was not substantiated. The referral involved a false allegation and a misunderstanding. Eighty-eight per cent of all neglect referrals were notified. Case 44 typifies non-notified referrals. It was referred by a separated father who had access twice weekly and was concerned that the children were not being looked after properly—abuse was not substantiated. Case 67 was referred by a social worker: the child had been removed from care in England and 'hidden among relatives'. Abuse was substantiated in the form of 'neglect due to poor parenting capacity', although it was not notified (see also Cases 80, 127, 178, 266 and 272).

Two of the eleven emotional abuse referrals were not notified. Case 41 was referred by a school citing emotional abuse by the father and was substantiated. Case 43, referred by the mother, concerned an access dispute between the father and herself, and emotional abuse was substantiated. Of the 36 cases where sexual abuse was defined as the main presenting problem, 90 per cent (n=32) were notified, four (10 per cent) were not. Of the latter, Case 37 was referred by gardaí, to whom a fifteen-year-old made an allegation of rape. The case was submitted to the DPP and although a prosecution took place, the DCC was not notified. The case was not previously known to the health board. Case 120 was referred by a mother because of concerns about her six-year-old son's sexualised talk, and non-contact sexual abuse was substantiated. Case 131 was referred by a neighbour concerned that the father was sexually abusing his three-year-old daughter, and emotional abuse and domestic violence were substantiated. Case 321 was referred by a mother, 'very anxious, child has been sexually abused, case has been dealt with, child was seen by CSA assessment unit, mother in need of additional support, not coping with disclosure'. Abuse was not substantiated, the child was referred for a CSA assessment, but was not notified to the CPN system.

Of the 19 domestic violence referrals to community care only seven were notified. Case 289, for instance, was referred by a hospital paediatric department alleging that a thirteen-year-old girl was terrified of her father due to his violent behaviour, and domestic violence was substantiated. Case 16 was also typical. It was referred by a hospital A&E department because the mother was badly beaten up by her partner while she had a one-year-old child in her arms. Severe domestic violence was substantiated, and yet the case was not processed through the CPN system (see also Cases 13, 28, 58, 59, 64, 65, 199, 288, 317). The clear pattern is that, with the exception of domestic violence, the majority of non-notified physical, sexual and emotional abuse cases were unsubstantiated. Substantiated domestic violence cases, on the other hand, are seriously 'under-managed' by the official child protection system. This is despite the fact that many cases include very serious violence and risks to women and children. Case 16 exemplifies this. It was referred by a radiologist in an A&E department. As the social worker wrote:

> 'mother beaten up badly by partner. She ended up in emergency unit of hospital. Severe bruising all over body and eyes. Also severe swelling of right eye which mother showed me later. Baby in mother's arms while she was beaten by partner. Baby with mother and other three children being taken care of by neighbour. Mother persuaded by hospital to contact gardaí and make statement and hospital contacted me.'

It 'was the worst beating [radiologist] had seen for a long time'. Domestic violence was substantiated for the five children, aged between one and twelve years. The family had been known to the health board for two years before the referral because of concern about possible physical abuse by the mother, who was under a lot of stress and was a suspected victim of domestic violence. A case conference was held and the case was viewed as high risk. The mother was viewed as a reluctant client: 'she didn't want us to have anything to do with her'. A new social worker experienced difficulties establishing a relationship with the family. The case was not active at the time of the new referral. The day after the new referral, the social worker accompanied the mother to court to obtain a protection order which was granted. She felt the mother carried through with this action because the baby had been in her arms when she was assaulted. However, having obtained the protection order she failed to attend court for her barring order application. The social worker did not liaise with the gardaí in relation to the mother's non-attendance at court because she doubted any good would come of it: 'I have learnt over the years that, well it's a bit like you can bring a horse to water but you can't make him drink'.

Following the mother's non-attendance in court her partner returned to the family home. Nine months later the mother referred herself. She rang *'in a state'*, informing the social worker that her partner was 'going mad' with violence. He had threatened to kill her if she contacted the gardaí, who she claimed were failing to respond to her calls any more because she always withdrew complaints through fear. The social worker again did not liaise with the gardaí, having 'let it slip'. On the ensuing home visit the social worker asked the children about the violent incident and they confirmed that their father had hit their mother and she was very frightened. When the social worker again brought up the option of a barring order, the mother became unco-operative and hard to see again: 'but that's her history and she's one of these people I'm not so sure she can live without him, not so much maybe without him but like she has to be in some kind of relationship and any relationship she's going to have with a man, there's going to be a certain amount of violence in it'.

Neither of these very serious referrals was processed through the CPN system because 'it was already in the system . . . the case was already there so I wouldn't have sent in anything in great detail'. Moreover, 'if I haven't the information I can't send in a CPN'. The social worker stressed that the senior social worker was made aware of the referrals and, although the case was not officially notified, the social worker thought that the senior brought it to the attention of the CPN meeting but was unclear of the details. The gardaí were notified of the initial referral by the mother prior to social work involvement, interviewed the suspect abuser and issued the protection order. They also 'warned' him again when the mother did not follow through with the barring order. The outcome was confirmed abuse with the case remaining open but inactive one year on from the initial referral: 'at the end of the day no matter how serious the situation is if you can't get some kind of co-operation even if it's only minimum you can do nothing with that family'.

This case was not, in fact, actually 'in the system' in any meaningful sense and only the social work team was accountable for it. The level of risk to the mother and children justified notification, especially in the light of the previous high risk definition. The social worker's attitude is less surprising when it is considered that, as Chapter 3 showed, a decision not to directly investigate a domestic violence referral was taken by a CPN meeting. Guidelines need to specify domestic violence as a notifiable form of child abuse. When referrals of previously known cases, or cases perceived to be 'already in the system' should be notified, also needs to be clarified. Where the level of risk to the children and/or their primary carer justifies it, all referrals should be notified whether they are previously known or not.

Social workers' operational perspectives on the CPN system

The vast majority of the area social workers interviewed saw the CPN system as 'supportive'. Positive views of the system ranged from 'supportive' to 'accountable' and a 'safeguard'. One went so far as to describe the CPN system as 'absolutely brilliant'. Negative views were expressed by a significant minority of social workers, ranging from 'a hindrance', to 'constraining' and 'automated'. As one expressed it, 'I don't actually know what the point of it is . . . just a cover for themselves, just covering themselves'. For another, it's 'just extra paperwork . . . it's off-loading in a sense'. Those social workers expressing negative views also expressed a positive view in all but one instance: 'I'm not so sure that the new systems in place are of any great benefit to the people that I'm working with. [It's] basically protection for the system and the whole process of notifications and CPN meetings, they're of no benefit to me or the people I'm working with'. She cited an example where she did not receive information that had come through the CPN committee on a family she had been working with for two months. For her, if communication breaks down, 'the system will find a scapegoat and that will usually be one of us at the end of the line'.

The provision of greater 'safety' in their practice by the CPN system loomed large in social workers' narratives: 'basically I think they are looking to keep the system safe in case something blows up . . . it is to secure that everything possible has been done', although it does not 'make work easier with the clients, the direct work'. As one social worker exemplified this view: 'I suppose it promotes safer practice. Things are documented, there's an obligation on you to make a formal referral, so things don't get lost. I think it makes practice safer and it's more structured, there are steps to follow and they're very clearly laid out'. And another said: 'you send in your CPN and there is a relief there, you have dealt with it appropriately'. The administrative function of the process was regarded as central by many social workers, where 'primarily it's just a way of collating new referrals and for statistical purposes . . . just another kind of supervision'.

Decisions are made at the local level on which referrals are to be submitted to the CPN meeting. Cases are usually discussed at the team meeting and 'our manager would advise us to send in a CPN and they probably decide then whether it will go further or what action is going to be taken and we get a letter back with instructions'. How cases are framed as child protection and how decisions are made to notify them are crucial issues. Views on best practice in the timing of CPNs varied significantly but two main approaches emerged. The first approach is to complete the initial investigation before submitting a CPN. Even though it was technically in breach of the Child Abuse Guidelines, this was the most common response, occurring in 56 per cent of the notified cases. Its perceived benefits are that it allows for as 'full a picture as possible', in that 'the decision then of the panel would be much more informed at that point than just throwing in something. The initial referral information can be quite different from the investigation'. This makes it possible to establish whether or not there is something to warrant a child protection concern before it is notified to the CPN system.

The second approach is to submit a CPN as soon as a referral is received 'to get it into the system' and then complete an initial investigation. This happened in 40 per cent of notified cases.[1] While this is procedurally valid, too often it related not just to notifications of suspected child abuse, but to all manner of child care problems. Some social workers resolve the dilemma of categorisation by notifying everything, thereby leaving the decision to the CPN meeting: 'what I would do is put everything in a CPN and then it comes back, if it's an inappropriate referral they'll clarify it then'. In some such cases, social workers wait for CPN direction before investigating, but invariably seek the support of a team leader or team meeting to legitimate the delay. As Chapter 3 showed, referrals notified to the CPN system generally received a slower response that those that were not. In others, social workers don't wait but go ahead and investigate as there 'are some cases where you can't wait for the process, where you go to management'. The role of the team leader 'to get immediate direction' is always viewed as central.

Here, CPN directions, when they do arrive, end up 'just sort of reiterating the route to go'. In many cases the directions made by the CPN meeting have already been completed by the time the social worker receives the response. This can cause frustration because it is the next step that needs attention: 'You'd get an instruction what to do but I've done that so what do you do next then?' It is 'quite annoying' to have 'already done something and you're being told to do it again'.

What, then, is the status of the CPN meeting response? How directive is it and what discretion do front-line professionals have to challenge the response? Views of the CPN meeting varied from 'open to alternative routes if you like or alternative suggestions . . . there would be times when the social worker would be asked for their own opinions and what advise should happen', to 'I don't think it's really encouraged [to work imaginatively within the health board] you know like there's certain types of responses you'll get'. One social worker—who is able to attend the CPN meeting and offer input—regarded the CPN system as 'flexible, it's not rigid'. At the other extreme a social worker felt that 'there's not a bit of scope and there are kind of procedures that are followed . . . I think you can become almost working in an automated sense'. On balance, most viewed the CPN direction as 'instructions', but they can be queried if the individual social worker does not agree. Examples of queries included questioning whether a case conference was warranted and the team leader deciding instead to hold a network meeting. In another case the CPN recommended a return home visit to 'a very aggressive client' who had almost hit the social workers when they did the investigation: 'we didn't feel it was appropriate to go back and provoke him further and we didn't do it'. Here, the system was described as 'flexible' because the area social worker can query the direction with immediate management: 'if you don't agree with those recommendations you can object and go back to your manager and say I don't agree'. Generally, though, the CPN meetings' directions are regarded as 'appropriate'. Indeed, some social workers had never disagreed with a CPN direction: 'I've never come across it I find them beneficial more than anything else'. A more ambiguous response is where 'if it reinforces what you've done already and points you in the right direction, then it is supportive, [but] if you don't agree with the response it can be constraining'.

More negatively, some CPN directions were seen as 'away with the fairies' and as 'stating the obvious . . . some of them I was going to do anyway'. Another point of tension is where social workers receive advice from their immediate manager that differs from that of the CPN meeting. When this happens, most approach the team leader to discuss the most appropriate form of action. One social worker viewed the CPN system as 'another form of supervision'. On occasion, social workers view a case as 'more serious' than the CPN meeting, for example, when the case can only be classified as emotional abuse and the CPN meeting is not as concerned as the social worker. Accountability and anxiety about possible system failure still drive practice to the extent that, as one social worker put it, 'you notify everything because you never know what's coming back or what might be significant later on'. However, there are signs that the system is calming down some-what and becoming more reflective after an initial rush to notify, partly out of lack of clarity about what should be notified and partly out of defensive practice arising from professional anxiety regarding system failures. 'Before we used to fill in everything, absolutely everything, but now we are just beginning to discuss what requires notification'. There is a need to 'tighten up' on what gets notified and this raises the very important question of what criteria should determine what gets notified, and when.

While social workers felt that the 'seriousness' of the case determines whether a CPN is submitted, in practice they were aware of the pressure to notify cases 'for statistical purposes, because if we don't and the figures aren't right, although we may be dealing with more cases if we don't pass them on they don't count—it might take resources away from us'. The taking and acceptance of referrals is now meant to be governed by what is and is not suspected child abuse: 'We're not meant to take referrals that aren't a type, that don't have a child protection element'. Social workers are acutely aware of how hard it is 'to decipher or decide what is a child protection concern'. This is borne out by significant variations in what gets notified. For in-stance, very similar neglect referrals were notified by some social workers and not by others. In Case 237, a ten- and seven-year-old were left unat-tended while their parents were in the pub and the social worker notified the case. In Case 304, with similar concerns for ten-, eight-, three- and two-year-old children, the social worker did not notify the case.

Although social workers have influence over decision-making, they feel they have much less influence 'in terms of policy and procedures or what the definition of abuse is'. Thus, 'managers would have more say in relation to the definition of child abuse and policies and what we deal with and what we don't deal with and what you see as a child protection concern and if they don't it won't be taken as one'. The power of the CPN system is significant in deciding what work should *not* get done: 'If it isn't seen as a child protection concern, and you're told not to become involved in this case, well then you don't become involved in the case'. Most felt that family support work was in danger of being squeezed out of child protection. The categories of child abuse on the CPN form were seen as limiting in that the broad range of concerns about real risks to children may not fit into the categories of physical, sexual, neglect or emotional abuse. As one social worker exemplified it:

'Children could be potentially homeless and it depends on whether you define that as a child protection concern or not, if they haven't got a roof over their heads then it is a child protection concern to a degree but it doesn't come under physical, sexual or emotional abuse. The ones under those categories get the most attention, because there has to be a cut-off line in the work as well, because you will find people calling with inappropriate things that we really have no control over, but sometimes it depends on people's opinions on what a child protection concern is, there are definitional issues there'.

This ignores the non-notified work that *does* go on outside the official child protection system. Social workers conveyed a powerful sense of struggling to have the necessary preventive family support work recognised. There is a feeling that this work is not legitimate, almost that it has to be done in a furtive, clandestine way. The official child protection system excludes some children in need who do not fit its categories, as social workers are told to close cases because there are 'no child protection concerns'. But this does not mean that no work goes on with such cases. What it does mean is that these cases have a perilous identity within the system because they are largely invisible behind the weight of official effort put into child abuse. As one social worker captured it:

'I think it's a reality we're going to have to address and say this is our caseload and the CPN means nothing, because they're very small in our caseload, and that the real work is done in the support element. Having been at a team meeting the other day, now they only want very few referrals, CPNs have to be child protection, but all the other support, all the other concerns other than child protection which is support, family support and really it's what the balance of our work is about, the majority of our work is about, but the emphasis and the energy and all the statistics goes on child protection.

There is at least some awareness that the decision as to what is notified is subjective and depends on what the social worker and the CPN committees regard as 'abuse'. The cases most at risk are those of practitioners who notify all referrals before doing an investigation. When social workers carry out initial assessments before deciding whether to notify, they leave themselves more discretion to provide services to non-abuse cases. But this also makes them vulnerable, without the security that being accountable and entering a case 'into the system' brings. There is a real tension within the system because of the way community care social work has effectively been reconstituted to deal with child protection while at the same time teams receive information and accept referrals applying to a broader range of problems. The criticial issue becomes what constitutes a child protection concern and how elastic is the notion of 'child protection'? There is now an organisational imperative to fit as much as possible into abuse and 'protection' categories so that as much as possible of the work going on is recognised at administrative level. Management tacitly acknowledges that cases that don't fit the strict definition of 'abuse' are being worked with but there is real concern about what happens, administratively and practically, to those cases which don't really fit the 'abuse' definition. How accountable are professionals supposed to be for non-notified cases? Understandably, many are afraid of the consequences of not notifying should something be judged, with hindsight, to have 'gone wrong'.

There are two main implications for notification and management practices. First, there is a need for stricter operational definitions of child abuse. Very similar referrals are notified by some social workers and not by others. At a minimum, the criteria for notifying to the CPN system should be harm or identifiable risks to children, especially where neglect is concerned. On the other hand, the findings suggest that a broader notion of 'a child protection concern' is operating in the Irish system, one which includes a concept of child welfare and family support work, and this needs to be respected. The critical issue is the type of service which follows from particular case designations and whether it meets needs. The notion of child protection in itself is unobjectionable so long as it can deliver what children and carers need. Second, the decision to notify or not is better taken *after* the social work team has assessed the case and assessed precisely what kind of service the child and family needs, child protection or family support.[2] Management structures need to be developed for family support/therapeutic work so that accountability for non-notified cases can be institutionalised. It must be emphasised that a decision not to notify does not necessarily mean that the case is not serious: it means rather that a different case categorisation is appropriate. The health boards—and the Department of Health—need to design categories capable of reflecting the child welfare work that is going on; this is an essential part of its development as a service.

Child protection and domestic violence: the role of the women's refuge

As noted earlier, 33 referrals were made to MWHB social workers based in a women's refuge during the sampling period April–June 1996. It was necessary to analyse these referrals separately because responses to them were quite different to the referrals made to community care. This is not an in-depth analysis of the operation of the refuge (for which, see Ruddle and O'Connor, 1992) but rather a much more limited evaluation of some aspects of the role of the health board social work service within the refuge setting, specifically of how it relates to the broader child protection system. Clearly, although employed by and accountable to the health board, the refuge social work response was governed by the organisational philosophy of the refuge. Cases that, in the community care setting might be considered protection are, for the most part, not processed through the official protection system by social workers meant to be operating under the Child Abuse Guidelines (1987; 1995). This is a key finding and further reflects the marginal position domestic violence has within formal child care and protection work, although, paradoxically, as this book shows, a huge amount of work is done with domestic violence.

As with the community care sample, there was a high rate of investigation of refuge cases, with almost 80 per cent (n=26) directly investigated by refuge social workers. In some, intervention took the form of telephone contact with advice given. In only one refuge case was the mother not directly interviewed or spoken to by telephone, and this case was referred by the refuge social worker to an area social worker in another health board region due to child protection concerns. Mothers were key referral agents to the refuge, making 70 per cent (n=23). The remaining ten were made by professional sources, although in eight of these the mother informed the referral agent of the violence. Hence in only two refuge cases was the mother not instrumental in the referral. A limited amount of formal multi-disciplinary work in terms of child protection went on in these refuge cases. One of the 33 refuge cases was processed through the formal DCC notification system and in four cases the gardaí were notified by the refuge. None of the refuge sample cases received a conference.

A range of child protection and child care difficulties, other than domestic violence, were brought to the attention of refuge staff in over half (18) of the referrals. Emotional abuse was cited in eighteen cases, physical abuse in three, neglect in two and sexual abuse in one. Parents under stress were cited in seven cases, as were parent/child relationship problems. Alcohol abuse by a father was noted in six cases and by the mother in two. Parental mental health problems featured in six, and financial/housing problems in nine. In 32 of the 33 refuge cases the concern expressed in the referral was substantiated on investigation. The other case was transferred to another health board due to child protection concerns. Domestic violence was substantiated in all 32 cases, for 79 children. Verbal/psychological violence by the male partner to the mother was the most frequent form of domestic violence substantiated, in 89 per cent of cases, followed by physical violence against women, in 76 per cent There was evidence of adversity/distress for children in 70 per cent of the cases. Twelve referrals resulted in an admission to the refuge, the length of admission ranging from overnight to several weeks. These twelve women and their children received treatment/support services from the social worker. Legal aid became involved in four cases and both a clinical psychologist and a psychotherapy group in one. Of the non-resident referrals, in one case the mother engaged with adult psychology. In nine cases civil legal proceedings were instituted. Barring/protection orders were granted to five women, and a safety order to one. In two cases judicial separations were applied for and in one case a custody/access dispute was settled by the courts. Care proceedings were not a feature of the refuge cases with no children being taken into voluntary or statutory care. The follow-up of all refuge cases one year on revealed that three were re-referred to the refuge, a much lower re-referral rate than the community care sample (see Chapter 9). The majority of refuge cases were closed at the end of the research period, with three remaining open and active. Research interviews included some with women who had entered the refuge, either during the research period or, more often, before it. These demonstrated that such services constitute a vital resource in woman and child protection, especially given the high prevalence of domestic violence in the cases coming to the attention of the board.

When child protection becomes child welfare: Case study 234

Case study 234 provides further evidence of the function and ambiguous role of the CPN system in case management especially with respect to defining cases and framing investigations and intervention in terms of child protection or child welfare. This account is based on interviews with the health board social worker, home help organiser (HHO) and public health nurse (PHN) and reading of the case file. The psychologist who worked with the family was not available for interview, and neither were the father, mother and children. The referral centred on suspected sexual abuse and neglect, with anxieties that the two teenage girls and their younger brother were getting out of their father's control. The case was initially defined and processed through the CPN system as sexual abuse and physical neglect. However, it was investigated and responded to essentially in terms of child welfare with the concerns of sexual abuse and, to a lesser extent, physical neglect, becoming peripheral. While family support work of some significance went on—one view was that this avoided the children going into care—this re-framing of the case and relegation of child protection issues to minor significance, resulted in a failure to investigate possible sexual abuse.

The referral and responses to it

The case was referred by a home help organiser, expressing concern for two girls aged thirteen and eleven and an eight-year-old boy.

> Mother has [left family home/living abroad]. Father has [health problems] Children receive little supervision and are out of control. Father sleeps with daughter and home help discovered used condoms in his bedroom (case file).

Neglect, sexual abuse and children out of parental control were cited as child care problems, with neglect considered by the social worker to be the most important. The family was known to the social work department prior to the referral due to the mother leaving the family home rather than due to concerns about the standard of child care. A network check was made with the PHN and HHO and this yielded no additional information. The social worker also contacted the family's GP on the same day as the referral; the doctor's view was that 'the [children] are out of control and that their father is incapable of minding them, he [GP] felt that the [children] should be in care' (case file). A professional network meeting involving the investigating social worker, PHN, superintendent PHN and HHO was held six days after the referral. It appears from the case file that the main concern of the meeting was that the children were frequently left unsupervised and that there was 'poor control in the [family] household and the [children] are left to their own devices'. Concern was also expressed at the meeting about the sleeping arrangements and that the home helps had found used condoms in the father's bedroom on three occasions. The consensus was that the father 'requires much help and support in his task of parenting' (case file). The decision was that the HHO would talk to extended family members and 'inform them of concerns and ascertain what kind of practical support they can offer'. The most appropriate form of action was viewed as referral of the two children for psychological services, and the social worker was to organise 'counselling' for the two children.

Although the focus of the network meeting was on the father's coping capacity and parenting in terms of supervision the social worker remarked in interview that, 'at the end of the meeting we weren't completely confident that there wasn't abuse happening, people just felt that this might be the proper course of action at that point'. Thus it was decided that the issue of the used condoms would not immediately be brought up with the father. The social worker did contact the child sexual abuse assessment team who 'would want something more weighty before proceeding with investigations and they would have agreed that the priorities with the children would have been around counselling around this time . . . It was just felt in this instance that it was rather vague'. Thus, a child sexual abuse validation assessment did not take place, as

> 'At the time, following the network meeting it was decided that concerns for the [children] were the issues around loss in relation to their mother [separating from their father] and in relation to their dad, who [was unwell] and we felt that they had established a relationship with somebody like the psychologist, then perhaps they would come to light. But really we couldn't have initiated a CSA assessment on the grounds of finding used condoms in a dustbin. The real concern there was the issues around loss for the [children] counselling around it and we investigated in as much as we could the allegations around CSA.'

However, the child sexual abuse issue was always going to remain 'vague' as long as no one did in fact directly investigate it. The father was inter-viewed 20 days after the referral by the social worker. The concern about the condoms and sleeping arrangements were not put to him. Nor were the children themselves even asked about it. The father was unwell and needed a great deal of support and part of the social worker's rationale was the fear that if the concerns were put to him, this might jeopardise the relationship he had with the home helps, especially since it was the home help who had referred the concerns to social work. Once again, further to the discussion in Chapter 2, as far as the social worker was concerned, the way in which the referral was made affected the response in that the home helps were 'not being clear themselves and not sure if they wanted to make a referral and wanting to remain anonymous and retracting, not retracting completely, but withdrawing'. This 'made it difficult because they weren't really prepared to stand over it.' The father was soon expressing concerns to the social worker about his eldest daughter's behaviour. The social worker spoke to the chil-dren and observed: '[they were] very pleasant and chatty, acknowledged dif-ficulty of home situation with [father] unwell and agreed to attend counsel-ling' (case file).

DCC notification

The case was notified to the DCC prior to the investigation; both sexual abuse and physical neglect were cited on the CPN form. The concerns of the HHO in relation to the condoms and the girls sleeping with their father and of the PHN that the children were not being 'adequately supervised' were outlined. The CPN meeting advised 'that the child protection concerns (e.g. alleged lack of supervision of the girls, allegation that they sleep with father, condoms on bedroom floor etc.) be discussed directly with the father. Reassess situation on completion of same. Review case with [area team leader]' (case file). The directions from the CPN meeting were not carried out; the social worker noted on the case file that, following a meeting with a line manager, it was decided that should she meet with the father regarding the condoms that he might become 'hostile' to the home help. The home help contact was extremely important and 'should they be refused entry the situation will inevitably deteriorate for the [children]'. As far as child sexual abuse was concerned it was noted on file that there was 'no evidence, only condoms which could mean anything, should CSA exist this hopefully will be picked up during counselling which is imminent'.

The social worker felt that 'it was difficult because what we decided to do was different to what came back from the CPN meeting'. She identified as a problem the way the definition of a case at the referral stage may change after the notification. A case may be notified as sexual abuse, for instance, prior to the investigation, but the presenting problem may change after the initial investigation. In the official statistics this case was categorised as sexual abuse but it is clear that on investigation the social worker did not classify it as such. Not complying with the CPN instruction 'was difficult' but the social worker felt justified on the basis that the case had been reframed as a non-child protection issue.

Gardaí notification

The gardaí were officially notified of the referral and were contacted by the social worker as part of a network check. A juvenile liaison officer (JLO) was contacted to ascertain whether he was aware of the family, because 'the allegations were that [child] was on the streets at night out of control, drinking, taking drugs and I just wanted to establish the truth of that'. Having made contact with the JLO purely to gather any relevant information, to the social worker's great surprise and annoyance, the JLO went to the child's school, called her out of class and interviewed her. The social worker felt that the JLO dealt with the case 'in a very inappropriate way. I wasn't comfortable with him going to the school and calling her out of class . . . and interrogating her'. The JLO 'cautioned' the child and it was never the social worker's intention that the case should be handled that way.

The PHN's role

The PHN discussed sleeping arrangements with the father and supervision of the children, and felt that the 'situation is stable'. But the used condoms were not discussed with him. The social worker met with the PHN again three months after the initial referral, by which time 'situation has deteriorated, no supervision again and children left to their own devices again' (case file). The PHN expressed concern about the eldest child's out of control behaviour. The PHN felt that there was 'not great liaison' between social work and public health. She 'gave an odd call to support family', which was now the limit of her role in the case. Following the network meeting the PHN called to the house more frequently and at the time of the interview was calling 'every few months'. Her relationship with the father was good and did 'not change' following the report of the condoms in his room; however, she became 'more observant'. She expressed dissatisfaction with the level of feedback from social workers and was unaware of the outcome of the case.

Home help organiser (HHO)

The social worker met with the HHO approximately three weeks after the professional network meeting. The HHO had by this time spoken to the father regarding the dangers of leaving the children unsupervised and the extended family 'have agreed to ensure adequate supervision of the [children]' (case file). The main concerns were with the eldest girl's behaviour 'not talking to anybody, she was just totally withdrawn into herself and keeping into her room and locking the door and keeping everybody out and we had concerns that she was out at night and going down town'. The HHO worried about the used condoms and had no hesitation referring the case to the social worker. However, the HHO's main concern was the father's need for support in parenting his children: 'we wanted somebody maybe that [child] could build up a relationship with that she could be comfortable with, talk with, because she must have had massive problems with her father's illness and her mother [gone]'. With respect to the condoms the HHO was of the view that 'that was sorted out by the social worker she [home help] didn't know where these [condoms] were coming from and she just came and spoke to me about it and I spoke t!o the social worker and they sorted it out'.

The home help 'monitors' the situation as the father is unable to cope and provides practical support. The HHO felt that 'only for she being there that family would be in care'. The father was parenting the two children 'to the best of his ability'; however, support systems were necessary. The HHO had very little contact with the social worker. The HHO expressed concern to the social worker that '[child] may become promiscuous and pregnant'. The HHO and social worker discussed the issue of the condoms five months after the referral and it was noted on the case file that 'home helps feel that [father] is not sexually abusing the girls but perhaps using condoms for masturbation, [father] does not have a girlfriend'.

According to the social worker the psychologist accepted the referral and 'established a pretty good rapport with the children'. She worked with them for six months and had contact with the father 'and supported him also'. The psychologist informed the social worker that the father 'presented as very caring and very concerned re girls and effects of mother's loss and his illness on children'. The social worker outlined the concerns re the condoms and 'advised [psychologist] that primary concern for girls seems to be in relation to losses they have experienced'.

The outcome of the case

The issue of the used condoms was eventually brought to the father's attention almost seven months after the initial referral. The psychologist expressed fears to the social worker that the father might be informed of the issue by family members as they were aware of the situation, and 'advised' the social worker to formally 'review the case'. A further network meeting was held between the social worker, psychologist, senior social worker and HHO and it was decided that the father should be approached about the condoms. This was 'because the HHO who was involved with the family had told people about the condoms, and had discussed what we had discussed at the network meeting with family members, so it seemed that everybody knew about the condoms except [father]!, it was discussed with him then'. The social worker expressed reluctance to the senior about discussing the reports of condoms with the father because it 'could cause [father] embarrassment, consequently it may impinge negatively on our working relationship', and 'it would be very difficult for him if he had to work with me afterwards.'

Another social worker in fact interviewed the father who 'appeared embarrassed' and said that the condoms 'were for his own personal use' (case file). This social worker assured the father that 'there was no difficulty' with his explanation. But quite what his explanation *did* mean is not clear to us as researchers. The case returned to the first social worker. Overall, the social work response to the father was made up of four interviews and focused on his coping capacity and parenting in terms of supervision of the children. A very cautious, non-investigative approach was always adopted by the first social worker, avoiding confronting the father about the 'used condoms'. She was aware of this, commenting that, 'it was rather unusual in terms of distinguishing whether or if there was a concern in relation to sexual abuse'. For her the big issues in the case were the children's loss due to their mother leaving the family and the father's health problems. The children's possible sexual abuse and the fact that the father sometimes sleeps with them were ultimately framed in terms of their need for 'comfort': 'it was a comfort thing and in relation to the condoms he would have stated that they were just for his own use'.

The social worker felt that the clinical psychologist did a lot of work with the children and saw the distinction between the social work role and the psychologist's as 'we have a kind of policing role and all of that whereas they have a very clear role and they just offer support or offer counselling in some supportive way'. The concern about the possibility of sexual abuse was not discussed with the girls: 'We didn't broach it with either of them because there was really nothing in relation to it, all it was, was evidence, circumstantial evidence, condoms in a bin and the children sleeping with the dad. Without his consent we couldn't have interviewed the children in relation to it'. Yet no one asked him for his consent. The social worker felt the children had a 'very good relationship' with their father who was 'very concerned about them'. He was open to intervention, 'very co-operative' and welcomed 'help' and 'support' for the children in terms of the psychological service. Thus, the more co-operative the parents, the more difficulty professionals have in viewing their moral character in a negative light.

The social worker described his/her inter-agency role as follows: 'Where there isn't a child protection concern you can withdraw sometimes you mightn't have active involvement, your involvement is just holding the case and just linking in with the psychologist'. In essence, the social worker acted as a case manager. The increase in home help services and the referral to psychology constituted the 'support systems' put in place, with the social worker liaising with and co-ordinating the services with little or no direct involvement with the children. The case was closed after eleven months as 'child and family needs met by other service' (research forms). The outcome of the case was unconfirmed abuse but confirmed child welfare problems. However, because the psychologist was involved 'it kind of provided some sort of safeguard so I felt happier knowing that was there'. The case was closed when the psychologist, who had worked extensively with the family, pulled out, with the proviso 'that if they felt that they needed further counselling or any other help to come back to us'.

Framing and managing child protection and child welfare work

Case 234 raises many issues about safe practice in child protection and welfare work. At the referral stage the concerns for the children were both child protection (sexual abuse/neglect) and child welfare (child out of control/poor supervision/vulnerable parent). The case was initially defined as protection and was officially categorised as such in terms of a notification to both the DCC and the gardaí. However, even before the investigation—and certainly during it—the case was re-categorised by the expert system at a network meeting and the social work response was framed in light of this re-categorisation. Social work intervention in this case could not be described as investigative. The social worker herself characterised it as to 'offer practical support' to the father and the children through increased home help and psychological services.

Undoubtedly, the mother's absence and the father's poor health, with the losses this meant for the children, required a humane response to the family. Indeed, the supportive work was in many respects exemplary child welfare practice, ultimately preventing the children from entering care and making some contribution to their healing. Yet, from the point of view of safe child protection practice, the lack of a direct investigation of the child sexual abuse concerns until seven months after the referral—and even then, a minimalistic approach was taken—cannot be viewed as anything other than highly questionable. When it is known that a man is sleeping with his teenage daughters and that there are used condoms in the bedroom, failure to investigate the matter with him is not justified because of fears that he might refuse to allow access to the support services who brought the matter to light. The reluctance of the social worker and other professionals to raise the sexual abuse concerns directly with the father appears to be avoidance. Their discomfort with talking to the man about his sexual practices is striking and suggests the need for sexuality awareness training for social workers and other professionals. This avoidance, together with a desire to preserve the man's privacy and dignity, and a particular ideology of child welfare practice with its emphasis on benevolence and support, lies at the core of the (non)response.

According to the senior social worker, 'medical advice' influenced the

decision not to take an investigative approach; however, there was no reference to such advice in the case file, nor did it emerge with any clarity during
the research interviews. Thus, while management's view was that the case
worker felt discomfort, it was the medical advice rather than the discomfort
that was the underlying rationale for not directly discussing the issue with
the father. This suggests a belief that a satisfactory balance was struck between the medical advice regarding the father's health and the monitoring of
the children through the increased involvement with the home help service.
Hence from management's perspective a balance was struck in terms of safe
child protection practices and a regard for the father's health. The key question is: where are the children and their welfare in all of this? Crucially,
viewed within child welfare work terms, the practice in this case should not
be seen as bad social work practice. The case exemplifies the shifting role
from social worker to case manager, a pattern that is clear in this study. This
is especially so in situations defined as involving few or no child protection
concerns. The fewer the perceived protection issues, the more limited the
direct social work role. As we have and shall see, the key work is done by
other professionals. The case also demonstrates some of the difficulties of
achieving effective child welfare and protection through inter-agency work.
Apart from the psychologist, the one professional who made a proactive
effort to engage with the children was the JLO. Ironically—in the light of the
child sexual abuse concerns—the garda took the child out of school to 'cau-
tion' her about her alleged unruly behaviour in an (unintended) and inappropriate manner, while the issue of possible sexual abuse was not raised with
her or her sister or brother at all.

This demonstrates the need for greater understanding by all professionals
of each other's roles and of the meaning of practices such as 'notification' to
the gardaí, and the CPN system. Viewed within the wider context of debates
about the balance of child welfare and protections systems, there is a para-
dox here. Despite the opportunities to define the case as child protection,
the professional community put huge effort into framing the intervention in
terms of the perceived needs of the children and father for support. The
control and supervision problems with respect to the girls were defined as neglect, but responded to in a most supportive, non abuse-focused way. But while
the child welfare work was quite effectively achieved, the specifics of the child
protection task were not. Professionals need to be aware of the dangers of seeing
the requirement for a welfare-oriented response as incompatible with direct
confrontation of a parent about child abuse concerns and attempts to engage
with the children directly about them. This does not mean that the child welfare

orientation is necessarily invalid. It depends on the outcome of the investigation into the risks to the children; where there are concerns about possible abuse, those have to be at the forefront of the investigation.

The limitations of the CPN system are apparent in the lack of accountability: while the social worker sought support from her line manager and accounted for decisions very well in writing in the case file, she did not have to account to the CPN system when directions were not carried out. Indeed, the very status of such CPN committee instructions (directives?) is unclear, as is the structural relationship between them and frontline managers such as team leaders and senior social workers. At present the CPN system is neither a relatively simple administrative system for collating data on child abuse referrals—notwithstanding the difficulties of deciding what they are—nor a meaningful actor in the management of cases. As this chapter has shown, what it does well is enable workers to feel safe, in the knowledge that at least some attempt is being made to track the (relevant) referrals entering the system and that frontline workers are not solely accountable for child protection. But where the system fails most is in the lack of any systematic mechanism for feedback and on-going monitoring of the progress of notified cases. While this chapter has shown that some social workers do go back to the CPN committee and challenge its directives, Case 234 illustrates the gaps in practice and management that arise because there is no formal procedure or obligation to review cases.

The structural relationship between CPN committees and frontline managers, such as team leaders and senior social workers, especially the extent of frontline managers' power and autonomy, need to be clarified. At the time of this study, only one of the three community care areas had a system in place for on-going monitoring of notified cases, where social workers were expected to provide reports on the progress of cases. This system was perceived as the most supportive by both the managers and social workers and was often intensively used. In one very high risk case (138), which will be discussed in detail in Chapter 6, no fewer than thirteen CPN communications were completed by the social worker in a two-year period (1995–7). This is meaningful involvement by senior management. There was recognition, however, that this more advanced system was in danger of being overwhelmed by the weight of work involved in administering new referrals and managing existing cases. This is especially so when CPN committees are being asked to decide what is a legitimate notification (a 'child protection concern').

We have recommended a more rational 'tightened up' system where *what* should be notified, and *when,* is clarified. We have also argued that the status and fate of cases not notifiable within the terms of the child protection categories need to be clarified, and the kind of welfare work that does go on accounted for, valued and developed. Managerialism and bureaucratisation are a double-edged sword. On the one hand, they promote efficiency and help workers to feel safe. On the other, they threaten to remove workers' discretion and introduce organisational criteria (such as child abuse categories) which threaten to determine the responses to children and families as opposed to a more authentic inclusive definition of client need. It is crucial that this tension be worked with creatively. Thus, while this chapter has argued that more, not fewer, management structures and practices are required to promote child safety and welfare, this must not be at the cost of eroding the discretion practitioners need to reach sound professional judgements and practice creatively.

Note

[1] The remaining 4 per cent (n=7) were notified directly to the CPN system by professionals other than social workers.

2 The 1999 Child Abuse Guidelines, which appeared after the fieldwork for this study was completed, broadly follow the wisdom of this approach and clarify that the correct timing of official notification of cases to the CPN system (in the person of the child care manager) should be *after* an initial investigation of the case (DoH, 1999).

5 Child Protection, the Law and Safe Practice

With the advent of the Child Care Act 1991, the law has come to play a much greater role in child welfare and protection. The relationship between child protection and social regulation has also been tightened through the 1995 *Guidelines on the Notification and Reporting of Suspected Cases of Child Abuse* and the 1999 Child Abuse Guidelines (DoH 1995) which require health boards and gardaí to notify all suspected cases of abuse to each other. In this chapter we consider aspects of the use of the criminal and civil law and the role of the gardaí in child care and protection. We begin by analysing how these procedures are operating in practice. We then consider those cases that end in legal action, focusing particularly on responses to sexual abuse. Two main issues are identified: the impact of legalism on child welfare systems, and the use of the law as an effective resource for promoting the safety and welfare of children.

Some 17 per cent of the children in this study received a care-based service during the study period (1996–7). However, as we shall see, the number of legal care proceedings is very small, and criminal prosecutions are very rare. Voluntary receptions into care are by far the most common outcome, although a proportion of those cases involved the threat of legal action should the parent(s) not consent to voluntary care. The impact of the law on safe practice is shown to be multi-dimensional: while in some cases it empowers and provides a means for victims/survivors to regain control and achieve justice, in others it de-skills and frustrates justice, safety and healing.

Health board–gardaí notification procedures

Fifty-four per cent (n=153) of all referrals to the three community care teams were formally notified under the 1995 guidelines. Of these, 24 were notified by gardaí to the health board and when these are excluded, 49 per cent (n=129) of all referrals were formally notified by the health board to the gardaí; the analysis focuses on these notifications. Fifty-two per cent were notified to the gardaí before the social work investigation. Forty-six per cent were notified after the investigation. No social work investigation took place in 2 per cent. Neglect was the most prevalent form of child abuse notified, accounting for 20 per cent, while 19 per cent were sexual abuse. The com-

Table 5.1 **Main presenting problem in referrals notified to the gardaí**

Main presenting problem	%	No.
Physical abuse	11	14
Neglect	20	26
Emotional abuse	3	4
Sexual abuse	19	25
Domestic violence	6	8
Child behaviour/control	18	23
Financial/housing	2	2
Parental difficulties	16	21
Parental addiction	2	3
Miscellaneous	2	3
Total	*100**	*129*

**Note:* The % total does not add to 100 due to rounding.

bined abuse categories of neglect, sexual abuse, physical abuse, emotional abuse and domestic violence accounted for 60 per cent (see Table 5.1), leaving a surprising 40 per cent (n=52) in the category child welfare. Of these 52 cases, 27 were also concerned with child protection. Hence 25 referrals notified to the gardaí were not defined as suspected cases of child abuse, although 'danger' to the child was perceived, while some of these children were 'out of control' and/or offending.

Section 3.1 of the 1995 guidelines states that 'where a Health Board suspects that a child has been physically or sexually abused . . . the Gardaí must be formally notified immediately' (DoH, 1995, p. 8). Hence, all physical and sexual abuse *should* have been notified to the gardaí in accordance with the guidelines. However, 22 per cent (n=7) of sexual abuse and 34 per cent (n=7) of physical abuse referrals were not notified to the gardaí and are technically in breach of the guidelines. The guidelines also cover suspected 'wilful' neglect, and 50 per cent (n=26) of all neglect referrals were not notified to gardaí. This should *not* be taken to mean that these cases were necessarily in breach of the guidelines as they include both wilful and unintentional neglect. As the guidelines do not define what constitutes 'wilful' neglect it is impossible to determine the extent to which they were technically breached here. In relation to emotional abuse, which includes 'exposure to ongoing domestic violence' and unintentional neglect, 'it is not envisaged that the Health Boards should routinely notify [such cases] . . . since the circumstances of such cases may not involve law enforcement issues' (DoH, 1995,

p. 8). This suggests a problem with the guidelines, rather than with health board practice: it is strange to exclude law enforcement from emotional abuse arising from domestic violence. In any event, the notification of emotional abuse, including domestic violence and unintentional neglect, is deemed to be discretionary.

Reasons for non-notification to gardaí

Over twenty categories of explanation emerged for not notifying referrals to the gardaí, the most frequent—in 58 per cent of cases—being 'circumstances of referral did not warrant such action', followed by 'insufficient evidence of abuse', in ten cases (see Figure 5.1; information was missing for 37 cases).

Figure 5.1 Reasons for non-notification of referrals by health board to gardaí
> Social work investigation not complete
> Joint decision between ASW and residential staff not to do so
> Awaiting decision from DCC
> Attempted but calls not returned/garda on border duty
> Mother co-operating—no need for gardaí
> Case transferred
> Will be notified when case conference is called
> Are already aware of family
> No child protection concerns
> Insufficient available data
> Could not be categorised as per guidelines
> Other professional monitoring situation
> No abuse took place in MWHB area
> Abusers in group housing scheme/avoid tension amongst residents
> Gardaí not notified of emotional abuse cases

With respect to physical abuse, Case 4 concerned a fifteen-year-old girl living with her grandmother and uncle. The child disclosed to a social worker that 'her granny hits her with a poker and makes her share a bed with her' (research forms). 'Child hit but no visible evidence of marks' was substantiated. A formal notification to the gardaí was not made as 'no physical evidence to suggest that a crime has been committed' (see also Cases 130, 153). Case 309 was referred by a school as 'child presented in school with bruising to upper thighs, school is concerned for possible NAI . . . child is on FPO [Fit Person Order][1] at home', and was not notified to gardaí as 'not confirmed abuse'. With respect to sexual abuse, in Case 39 the mother of three children aged six, five and two, expressed concern about 'simulated sexual activity' and 'inappropriate sexual talk'. It was not notified to the gardaí as 'did not warrant it'. Case 131 was referred by a neighbour, 'concerned that father is sexually abusing child . . . neighbour heard child screaming "get off me daddy" at 2.30 am'. Emotional abuse was substantiated and the social worker deemed garda notification 'not necessary' (see also Case 143) (research forms). Of the neglect referrals, Case 3 was referred by an anonymous source claiming that 'mother is very scatty and child presents as being very nervous, she also said that believes mother is on drugs.' 'Child neglected due to poor parenting capacity' was substantiated. The child was deemed as at high risk. Despite this, the gardaí were not notified as 'there was no suggestion from the referrer that child was physically or morally at risk'. Case 102 was referred by the grandmother who 'claims that her daughter held one of the children over the balcony . . . there is ongoing friction between grandmother and daughter'. The gardaí were not notified as 'referral did not justify such action' (see also Case 44). Case 162 was referred by a PHN because 'parents had refused to have children vaccinated and failed to attend clinic appointments . . . children [ten-, five- and three-year-old boys] are not attending school'. The gardaí were not notified as 'PHN elicited a response from mother and is monitoring situation through home visits and clinics' (research forms).

Decision-making in health board–gardaí notification practices

Of the 129 referrals not notified to gardaí, 44 per cent were processed through the CPN system. Hence in 56 per cent of referrals not notified to gardaí, the decision was made at the frontline. To facilitate a deeper understanding of how the notification guidelines actually operate in practice, and to establish whether a threshold between garda notification and non-notification exists, referrals were examined in relation to the following key criteria: (a) age of the child(ren); (b) referral source; (c) case substantiation; (d) previous health board involvement and (e) abusive incident.

(a) *Age of the child(ren)*

A total of 365 children were cited in the 129 referrals notified to gardaí, 3 per cent of whom were under one year of age, 36 per cent aged between one and six, with 15 per cent between seven and nine years, 17 per cent between ten and twelve, and 29 per cent between thirteen and eighteen. Fifty-four per cent of children were under ten. In referrals not notified to gardaí, 4 per cent (n=14) of the children were under one year of age, 33 per cent were between one and six, 15 per cent were between seven and nine, 18 per cent between ten and twelve and 39 per cent between thirteen and eighteen. Fifty-two per cent were under ten. Thus, in general terms, the age of the child(ren) does not have an impact on garda notification.

(b) *Referral source*

Forty per cent (n=52) of notified referrals were by a lay source, 60 per cent by a professional, while 38 per cent (n=49) of non-notified referrals were referred by a lay source and 62 per cent by professionals. In total, 52 per cent (n=55) of all lay referrals were notified to gardaí and 48 per cent (n=77) of all professional referrals. The source of the referral does not appear to affect the decision to notify the gardaí.

(c) *Notification and substantiation*

Of the 160 cases substantiated as a result of the social work investigation, 58 per cent (n=93) were formally notified (this includes 16 notified by gardaí). Sexual abuse was substantiated in 21 per cent (n=16) of substantiated cases notified by the health board to the gardaí, neglect was the substantiated concern in 42 per cent, emotional abuse also featured strongly, substantiated in 26 per cent of such cases. Eleven per cent (n=2) of all substantiated sexual abuse cases were not notified to gardaí. 'Suspect non-penetrative sex' and 'suspect non-contact sexual abuse' were the forms of abuse in question, one involving children behaving sexually inappropriately for their age, 'the circumstances of the referral did not justify gardaí notification'. The second case involved inappropriate sexual conversation and 'social work investigation not completed' was the reason outlined for non-notification. Fifty-four per cent of unsubstantiated cases were notified to gardaí, only 4 per cent fewer than substantiated cases. This suggests that substantiation is not a factor affecting notification of gardaí.

Some 88 per cent of substantiated sexual abuse cases were notified compared with 86 per cent unsubstantiated. Over half—51 per cent—of substantiated neglect cases were notified compared with 60 per cent unsubstantiated, while 70 per cent of substantiated physical abuse cases were notified, compared with 67 per cent unsubstantiated. Over half—52 per cent—of substantiated domestic violence cases were notified. Whether or not a case was substantiated did not affect notification to the gardaí, in accordance with the notification guideline which states that a health board 'must not await confirmation of such abuse' (DoH, 1995, p. 8).

(d) *Previous health board involvement*

Previous health board involvement did not generally affect notification. Sixty-six per cent (n=85) of referrals notified to gardaí were previously known compared with 60 per cent (n=76) of non-notified referrals.

(e) *The abusive incident*

The nature of the 'abusive incident' in the referral does affect notification. Of the fourteen referrals primarily defined as domestic violence and referred by a non-garda source, eight were notified to gardaí. In none of the six non-notified cases, was a specific incident of violence cited. The referral could then be described as less serious in terms of potential harm to the children. For example, in Case 248, 'mother and child spent some time in [the women's refuge]', was the only reference to domestic violence in the referral. Similarly, in Case 317 a concern regarding domestic violence was raised but no specific violent incident was cited. By contrast, in six of the eight notified domestic violence referrals, a violent incident was cited. For example, Case 169 included 'mother living in family home with her father and two brothers, a brother came home drunk and began hitting her. He then snatched the baby and took him through the fields. Baby was found with uncle by gardaí three hours later' (see also Cases 16, 64). Notified domestic violence referrals were also more likely to directly express concern for the children than those not notified. In Case 165, 'children are exposed to violence, fear that may result in NAI to children because of impatience with them'. Case 288 expressed concern for the children as they were present in the home during a domestic violence incident (see also Case 59). In only one non-notified domestic violence referral were the children mentioned in the referral. In five the referral was not processed through the CPN system, hence in only one was the decision not to notify the gardaí made by the CPN meeting.

The decision to notify sexual abuse referrals is also affected by the reported 'abusive incident'. All sexual referrals citing a specific allegation and naming an alleged perpetrator were notified to the gardaí. The details in non-notified sexual abuse referrals could be interpreted as 'less serious', in terms of harm to the child or absence of an alleged perpetrator. In two, the child was exhibiting inappropriate sexual behaviour and conversation and an alleged adult perpetrator was not identified. Another non-notified sexual abuse referral was concerned with previously confirmed sexual abuse and the child and family's need for more support in overcoming it. In only one non-notified sexual abuse referral was a specific allegation made and a perpetrator named: a neighbour reported hearing a child screaming in the middle of the night and was concerned that the father was sexually abusing the child; on investigation the allegation was not confirmed.

By contrast, in non-notified physical abuse referrals distinct patterns concerning the abusive incident are not evident. In three, the child made a specific disclosure, in another three reference was made to bruises, marks or burns, while in one case the father made an allegation that the mother's new partner had hit his child. All the non-notified physical abuse cases made specific references to suspected harm to children and there appears to be no justifiable reason for not notifying the gardaí.

The notification or not of neglect appears to be ad hoc, and is problematic on a number of levels. The key questions are: what constitutes 'wilful' neglect, when is neglect 'unintentional' and who makes that decision? The analysis of all the neglect referrals suggests six broad categories: home alone/ children unsupervised; poor housing/material conditions; poor hygiene/neglect of physical needs; alcohol abuse; non-attendance at school; and neglect of the child's medical needs. No patterns were found suggesting that particular forms of neglect are more likely to be notified, with no significant differences apparent between notified and non-notified neglect cases. Good examples of the discretionary nature of notification can be seen in Cases 239 and 304, both of which involved children reported to be left unattended and unsupervised. One case was notified to the gardaí (239), and a joint social worker/gardaí investigation ensued; the parents were warned about their behaviour and consequences should it recur; in Case 304 the gardaí were not notified. The social worker made a home visit alone and 'the concerns were presented to parents'. In both cases the children named in the referral were under ten years of age.

Neither the age of the child, referral source, case substantiation or previous health board involvement appear to have any major impact on the decision to notify a case. However in some categories of child protection, the actual abusive incident does affect the decision. In domestic violence referrals, specific references to concern for the child(ren) appear to have a bearing, similarly in sexual abuse cases the more 'serious' sexual abuse cases were invariably notified. However, the severity of the reported incident in physical abuse cases does not appear to affect the decision to notify, with ostensibly quite serious referrals escaping the notification system.

Garda investigations

Twenty-six per cent of all these notifications—34 cases—were actually investigated by the gardaí. Sexual abuse was the main presenting problem in nine, five were physical abuse, five neglect, one emotional abuse, six domestic violence, six behaviour/control, and two parental difficulty. Thirty-two of these cases were substantiated, with sexual abuse being the most common form investigated, followed by domestic violence and emotional abuse, and then neglect (see Table 5.2). Thirty garda-investigated cases involved substantiated child abuse, while four were solely concerned with children's behaviour/control problems, in particular, criminal offences and substance abuse. Some of the substantiated child abuse cases were investigated, not simply for possible criminal offences by parent(s), but also to ensure immediate child protection. Cases 237 and 239, for instance, involved reports that the parents were leaving children under ten years of age unattended very late at night. The gardaí were notified by the health board, made a home visit and found the children alone and unsupervised. Both the social worker and garda made another home visit to interview the parents. The garda 'cautioned' the parents and 'warned them of the consequences' should they leave the children unattended again. Eleven joint social work/gardaí investigations took place, involving physical abuse in two cases, neglect in two, emotional abuse in one, domestic violence in one, sexual abuse in three, and two were primarily defined as behaviour/control problems. In seven of the cases investigated by gardaí, care proceedings were taken by the health board and the children placed in residential or foster care.

Table 5.2 Nature of substantiated abuse in cases investigated by gardaí

Nature of substantiated abuse	%	No.
Sexual abuse	39	13
Neglect	26	9
Emotional abuse	32	10
Parents under stress	3	1
Physical abuse	19	6
Domestic violence	32	10
Homelessness	3	1
Substantiated abuse	3	1

Note: The % total adds to more than 100 due to multiple responses.

A wide range of reasons were given by social workers for the non-occurrence of a garda investigation in notified cases (see Figure 5.2). The most common was 'investigation unwarranted', followed by 'lack of evidence' and 'no statement'. One clear implication is that, in most respects, garda investigation is a discretionary act based on negotiated outcomes between the gardaí and the health board.

Figure 5.2 Reason for no garda investigation in notified cases

Reason	No. of cases
Investigation unwarranted	16
No statement	5
Lack of evidence	5
Notification purposes only	3
Monitoring of situation	4
Case supervised by other professionals	2
Prior investigation to this referral	1
Co-operation with social workers	2
No criminal offences	2
Child now in place of safety	1
Awaiting assessment	2
Suspect abuser out of country	2
Parents requested not to do so	2
Child involved in JLO	2
Child did not want to proceed	1
Child unable to disclose name of alleged abuser	1
Witness withdrew allegations	1
Awaiting case conference decision	1
Decision not to investigate at this stage	1
Child now over 18	1
Awaiting medical examination outcome	1
Family moved from area	1
Child protection meeting decision	1
Parents were hospitalised	1
Gardaí contacted to establish facts	1
Parents would not allow interview of young child	1
Concern in referral had no foundation	1
Abuses whereabouts unknown	1
Good professional support	1
Missing information	20

Legal proceedings and outcomes

Legal proceedings took place during the initial sampling period (April–June 1996) in 15 per cent (n=44) of the 286 community care referrals. This analysis concentrates on legal proceedings during this period only, while longer-term legal responses in terms of care proceedings are examined in Chapter 7.

Legal proceedings in these 44 cases took civil and criminal forms. Voluntary receptions into care were by far the most common 'legal' route in civil cases (see Figure 5.3). At the end of the initial sampling period 13 per cent (n=36) of all referrals resulted in children entering care. A total of 53 children were involved, 6 per cent of all the children named in referrals. The reasons for reception into care were defined in 19 per cent (n=7) of cases as neglect, in 14 per cent (n=5) as physical abuse, 3 per cent (n=1) sexual abuse, 3 per cent (n=1) domestic violence, 31 per cent (n=11) behaviour/control problems, 19 per cent (n=7) parental difficulties, 6 per cent (n=2) parental addiction, and 3 per cent (n=1) financial/housing. This again demonstrates the range of protection and welfare concerns which characterises child care practice.

Figure 5.3 Legal proceedings

Legal action	No. of cases
Emergency care order only	1
Care order only	2
Supervision order only	2
Barring/protection order only	7
Voluntary reception into care only	21
Custody and access only	3
Hague convention	1
Court proceedings against abuser	1
Child was already under care order	1
Emergency care order, interim care order and voluntary reception into care	1
Emergency care order, interim care order and care order	1
Court proceedings against abuser & voluntary reception into care	1
Emergency care order, care order and barring/protection order	1
Emergency care order and care order	1

Foster care was the most common immediate placement for these children. In 13 of the 36 cases children experienced a change in placement during the sampling period. This included some who returned home, while others went into other forms of care. Eighty-six per cent (n=31) of the cases of children entering care had been previously involved with the health board. Seventy per cent (n=11) were notified to the gardaí and 77 per cent were notified to the CPN system.

Three cases resulted in a file being sent to the Director of Public Prosecutions (DPP) during the sampling period April–June 1996, one file was in the process of completion, and a further two cases were sent to the DPP during the follow-up period July 1996–July 1997. In five of these six cases a prosecution followed, in four the hearing was still pending at the end of the study period, in three of which the prosecution related to sexual abuse, and in one to domestic violence. In one case the defendant, a mother, was found guilty of not sending her fourteen-year-old son to school for four years. The child was placed in an assessment centre and subsequently in foster care. The DPP made the decision not to prosecute in one sexual abuse case. The social worker was not told and remained unaware that a prosecution was not going to take place four months after the DPP decision was made known to gardaí. This is contrary to the 1995 notification guidelines which recommend that both the health board and gardaí 'should notify each other of the progress of cases; for example, where the case has been referred to the Director of Public Prosecutions and the outcome of such referral' (1995: 13).

In addition to the 44 cases resulting in legal action, and the six cases submitted to the DPP, it is important to note that some cases were processed through the criminal justice system prior to the referral included in the sample and it is possible that other cases arising out of other referrals were sent to the DPP after July 1997. These 44 cases offer only a snapshot of legal outcomes within the time frame of the research.

Social work perceptions of the health board/gardaí relationships

Against this background of legal outcomes, a range of qualitative issues arise concerning the use of the procedures and the law. Social work perceptions of the health board/gardaí relationships notification system varied considerably. Several social workers viewed their relationship with gardaí in an extremely positive light. One said, 'we have an excellent relationship' and related this to the rural locality where it was felt co-operation is easier. Another regarded her relationship with the gardaí as 'fantastic . . . I find them very supportive'. The health board–gardaí notification procedures were also generally viewed positively. The decision to notify the gardaí is made at the CPN meeting which means that only CPN-notified referrals are considered for gardaí notification. On occasion the social worker will informally notify the guard of an urgent matter prior to the official notification in order to 'speed things up'. The consensus seemed to be that the 1995 guidelines had introduced a new level of accountability and transparency into the system: 'the system has tightened up a fair bit'. This social worker noted that 'we're actually more accountable now than we were before to external agencies like the guards and the guards are more accountable to us as well, in that they have to notify us as much as us notify them'.

There is tension between the more investigative, forensic nature of the social work role entailed by routine notification of child protection concerns and the role of the gardaí. What level of trust can social workers and gardaí have in one another when notifying cases? Indeed, what does 'notification' mean to the respective agencies in terms of good practice and the kinds of responses expected? As one social worker expressed it:

> 'In some cases I feel it is quite appropriate that the Gardaí take a role as well, that they investigate and take some of the policing role off of us as well, depending on what case. For example, in a non-accidental injury I would feel it is inappropriate for us to investigate because we are not the Gardaí, we are social workers and that some of our cases are very conflicting, our role is conflicting because we are the ones who bring people to court, at the same time we are expected to have a relationship with those people.'

While social workers clearly agonise about new child protection procedures constructing them as 'quasi-gardaí', much of their criticism concerned police not doing *enough* to investigate, leaving social workers to take a more forensically investigative role themselves. Several identified difficulties in communication between social work and gardaí. Case 234 (see Chapter 4) has already provided a classic example of breakdown in understanding between professionals where the JLO responded to the notification by taking the young person out of school to question her. Other problems included a perception that the gardaí were using the social work department to do their job, or to try to retrieve bad practice situations. In Case 172, the gardaí made the referral to the social work department, which was primarily concerned with the child's criminal behaviour: 'the child was in trouble for years before the gardaí had the sense to do anything about him, they couldn't get their act together. I mean there were too many gardaí involved'. The social worker suspected the child had committed many burglaries, both alone and with his friends, to the value of thousands of pounds. The referral from the gardaí was "passing the buck". . . He was extremely criminalised and the gardaí hadn't done a thing about him, they wanted me to lock him up and I pointed out that we don't detain children'.

Social workers complained about the notified guards not coming back to them to seek follow-up information. This is exemplified in Case 305, where the social worker was not informed by the gardaí of the DPP's decision not to proceed with a prosecution in a child sexual abuse case. There was a perception that the gardaí rarely investigate cases. Case 283, for example, was formally notified to the gardaí but the social worker 'never heard a thing', which he regarded as 'not satisfactory because what happened was it was left to ourselves to address the inappropriateness of this physical abuse. It was left to me, well, myself and another colleague were left to go in and out to them and get the response of the parents . . . It would be important for the guards to go in and carry out their own investigations, maybe the guards did go in and carry out their own investigation, but I am unaware of it'.

The police were viewed as 'amazing when it comes to CSA' but less responsive to other forms of abuse. The irony of this, however, is that the more legalised, forensic response to sexual abuse cases that this reflects results in a much tighter, more circumscribed social work role. The looser, less legalistic response by gardaí to physical abuse and neglect cases leaves open a discretionary space where more supportive/therapeutic practice becomes possible. Yet some social workers clearly want the gardaí to take on a more active investigative role in such cases and are frustrated when they do not. But even responses to sexual abuse cases can be problematic. Case 244 concerned a four-year-old girl who disclosed to her parents that the fifteen-year-old male babysitter had 'stuck his finger in my bum'. Following the social work investigation it transpired that the fifteen-year-old had admitted to his parents that he had 'fondled' his ten-year-old sister. 'Non-penetrative sex' was substantiated for the four year old and ten-year-old. The case was formally notified to the gardaí but it took over two months for the officer to get in touch with the social worker, who commented:

> 'The automatic referral to the gardaí, that we have, the system of reporting all cases of abuse to the gardaí, it created slight problems here in that a couple of months after the original distress to the family, the guards were unclear as to what they were to do. They got the notification and were ringing me and saying do we do a home visit, and at that point we had to tell the parents that they might insist on visiting themselves. We can't tell them not to and it just seemed a bit messy . . . but the guards weren't quite clear as to what they were to do. We eventually told them that we wouldn't be recommending it but that we couldn't stop them. But I just thought that some tightening up of that relationship wouldn't go astray between us and the guards and clarity about who was to do what. It's not the difficulty of visiting per se that I would have problems with, it's just that the timing of it, that it takes a while for that to go through the system. [It would be] better if they were involved when the initial crisis was there . . . a huge aspect of this case was the relationships in the neighbourhood, the pain it caused and the idea of the guards coming after a few months really terrified and upset them dreadfully.'

There is, then, a need for a more clearly articulated joint policy, and training, on if and when it is appropriate for the gardaí to investigate. The gardaí were seen by at least one social worker as being biased in their approach to some families. In Case 198, the referral concerned physical abuse and the social worker felt that the father is on 'friendly terms' with the local sergeant who, according to the father, told him that 'there's no harm giving them [mother and son] a clip'. While the social worker could not be sure the sergeant had made such a statement, he felt that 'you just don't know where you are with the gardaí'. Domestic violence was also a feature of the case and the social worker maintained that when the violence occurs 'two days or two months later I'm told about it and expected to go in and wave a wand and solve it'. The gardaí allegedly do not notify her of the occasions when they are called to the house. The mother was hospitalised because of her partner's violence and according to the social worker, 'I haven't been able to prove them but it's not my job to prove it, the gardaí would have a lot of stuff but they won't keep a record of it'. In a criminal, forensic sense, the social worker is, of course, correct that it is not social work's job to 'prove' abuse has happened. However, child protection does involve substantiating concern—especially in a context where the health board has new powers under Section 6 of the Domestic Violence Act (1966) to apply for remedies such as barring orders (Ferguson, 1997b). These examples illustrate the tensions that exist today in the social work role between forensic investigation and a welfare approach.

Garda perceptions of health board/gardaí relationships

Several gardaí commented that they enjoyed a good working relationship with social workers. Overall, gardaí perceptions of the notification system were positive, ranging from, 'I think it's great . . . it works well', to 'the new notification procedures are quite good'. One saw them as 'very basic proce-dures. . . I do think that they tend to work pretty well with a reasonable amount of co-operation . . . [and] helps streamline' child abuse investiga-tions. For some, it has increased their workload but 'you wouldn't mind that'.

However, several gardaí noted problems in the operation of the notifica-tion system with over-bureaucratisation and information flow stating that it actually 'slows' down communication. As one garda said, if a concern comes to her attention, she completes a notification form and sends it to the dis-trict office, which in turn sends it to the DCC: 'they in turn have to turn around and send it to the social worker in the area that's dealing with it, that itself is a slow procedure because if I get my notification here of a Friday evening at 5.00 pm, the District Office isn't open until Monday so you're talking even by the quickest post it's gone out of here Monday evening 5.00 pm, it's still going to be Wednesday morning before the DCC gets it so you're probably talking about a week's delay for the actual notification to get on the table of where it should be.' To address this delay, this garda will normally ring the social work department to inform them of the notification. There can also be a delay between the case being reported and receiving the notification: 'we would have some of the notifications come in one month after. At their [health board] end it seems to take longer to come through their channels'. Difficulties in post-notification communications were also identified; unless there is a case conference very little communication with social workers takes place. A 'drawback' with the notification form is that the referral source is not cited. If the guards knew who actually referred the case to the social work department it would enable them to talk to the referral agent and 'at least you'd have a background', without which the investigation occurs in a vacuum.

Several gardaí experienced difficulties in terms of what to notify and how to respond to certain types of notified cases, especially in defining neglect and emotional abuse, which are seen as 'less tangible', and 'more of a social worker's area': 'compared with sexual or physical, they are cut and dried . . . we know where we're going and we know that we're looking for, towards emotional. You need more contact with the family on a more regular basis, which is something which we can't really do, that is really what a social worker should do'. Another guard said: 'if I got a notification that somebody was being emotionally abused, I would honestly sit back in amazement looking at it'. Conversely, one garda felt that the inclusion of emotional abuse in the notification guidelines was positive: 'it has increased our appreciation of the whole issue'. Other difficulties in notifying emotional abuse arise because it is rarely notified in its own right, usually being cited in addition to another problem, especially domestic violence: ' you're only going on what you see when you get there and normally when we would get to the scene of a domestic violence, it is either finished or on the verge of finishing, and what you're really looking at is what you see when you get there and when we're thinking of emotional, we're really thinking of a young child sitting in the background and what they've seen in the night, but you really can't decide whether there is [emotional abuse]'. This garda felt that in domestic violence cases 'all we can do is let the social workers know what we have seen and whether we feel that there was going to be an effect on the child or not but it's a very dodgy issue, unless we know there's a re-occurrence of it because otherwise, one row, is that emotional abuse on the child? You really can't depend on just one incident to say you have an emotional case or that you have good grounds to say that you have kids that are emotionally affected by it'.

Even though 'in the end of the day we are all really trying to achieve the one thing', several gardaí said that the 'agenda' differs between the gardaí and social work investigation following a notification—the former's being 'gathering evidence', the latter's 'therapeutic'. The feeling was that 'the two don't come together very often'. However, in most respects, joint social work/ gardaí investigations were seen to 'work very well'. Tensions arise when social workers try to determine the garda response to notifications: 'what we often see on a notification is don't make contact with the family until you make contact with [social worker]. But I mean that is fine if you can get to your social worker or whoever is dealing with it quick enough'. Some also objected to social workers informing the guard that the family do not want gardaí involvement because the gardaí have to decide for themselves whether to investigate—to 'cover your own head at the end of day'. Since the introduction of the notification guidelines, there is an impetus to record reasons why an investigation did not take place. Some professionals fear litigation: 'I think people are very conscious of that . . . I suppose it's all the cases that have come to light that were brushed under the carpet and nothing was done with them, and because of that you're very conscious of how you deal with a case now, you're not going to leave it uninvestigated'. Some felt that the garda investigation should take priority over the social work investigation, perceiving a lack of understanding on the social workers' part of the importance of the garda role: 'a lot of social workers don't see our role as being priority and would often see us as interfering, you know where we would interview young kids they would see us as interfering with their side of the territory and that we'd get in too early and we do, it doesn't always suit to sit back and wait, you know'.

The 'contamination' of child protection: working with child sexual abuse

One of the most strident criticisms of advanced child protection systems is their legalistic nature. A shift has occurred, it is argued, from 'child abuse' as a 'socio-medical' problem to the construction of 'child protection' as a socio-legal problem (Parton, 1991). Where the police—and the courts—used to be an agency of 'last resort', they are now institutionalised into child protection. This is seen as part of the bureaucratisation of child welfare (discussed in the last chapter) resulting in social workers ceasing to be 'family caseworkers' imparting parenting skills and working with the whole family to create a better environment for the child. Today, this 'bureaucratisation of social work' thesis argues, 'dangerous parents' are the subject of intervention dictated by managerialism and the courts where the emphasis is on 'forensic' practices which seek out evidence of parental deviance. Following the child abuse inquiries, social work in particular, and child protection judgements more generally, are firmly in the public domain with a resulting loss of discretion for practitioners in what were once essentially 'private' encounters with clients. In the process, child protection becomes redefined as a measure of administrative competence rather than an ability to make individual decisions and provide therapy for children and families (Howe, 1992).

The findings from this study show that the law is indeed playing an increasingly significant role in child protection, both directly through the courts and indirectly through the impact of the 1995 guidelines. As has been shown, the use of the law in practice occurs in a relatively small number of cases. Crucially, however, the impact of bureaucratisation and legalism is not equal across all forms of child abuse. It only has a direct relevance to neglect and emotional abuse in extreme cases where care orders or supervision orders are used. Domestic violence is more directly subject to legal intervention and health board professionals are generally perplexed by the *under*-use of the law by the gardaí in such cases in terms of arrest and prosecution of suspected offenders. As has been shown, it can be argued that, rather than limiting the therapeutic role of social work, the systematic inter-agency relationships brought about through the 1995 notification procedures has sharpened the garda investigative role leaving social workers with considerable discretion as to how cases should be defined and a clearer 'non-forensic' investigative and therapeutic role.

With child sexual abuse, however, social workers, other child care professionals, as well as non-abusing parents, feel very constrained by legalism, and with justification. Huge efforts are put into gathering evidence that is 'forensically' sound with minimal beneficial outcomes for children and families. Intervention makes matters *worse* in some child sexual abuse cases as the children and (non-abusing) parents are left (alone) to carry the burden of cases proceeding very slowly through the criminal justice system and rarely ending in prosecutions. Parents are, rightly, perplexed at the extreme caution with which the legal system and the health board approach suspected abusers and the fact that nothing seems to be done to protect the children with whom the suspect abusers continue to have contact. Responses are dominated by the rigours of the criminal law and a forensic, legalistic response so that community care social workers fear being perceived to interfere by saying the wrong thing to a child and 'contaminating' evidence thereby rendering the child's statement inadmissible in court. Because of this fear the social workers may not really engage with the children or support their parents. This is left to the tightly bound parameters of the child sexual abuse assessment process which is carried out by specialist teams or units established since the late 1980s (McGrath, 1996). The ultimate source of these difficulties is an adversarial legal system that is anti-child, or at least pro-adult, and needs major reform so that frontline professionals can be enabled to work to promote the best interests of child victims and their families.

These issues will be highlighted here through three case studies (167, 293, 305) of extra-familial child sexual abuse. Case 293 involved interviews with the area social worker, garda, a specialist CSA assessment social worker, and the mother. The father did not wish to be interviewed and the parents did not consent to the child being interviewed by us. The case was referred by the mother whose eight-year-old daughter disclosed that her aunt's husband sexually abused her. The mother initially contacted a PHN who immediately referred her to the social work department:

> mother presented herself to the social work department, distressed and requesting help. Mother reported that child disclosed previous evening that whilst bathing the child . . . child disclosed whilst staying at her father's sister's house approximately two months ago, her partner came into the room. Child was sharing a bed with her younger sister. Man moved her sister away from her, pulled up the sheets and her nightdress and kissed her on the private parts . . . mother did ask child if man got on top of her, child stated 'No'. Child behaviour mother had noted mood swings, not wanting to go up or down to school on her own (case file).

The mother was 'anxious and upset but appeared to respond appropriately' to the child's disclosure. Her daughter had become 'aggressive towards her sister and defiant'. The social worker advised the mother not to 'question' the child further, but to 'listen' to her should she make further disclosures. The mother was 'open for a validation assessment' and was advised that a referral would be made for a CSA assessment. She was also advised not to approach the alleged perpetrator (case file).

A medical examination did not take place as the 'disclosure of incident occurred two months after alleged incident, child had no contact with alleged perpetrator since that day . . . mother did not want medical as she felt that it would further traumatise child' (case file). The case was formally notified to the CPN system on the same day as the referral and concern was also expressed as two 'small children' were resident with the alleged perpetrator. Approximately two weeks after the notification, the social worker received direction from the CPN meeting to 'call a case conference, refer . . . for assessment, liase with team leader, notify gardaí'. The child was, in fact, referred for a child sexual abuse assessment one week prior to the CPN direction, when her reaction to the alleged abuse was that she 'seemed withdrawn, does not want to walk to and from school on her own, a bit clingy, has mood swings . . . attention seeking, for example pretending there is something physically wrong with her. Tending to pick fights with her sister. Does not want to kiss her mum or dad or show signs of affection' (case file).

One week after the referral a fight broke out between the alleged abuser and the child's father who threw a brick through the window of the alleged perpetrator's car and the gardaí were called. The mother had by now reported the disclosure to the gardaí. Two days later the mother called again to the social worker stating that her daughter did not want to see a social worker on her own and was 'anxious to know if the gardaí will be involved'. The social worker informed them that the gardaí would indeed be notified but that it would be 'best if they did not speak with [child] until validation occurs'. A case conference was held and attended by the director of community care (DCC), team leader, CSA assessment social work team leader and the area medical officer (AMO). According to the social worker (the case conference minutes were not in the case file), the conference focused on whether a validation assessment would take place. Over four months after the referral, within the period of four weeks, the child was interviewed on three occasions by the child sexual abuse assessment team, and both parents were interviewed on one occasion. The assessment team reported that '[child] was clear and consistent throughout the assessment and indeed other statements . . . [child] was consistent in the location, the individuals present . . . her narrative was characterised by spontaneous reproductions of events'. It was concluded that 'on the balance of probability [child] was sexually abused by [alleged abuser]'. The report recommended that the case conference 'give due consideration' to the children of the alleged abuser (case file).

A network meeting was held one month later to discuss the outcome of the assessment and the prospects for a criminal prosecution, which may not be pursued 'due to lack of corroborative evidence'. Again the question was raised as to whether an assessment would take place of the alleged abuser's children. A second case conference was held one month later, but again the case file does not contain the minutes. The handwritten notes by the social worker suggested that the possibility of a prosecution was considered to be 'very slim' as there was 'no physical evidence'. The team leader would seek legal advice regarding the concerns for the alleged abuser's children and a network check would be completed on the alleged abuser's family and the parents provided with feedback on the case to date. According to the area social worker, this case conference focused on the board's responsibility to the alleged abuser's children and it was decided 'to hold off' on an investigation because 'basically, although the abuse was substantiated there was still a few grey areas, they didn't know if it would go to a prosecution, this man had been met and denied it'. Thus, now—some eight months after the initial referral—responses to the alleged perpretator and other children at risk still remained uncertain.

Avoiding direct social work involvement with the child

Although having direct contact with the family, the area social worker did not interview or speak with the child about the alleged abuse. The social work response to the child consisted of the CSA 'validation' assessment.

> 'I didn't see a role there for myself after the initial work had been done. Now having said that, after talking to the parents, they needed support and perhaps in retrospect I could have been more supportive to them around the whole issue of the sexual abuse and so in retrospect I could have been more supportive to the parents. In relation to the child as I say I'd really no involvement as such, except to just engage with the child and the reason for that was because the validation would take place and you didn't want to contaminate anything and I was conscious as well that that particular week was her communion coming up when the disclosures were made. But normally I wouldn't do that, talk to the child unless I was asked to by the [specialist child sexual abuse worker] to get more information. And that is really not to contaminate the evidence for one, and to put the child through saying a statement a number of times.'

The social worker conceded that she didn't give much time to the case in comparison to others. 'The essential things were done in this case, rather than the beneficial things'. She perceived the specialist child sexual abuse services to be supportive in nature, although long-term support services were not offered to this family. One year after the initial referral the social worker felt that the parents were open to the child being seen by a psychologist: 'so we may be able to offer them something a bit more'. It wasn't that she had a difficulty working with sexual abuse, 'there's more a fear of contaminating evidence if this child goes for validation. I mean if a child came to me themselves, fine, that's different. But I wouldn't approach a child.'

Both parents were open to counselling to explore their own feelings about the abuse, however the social worker felt that another agency would be better equipped to do this—a response that typifies the absence of long-term support work with parents of child sexual abuse victims, who 'are forgotten about'. This was despite both parents being 'very co-operative and very concerned . . . very open to the service' and the father being traumatised by the alleged abuse. 'He finds it very difficult to be natural with the children, to show them physical affection, things involved in their physical care or showing them affection, normal natural things a father would do, he feels he's backing off. Maybe he just feels vulnerable because in case anything he does would be misconstrued or whatever'. Following the child's disclosure of abuse the family applied for a housing transfer as they live in close proximity to the alleged perpetrator and a lot of the social work contact was about supporting their move. The child was considered to be at 'low risk', one year on from the initial referral. However the children of the alleged perpetrator were considered to be at 'greater risk'. The alleged abuser's partner had been made aware of the allegation but was 'in denial'. The outcome of the case at the end of the research period was confirmed abuse. The case was open with the alleged abuser awaiting prosecution. All that remained was 'closing it properly and just letting them know there's further support if they need it'. The social worker expressed concern about the delay in the court case and questioned the value to the child of once again having to give evidence, this time on video link in court.

Garda involvement

The case was notified under the 1995 guidelines by both the gardaí and the health board. The alleged abuse initially came to the gardaí's attention following the incident between the child's father and the alleged perpetrator. The garda had a very direct involvement with the child and accounts well for the process of engagement: 'I spoke to [child] for a while and I told her why I was there and I told her that I wouldn't talk to her about it that day, but that I would have to come back again to see her and would she talk to me about it then'. The child 'had no problem' talking to the garda 'until it came to the actual incident', when she 'clammed up'. When the garda asked the mother to leave the room the child then made a full statement. The garda felt that there was no difference between them and social work in terms of 'relaxing the child', but they are 'totally different as regards the time frame they have to work under and the time frame we have to work under'. It usually takes about six weeks before a child is seen by the CSA assessment workers and several more weeks before the assessment is completed. The gardaí would be trying to 'get the child as relaxed as possible to talk to us and then to get enough in the statement that we'd be able to arrest the perpetrator'. Her first contact with a child in sexual abuse cases would be 'to put the child at ease and have the child get to know me, be on first-name terms with the child and for them not to see me as a guard'. She would always try to interview children in plain clothes. The alleged perpetrator was arrested and interviewed by the gardaí. He was 'very dogmatic, very polite, didn't lose the cool, only once or twice, but was very adamant that he hadn't done anything. But he had his facts wrong. Like he said the child stayed at the house again after this incident, where it was the last time the child stayed at the house, she refused to stay there any more. Things like that were different but he still wasn't budging in his story, that it didn't happen'. There was in this case, 'no corroborating evidence at all, it was her word against his'. The social work report was included in the file sent to the director of public prosecutions (DPP)—the first time the garda had seen this happen—even though the social work report 'has no relevance whatsoever' and is never included in the book of evidence. Social workers regarded this child as 'one of the most truthful children they had ever come across'. The garda stayed in contact with the family while the file was with the DPP, in an attempt to allay their anxieties about why it was delayed for so long. The garda attended the second case conference on the alleged perpetrator's children and felt that the social workers were 'powerless' in investigating these children because as yet there was no conviction: 'it was just a case of waiting for it, if it was going to happen, waiting for it to blow up in the sense that one of the children would say it'. Overall, the garda was 'happy' with the multi-disciplinary work in the case but expressed annoyance with a social worker who informed the parents that a prosecution would be taking place prior to the DPP's decision: 'this was out of line because she had no way of knowing any more than we had. She was aware herself of how little evidence there actually was'. At the end of the research period, the court case was pending and the decision made for the child to give evidence by video link with a garda acting as mediator.

The mother's and the family's perspective

The mother spoke at length about her daughter's disclosure, the manner in which it was made and its effect on the family: 'We looked at each other and said no way, it couldn't have happened, it took him [father] a day to kind of sink in. He cried bitter tears, he went whiter than white, the blood just drained from his body and he just looked and started crying and saying what am I going to do, am I supposed to go up there and deal with him myself or what? They were 'having problems' with their daughter since the abuse took place in terms of her behaviour, and her daughter was 'bitter towards them all'.

The mother had considerable faith in social workers when she first made the referral to them: 'I knew [social worker] would be able to advise me about what to do'. But one year on, she expressed great dissatisfaction with the service: 'I have to get in contact with her [social worker] the whole time, she does not get in contact with me . . . I had to keep going to them [social workers] because I was not hearing anything from [social worker], there was no one coming near me, there was no one doing nothing. I sat here in this house day after day [and] heard nothing, nothing about the case, did not know if the case was going to court or what was happening. She never came near us . . . I have to do all the chasing and running'. The mother was, however, content that, while the social worker saw the child, she did not discuss the abuse with her, because 'if too many people ask her you would only be upsetting her more and prolonging it more'. She feels 'let down' by social workers 'in an awful way, because I have been always led to believe that they are there to help'. The father even had to ask the social worker about the possibility of receiving counselling which was eventually offered about a year after the referral. If a friend or relative had to go through a similar abuse experience she would advise them 'not to go near social workers because I don't think social workers actually do their job properly'. She did, however, feel that the social worker helped with the housing transfer.

The mother contacted a local politician in order to speed up the criminal proceedings case and was informed that it would be heard in two weeks time, which she 'couldn't believe'. She felt that the garda response to the allegation was much better than the social work response: 'Oh yes, definitely, they took it more seriously and everything'. The garda was 'like an auntie' to her daughter and met with her on several occasions before taking a statement in order to develop a relationship with the child. Her relationship with the garda was 'brilliant, just brilliant'. The garda was also the only person to update the family on the progress of the case. It was the garda and not the social worker who invited the mother to the first case conference. She was aware the second case conference was taking place but was not invited to it. The mother felt that the health board should have 'checked out' the alleged abuser's children who she fears were being abused. She 'fought hard with the social workers, I created war with them. I said it to them how come nothing is being done about the two kids over in that house. They keep telling me that they can't do nothing until the case is finished . . . nearly too late by then'. The mother had lost trust in social workers. For health board social workers to restore trust, 'what they need to do is to show people that they can be trusted to show a bit more sympathy or kind of listen more about what has happened and to let them know more what is going on because they are not doing that'.

Cases 305 and 167

The other two case studies are remarkably similar. Case 305 was referred by a school because an eight-year-old 'child made a CSA disclosure'. The child's uncle was the suspect abuser. Several attempts were made to get the child and parents to consent to a child sexual abuse assessment but the child refused: 'the parents were saying that she didn't want to be interviewed and they were not going to force her.' Due to 'contamination' fears, the social worker did not explore the allegations with the child; the gardaí took a statement but otherwise no professional discussed the disclosure with the child. The impact on the family was huge; the father started drinking again and threw a stone through the alleged abuser's house. The alleged perpetrator had children and, again, the feeling was, as the social worker put it, that 'it has to be validated first before the health board can move. If there is a prosecution we can move in then'. The case was open for approximately one year. The outcome was 'unconfirmed abuse'. A file had been sent to the DPP and the social worker believed that the DPP had yet to make a decision regarding a prosecution. However, following the research interview with the detective sergeant, it transpired that the DPP had made the decision not to prosecute the suspect abuser some months previously, but the social worker was not informed by the gardaí of the decision.

Case 167 was referred by a paediatrician, concerned that a 'child aged three and a half complained of having a sore bottom. When examined mother found she had blood on her thigh, mother took child to GP who diagnosed a tear on her vagina. He referred her to the paediatrician who confirmed same'. The paediatrician 'diagnosed sexual interference possibly with a blunt instrument' (case file). The child attended a nursery which had 23 children, aged from three months to eight years (the older children attend after school). The child is alleged to have named an older boy who 'put his finger in my bum' (case file). The nursery was staffed by a husband and wife team. Although a suspect abuser was not explicitly identified, 'suspicion was placed on male staff at nursery' (case file). Both the area social worker and team leader carried out the investigative assessment and reported two months after the referral. The child was met by them on five occasions, the garda was present for one of the interviews, and both parents were met twice. The child was 'not willing to engage in disclosure work'. She 'was easy to engage when trying to assess her comprehension, she presented as distressed, tired, angry or deliberately distracting when trying to discuss her previous childminders . . . she never wanted to talk about the doctor at the hospital . . . sore bums or anything . . . she was not willing to engage in this work' (case file). The outcome of the case was 'unconfirmed abuse' with the case closed because there was no named perpetrator 'and we got legal advice: nothing could be done'.

In relation to her initial contact with social workers the mother felt 'we had no choice to start with, whether we wanted the health board or not. We came into it green anyway for a start'. She expressed dissatisfaction because social workers did not contact her for a week after the paediatrician referred the case. She rang them every day. The impact of the alleged abuse on the family was such that 'we lived and breathed this flipping thing'. The social worker fully recognised this: 'I mean their reaction to it I suppose was the most damaging, I'd say was more damaging than the actual incident to the child'. The mother was aware that several case conferences and network meetings had taken place, however she was not invited to any of them. She felt that the 'system' was at fault more than simply the health board. The mother eventually formally complained to management about how social work handled the case.

> 'They did not do anything. They investigated us in the sense they brought us in and asked us about our families and whether any of them were alcoholics or was any of them flipping abused or did any of them abuse, things like that. But that was it. As far I am concerned, okay I know I am only coming in off the street, I know they don't know me no more than they know the man next door, and I know they are only taking what I am telling them. I know they can't take it as gospel but surely they can investigate it somewhere along the line.'

The mother could not understand why if the gardaí were legally in a position to question the suspected perpetrators social workers could not have investigated them. The playschool was closed down. A file was sent to the DPP and the gardaí were awaiting the DPP's decision. For the mother it came down to defensive practice by the board, which was anything other than child-centred:

> 'I know the laws are terrible. I think the health board should not care whether they are sued or not. I think kids should be the priority and let them sue me if they want me . . . they keep telling me there is laws around but there is no law there to protect the child. I am sick and tired of fighting with people, I really am so fed up with fighting with everybody cause I really feel with the health board and with everybody that you are banging your head against a brick wall. They would all love if I had forgotten about this twelve months ago, I would be giving them all an easy time. And it would be just another statistic and nobody would ever know, maybe when she was fifteen or sixteen she might need counselling but in the meantime we will forget about it and carry on.'

But, she asks, How do you forget about it when there is a man down there that you know in your heart and soul did it and had access to twenty other kids every day of the week?'

Conclusion

It is clear that the legalistic nature of CSA work over-rides the ways in which the services were organised locally. In spite of the fact that two community care teams had specialist CSA assessment workers, there is little evidence that outcomes differ as between teams. The problems, then, are clearly structural in nature and include the lack of medical evidence to substantiate sexual abuse but, more important still, a socio-legal system which does not work in the best interests of children. Specialist CSA social workers are painfully aware of these problems. One considered the lack of prosecutions to be 'frustrating'. It is common for cases to be confirmed by them, yet the alleged perpetrator is 'not approached'. In terms of dealing with this frustration:

'I don't know really how to put it. It doesn't affect me in my day to day work, it doesn't affect me with work with the kids or the families . . . But there are huge resources going into investigating child sexual abuse, so we'll investigate it and do legalistic interviews and they're video recorded and they can be used as evidence and very forensic. I mean there are questions we can ask and there are ways we can go but we cannot do x, y, z. So you have all this lovely, nice little package and then we have a confirmed outcome and it goes nowhere. Why is there this huge emphasis on investigation and this legalistic framework when you know fundamentally in terms of court it rarely goes that road, and I suppose personally the other side of that is I would much rather see an equal amount of resources and time or whatever going into the after care.'

Particular concerns were raised about the broader family and siblings in sexual abuse cases, who can be hugely affected, feeling guilty and responsible for their siblings having been abused, and 'we don't have the time or the scope or the staff to get into that'. 'Contamination' of evidence fears have such an influence that social workers who specialise in work with CSA are deeply concerned about how to conduct interviews in a legally acceptable way, to the extent that they even feel restricted in offering comfort to suspected abused children:

'It seems to be a very prescribed way of working with the children. Not so much with the families, but with the children it's very prescribed and then at times I would question because we have to be so careful what we say that we don't contaminate a child's statement. We have to be careful how we present. If a child is crying really and truly we could be strung up if it ever went to court anyway, which it rarely does, but we could be strung up if, for instance, we offered them comfort. If we touched them, if we say are you all right, you know if we offer them a drink. So in that sense it's restrictive and constrictive, the type of practice and that can be frustrating when you see that we're so very very careful and we're so very precise and we're so very legalistic you know. God forbid that we would contaminate a state-ment, but then if we're doing all of this and you know it's not going to court or it's not going to have a huge impact on this child or family at this time anyway.'

While in some instances the gardaí are involved in a joint interview process, there is no protocol for garda/health board joint interviewing, 'it's been on an ad hoc kind of case by case basis'. Nor is there a structure in place to receive feedback from gardaí or area social workers in terms of prosecution.

This chapter has shown that the law plays a crucial role in attempts to protect sexually abused children, but with poor outcomes in terms of crimi-nal prosecutions and the promotion of child safety and the victim's welfare. While just over half (54 per cent) of all referrals to the health board were formally notified to the gardaí under the 1995 Guidelines, a quarter of these (26 per cent) were directly investigated by the police, while just 13 per cent of investigated cases actually result in prosecutions, of which only a handful result in successful convictions. Intervention even makes matters *worse* in some child sexual abuse cases, as the children and (nonabusing) parents are left (alone) to carry the burden of cases that take an extremely long time to process through the system. They are rightly perplexed at the extreme cau-tion with which health boards and the legal system approach suspected abus-ers and the fact that little seems to be done to protect children with whom they remain in contact. Health boards and the wider professional system need to recognise the impact of legalism on child protection practice and outcomes. Social workers' fears of 'contaminating' possible forensic evidence by engaging with children should not be allowed to hinder support for the child or non-abusing parents. The immediate needs of the child for comfort and security must be put before the dictates of a legal system which, even when used to the letter of the law, in any case produces such poor outcomes in terms of actual prosecutions. Health boards need to develop a regional protocol for garda/health board joint interviewing of children. A structure should also be put in place to facilitate feedback from gardaí to area social work teams about the outcome of cases referred to the DPP.

Area social workers are so overcome with fears of 'contaminating' evidence in child sexual abuse cases that they avoid engaging with children altogether. The system needs to resolve the structural tensions which lead to such radical non-intervention. One way would be to put in place a system of child advo-cacy which focuses on children's immediate therapeutic needs for support and healing and provide this in a way that is quite separate from the legal process. Non-abusing parents in sexual abuse cases also feel ignored by so-cial workers and disenchanted with the health board and criminal justice response, not least because it is tortuously slow; one year on from being referred just one prosecuted child sexual abuse case had been completed. Non-abusing parents experience a form of secondary victimisation in the way the system fails to respond to their needs for support and fails to see that justice is done. A system of advocacy and support for such carers needs to be put in place.

More generally, this chapter has shown that the majority of child abuse referrals were notified to gardaí, but a significant minority were not processed through the formal notification system. This is not to say that informal contact with the gardaí did not take place; however, the system of notification is crucial in terms of formalising communication and clarifying each agency's role in investigating suspected child abuse. A number of difficulties in communications were identified by social workers and gardaí, and there are particular problems with definitions of physical abuse and neglect. Clearly, guidelines are not being followed in all cases, with 'quite serious' allegations of physical abuse not being formally brought to the gardaí's attention. This partly reflects the felt ambiguities as to whether the police have a systematic role to play in suspected physical abuse cases, a question which should be a matter for systematic review by health boards and the gardaí.

Real difficulties are also evident for practitioners in deciding what types of 'neglectful' behaviours warrant garda attention. The notification of domestic violence (if not always the *investigation* of it) is less problematic, in that the decision to notify the case appears to be based on social work concerns for the children's safety. The gardaí play only a modest role in neglect cases, and this is as it should be. There is a need for stricter operational definitions of child abuse in the notification guidelines, which provide clearer specifications of the harms to children which require notification. This is of particular relevance to neglect, where what constitutes abusive neglectful behaviour is left to the individual social workers and CPN committees to decide. Tighter definitions of both wilful neglect and unintentional neglect are required. Domestic violence needs to be seen as a notifiable problem in its own right and not simply submerged as possibly notifiable under the label of emotional abuse. Tighter *post*-notification procedures and communications are required between gardaí and community care, roles need to be clarified and the outcome of cases communicated. There was little evidence in social work case files that post-notification decisions are recorded and this needs to be put right.

Note

[1] The Fit Person Order under the 1908 Children Act was replaced by the provision of the Care Order under the Child Care Act 1991.

6 Case Conferences and Formal Inter-Agency Decision-making

Since the emergence of child abuse guidelines in the late 1970s (Ferguson, 1996a) case conferences have assumed a vital role in the management of suspected child abuse and decision making processes. We have seen that inter-agency work is fundamental to effective child protection and in this chapter we examine aspects of multi-disciplinary work and the achievement of safe practice through case conferences. Child abuse inquiries have demonstrated the potential for system failures when there is a lack of formal co-ordination of information and coherent case planning with clear roles, relationships and objectives. Little wonder then that the *Report of the Kilkenny Incest Investigation* (McGuinness, 1993) gives such a pivotal role to case conferences, recommending that reasonable steps be taken to facilitate the attendance of relevant persons, that accurate minutes be kept, that the reasons for decisions not to hold case conferences be clearly recorded, that key management personnel be given training on chairing case conferences, and that the attendance of parents/guardians be the norm 'unless there are substantial grounds for their exclusion'. Where they are excluded, parents or guardians should be advised in writing of the reasons. All of this 'will require careful preparation and training for those involved' (McGuinness, 1993, pp.103–5).

Studies of the reasons for failures of the system to protect known abused children have also begun to recognise the complexity of inter-professional collaboration; they have demonstrated that structures to facilitate inter-agency work and the holding of case conferences do not in themselves guarantee good practice. The ways in which involved parties communicate, and family systems and professional systems interact, can lead to a loss of focus on the child; they are crucial variables in the outcomes of cases (Reder, Duncan and Grey, 1993). It was beyond the scope of this study to analyse the dynamics of case conferences through participant observation. It was possible, however, to represent important aspects of the relational dynamics of case conferences through the case study in the final part of this chapter and the use of qualitative data here and throughout the book.

The methodology employed has allowed a systematic analysis of the use of case conferences as a tool for inter-agency co-ordination. We were particularly interested in discovering the role that case conferences play in decision-making and the degree to which inter-agency child protection work is planned in formal ways—something that is essential to safe practice. In theory, according to the Child Abuse Guidelines (1987), all cases involving suspected or known risk of child abuse require a planned inter-agency response which should take place through the formal mechanism of the case conference. As one social worker in the study put it, 'you are meant to call a case conference for any risk situations'. In practice, however, this chapter will show that decisions on case conferences involve a filtering process in which only some cases survive to conference stage. We examine the reasons why some cases result in a case conference and others do not, compare the practice here with international data and consider the implications for safe practice. We show that Irish practices on the inclusion of parents or guardians in case conferences fall far short of what is regarded internationally as best practice. The final part of the chapter further illustrates the issues involved in achieving safe practice in terms of the dynamics of case planning, management and inter-agency work through a case study of a very high risk case involving physical child abuse and domestic violence.

Case conferences: an overview

Eighteen per cent (n=51) of the 286 MWHB community care referrals proceeded to case conference as a result of the concern expressed at the time of the referral (April–June 1996). Case conferences were held for a further 23 referrals during the follow-up period of July 1996–July 1997. Here we examine the 51 April–June 1996 case conferences to elucidate the filtering processes and the decision to hold a conference at the investigative stage. The decision rate is quite consistent across the three community care areas, with Clare having a slightly lower rate, at 15 per cent, than Limerick and Tipperary (NR)/East Limerick teams, where a decision to hold a case conference was reached for 19 per cent of referrals in each area.

Conferences played a relatively small role in emergency cases and at the early stage of a case career, especially for new referrals where the family were not previously known. Some 31 per cent were held within two working weeks of the initial investigation, of which five were held within one working day[1]; 22 per cent were held between two and four weeks, 11 per cent between five and six weeks and as many as 36 per cent (n=16) were held six working weeks after the investigation. Child protection was the main issue in over 60 per cent (n=31): 26 per cent were defined as neglect, 18 per cent (n= 9) sexual abuse, 16 per cent (n=8) physical abuse and 2 per cent (n=1) emotional abuse. This does not mean that domestic violence did not feature in any of these cases, as it did appear as a 'secondary' problem in combination with the main presenting problem. Significantly, none of the referrals primarily defined as domestic violence received a case conference. This is yet another example of the failure to take the opportunity to process domestic violence cases through the formal child protection system, despite the high levels of risk and need in such cases which should result in formal inter-agency assessment and planning. Just under 40 per cent were primarily concerned with child welfare: behaviour/control difficulties was the main problem in 22 per cent (n=11), parental difficulties in 10 per cent, parental addiction in 4 per cent and in a further 4 per cent (n=2) financial/housing difficulties and miscellaneous problems.

Factors associated with holding case conferences

The likelihood of a case conference being held varied considerably according to the different categories of case. Thirty-five per cent (n=8) of physical abuse referrals resulted in a case conference, 25 per cent (n=9) of sexual abuse, 22 per cent (n=13) of neglect and 9 per cent (n=1) of emotional abuse. As already stated, no domestic violence referrals received a case conference, while 18 per cent (n=11) of child behavioural/control, and 11 per cent (n=5) of parental difficulties referrals did. Thus, although neglect was the problem that appeared most frequently in case conferences, physical abuse and sexual abuse were the most likely to result in a case conference, with domestic violence being the least likely. We can see that it is variables other than a suspicion of abuse or a serious child care problem that trigger a conference.

Filtering processes at the case conference stage of investigation

What then are the factors that lead to case conferences being held for some referrals but not for others? The question is whether routine filters are applied at the investigative/initial assessment stage and, if so, what are the implications for safe practice? Gibbons et al (1995), in *Operating the Child Protection System*, examined differences in cases reaching conferences. Factors relating to the child, the abusive incident, previous involvement, family poverty and parental deviance were examined. The authors concluded that cases were more likely to be filtered out of the system without a case conference if: (1) there were only girls in the family; (2) the allegations concerned neglect or emotional abuse; (3) the alleged abuse or neglect was less severe; (4) the perpetrator was not in the household; (5) there had been no previous investigations; (6) no parent figure had a criminal record, a history of substance abuse, a psychiatric disorder, a history of domestic violence or been abused as a child.

Having identified the factors associated with cases that reached a conference, the authors selected criteria to measure 'need for protection' in terms of a case conference. They felt such criteria were necessary because of the absence of any guidelines. The criteria included possible future risk to the child, the seriousness of the referral incident, the age of the child, alleged perpetrator's presence in the home, previous social work investigations, parental behaviour which might affect capacity to parent such as substance abuse, violence, criminal record and psychiatric illness. A substantiated case with 'many' of the risk factors was considered to be in more need of protection than an unsubstantiated case with few risk factors. These criteria were applied to physical abuse, sexual abuse and neglect referrals. The authors concluded that unsubstantiated physical abuse cases were very unlikely to reach a case conference no matter what the level of risk. Of the cases that were substantiated those with higher risk factors were more likely to be the subject of a conference. High risk sexual abuse cases, that is, sexual abuse cases with many of the risk factors, were more likely to reach a case conference than physical abuse cases even when the concern was not substantiated. Neglect cases, substantiated or not, were less likely than physical or sexual abuse cases to reach a conference. Gibbons et al concluded that very few unsubstantiated cases with few risk factors reached a conference, and neither did a significant minority of substantiated cases with many risk factors.

Applying this methodology to our sample shows that:

(1) Previous health board involvement, with at least one social work investigation, was a highly significant factor in cases that reached a case conference.

(2) Referrals made by the expert system were over-represented in case conferences.

(3) Physical abuse and neglect referrals that are substantiated are far more likely to reach a case conference than unsubstantiated cases.

(4) For sexual abuse cases, substantiation makes little difference.

Previous health board involvement

The family had been previously involved with the health board in 82 per cent (n=42) of the cases that received a conference, and in 57 per cent (n=134) of those that did not. In 30 per cent of conferences the involvement had been for under one year, in 70 per cent for over one year. Three cases had been known for over ten years, one for seventeen years. A large majority of 74 per cent (n=31) of the 42 conferences of cases with previous health board involvement were open at the time of the referral. Furthermore, some 38 per cent of these 31 cases were re-referred during the follow-up period to July 1997 (see Chapter 10). Hence 31 per cent (n=16) of referrals that received a conference were known to the social work department at the time of the referral and were re-referred during the follow-up period. Forty per cent (n=17) were known for either confirmed or suspected abuse/protection concerns. These included eight with substantiated domestic violence, which is interesting considering domestic violence was not the main presenting problem in any of the 51 case conferences.

The significance of previous health board involvement in cases selected for a case conference varies between the three community care teams. The family was previously known to the health board in 92 per cent (n=12) of conferences in Clare, in 83 per cent (n=15) in Limerick, and in 75 per cent in Tipperary. This again shows how rarely conferences were used when the children and family were previously unknown, accounting for just 8 per cent in Clare conferences, 17 per cent in Limerick conferences and 25 per cent in Tipperary/East Limerick. Thus a key finding is that case conferences play only a minor role in filtering referrals out of the system—such decisions are made elsewhere—their primary function being the management of well-known high-risk cases. The fact that in Ireland risk assessments, especially in new cases, do not routinely include conferences may be related to the absence of child protection registers; here it is a CPN which launches the case into the official child protection system.

Referral sources

Referrals by professional sources stand a better chance of receiving a conference than those by lay persons, 21 per cent (n=38) as compared with 13 per cent (n=13). The medical profession—including PHNs—was the largest source, referring 13 of the 51 cases. Thirty-eight per cent (n=89) filtered out were referred by laypersons,and 62 per cent (n=146) by professional sources. Twelve per cent (n=13) of lay referrals received a conference, compared with 21 per cent (n=38) of professional referrals. Garda referrals were the most likely of the professional referrals to receive a case conference, at 30 per cent (n=7). Sixteen per cent (n=9) of parental, 20 per cent (n=5) of social work and only one of the anonymous referrals (8 per cent) received conferences.

Case substantiation and risk

Thirty-nine (76 per cent) of the 51 cases that went to conference were substantiated, while ten were not. The social worker believed that the concern expressed in nine of the latter had some foundation—the level of risk was 'high' in seven and 'very high' in one. Thus the suspected level of risk to children affected the decision to hold a case conference. Fifty-eight per cent (n=121) of the cases that did not reach a conference were substantiated.[2] In the Gibbons study, 33 per cent of substantiated low-risk referrals, and 53 per cent of substantiated high-risk referrals reached a case conference. In the present study, 70 substantiated cases were considered to be high risk; for 33 per cent (n=23) of these a case conference was held, 14 per cent (n=8) of substantiated low-risk cases received a conference.[3] Thus, as compared with international data, fewer substantiated cases reach conferences in Ireland which again suggests that decisions are made elsewhere. The fact that so many substantiated high-risk referrals do not receive a case conference is especially significant, and indeed worrying in terms of the apparent absence of a formal inter-agency response.

A crucial issue, then is the reason why conferences were not held for substantiated high-risk cases. The most frequent response by social workers—37 per cent (n=17)—was 'intervention plan already formulated'; for 35 per cent (n=16) it was 'good informal inter-professional work took place'. 'Insufficient information to proceed with case' was the reason for 13 per cent (n=6) and 'insufficient time to hold one' for 13 per cent (n=6). For 11 per cent (n=5) the social worker noted that a case conference was to be arranged but it was not held during the sampling period. Other reasons included 'insufficient personnel involved in case', 'insufficient information to proceed with case', 'level of severity /concern did not justify it' and 'family moved from health board area'.[4] This implies that a high level of informal inter-agency planning was the most significant reason for the absence of a case conference in substantiated high-risk cases. A crucial question is how the decision was made. An important—if somewhat crude—indicator is that 73 per cent (n=32) were notified to the CPN meeting. While we do not suggest that the holding of CPN meetings led to the decisions not to hold case conferences, it is clear that these cases were known to higher management and they were accountable for them. Thus the decision not to hold a case conference for the remaining 27 per cent (n=12) of such cases was made entirely at the local level of social worker/line-manager/team meeting—the referral never having reached the CPN meeting.

Thus, greater clarity is required in the decision-making process on case conferences, especially for substantiated high-risk cases, so that the circumstances where conferences are deemed (1) essential or (2) discretionary, are absolutely clear. This should include specifying who is responsible for calling case conferences, the role of the CPN system in this and the relationship between decision-making and planning at CPN meetings and case conferences. The difference between a case conference and a 'network meeting' also needs critical attention; it needs to be clear which decision-making format is appropriate for the management of different levels of risk.

Application of research criteria to child protection categories

We now develop the analysis further to examine decision-making and the role of case conferences with respect to different forms of child care problems/abuse. We applied the key criteria of previous health board involvement, referral source, case substantiation, and risk assessment to each category of protection problem to establish the differences between the categories that were the subject of case conferences and those that were not.

Physical abuse: Eight physical abuse referrals reached a case conference, all of which had previous health board involvement. One of these cases was of confirmed abuse, four of suspected abuse, three domestic violence and five child behaviour problems.[5] Seven of the eight physical abuse referrals that received a conference were referred by a professional, one by a layperson. Just under half of the physical abuse referrals which did not reach a case conference were previously known to the health board and were referred by a professional.

Six of the eight physical abuse cases that received a conference were substantiated, compared with only three of the fifteen that did not reach a case conference. Of the six substantiated cases, three were considered to be high-risk at the time of the conference, one to be low-risk and one to have no risk. Although two cases that received a case conference were not substantiated they were considered to be high-risk. In all, nine physical abuse referrals were substantiated, of which six received a case conference; a further nine were classed as high-risk, of which five received a case conference. However, the four high-risk physical abuse referrals that did not receive a case conference were unsubstantiated. Although the number of physical abuse referrals is relatively small, those that were substantiated and high-risk were more likely to receive case conferences than unsubstantiated low-risk referrals.

Neglect: 85 per cent (n=11) of the neglect referrals that resulted in a case conference were previously known to the health board, of which 77 per cent (n=10) were referred by professionals. Sixty per cent (n=28) of the referrals that did not receive a case conference were previously known, of which 66 per cent (n=31) were referred by professionals. Eighty-five per cent (n=11) of the 13 referrals that received a case conference were substantiated compared with 49 per cent (n=22) of those that did not reach a case conference. Of the eleven substantiated cases that reached case conference, one concerned a child considered by the social workers to be at very high risk, seven cases were high-risk, and two low-risk. Although the concern expressed in the referral was unsubstantiated in two of the cases that went to conference, the risk posed to the children was assessed as high. Of the total of 33 substantiated neglect referrals, two were classed as very high risk, one of which went to case conference. Nineteen were considered to be high-risk, with 37 per cent (n=7) reaching a case conference, eleven low-risk, with 18 per cent (n=2) resulting in a case conference. By comparison, in six unsubstantiated neglect referrals the children were considered to be at high risk, but only one reached a case conference. Four unsubstantiated neglect referrals were classed as low-risk, and none reached a case conference.

Taken together, some 85 per cent (n=11) of the neglect referrals that reached a case conference were previously known to the health board and were substantiated, 77 per cent were referred by a professional. These three factors were present in only 26 per cent (n=12) of the 47 neglect referrals that did not reach a case conferences, leaving a relatively high number of substantiated high- and low-risk neglect cases without a conference.

Sexual abuse: Previous health board involvement is less significant in sexual abuse referrals that reached a case conference than physical abuse or neglect referrals. Of the nine sexual abuse referrals that resulted in a case conference, 55 per cent (n=5) were previously known compared with 52 per cent (n=14) of the 27 sexual abuse referrals that were filtered out without a conference. Likewise, the referral source is not as significant as in other categories: 66 per cent (n=6) of the cases that reached conference were referred by the expert system, as were 66 per cent (n=18) of those that did not. Six of the referrals that reached a case conference were substantiated, three were not. Forty-four per cent of the cases that did not reach conference were substantiated. Of the six cases that reached a case conference the risk was high in one, low in one, and very low in one.[6] Of the three unsubstantiated cases that received a conference risk was assessed as high in one, low in the second, and was not assessed in the third. Overall, eighteen sexual abuse referrals (50 per cent) were substantiated on investigation, nine of which reached a case conference. In one substantiated referral the risk was measured as high and a conference was held, in seven the level of risk was assessed as low, and one reached a case conference. In four substantiated referrals risk was considered to be very low, and two received a conference. Of the unsubstantiated referrals five were classed as high-risk, only one of which reached a conference, three were low-risk, and one reached a case conference. Thus, the findings again show that the designation high-risk does not of itself determine the calling of a case conference, other factors also need to be present.

Emotional abuse and domestic violence. One emotional abuse referral that received a case conference was previously known, was referred by a professional, was not substantiated but was classed as high-risk. Case conferences were not held for the 19 referrals primarily concerned with domestic violence. Twelve of these cases were previously known, twelve were referred by professionals and fifteen were substantiated. Of the latter, eleven were classed as high-risk, one as low-risk and two as very low-risk. It is again clear that case substantiation, level of risk, previous involvement and referral source do not affect the decision to hold a case conference for a domestic violence referral.

Summary of implications

Our findings, like those of Gibbons et al, indicate that although the vast majority of referrals that reached a case conference were both substantiated and high-risk, a considerable number of such cases did not survive the filters to reach a case conference. A significant number of high-risk substantiated cases that could, or perhaps should, have reached a case conference did not do so. A full 67 per cent (n=47) of substantiated high-risk referrals did not receive a conference.[7] Twenty-five of these concerned child protection (two physical abuse, twelve neglect and eleven domestic violence). The remaining 22 were classified primarily as child welfare referrals, even though some also had child protection concerns. Thus it seems that in the Irish system referrals that reach a case conference are nearly always high-risk substantiated cases: only one unsubstantiated low-risk case made it to a case conference. Cases with a lower threshold of risk/need are either filtered out of the system altogether or—more typically—worked with without a case conference, which implies that risk assessment or planning does not occur at the formal multi-disciplinary operational level.

When the question is asked whether routine filters are applied to all referrals certain anomalies appear. In relation to child sexual abuse, all of the substantiated high-risk cases received a case conference, so it appears that such referrals routinely receive a case conference. However, different criteria apply to physical abuse, neglect and domestic violence referrals and significant numbers are filtered out of the system and some substantiated high-risk cases do not receive a case conference. These findings have significant implications. Case conference resources are targeted at substantiated high-risk cases with histories of health board involvement, leaving a significant number of high-risk substantiated cases without a formal inter-agency response. More case conference resources need to be made available to target those substantiated high-risk cases that do not survive the case conference filter.

Case conferences and the provision of long-term services

The implications of these findings are more significant still when the long-term outcomes and the influence of case conferences on the provision of support and treatment services are considered. Eighty-eight per cent (n=45) of cases that reached a conference were provided with a long-term treatment/support service, compared with 58 per cent (n=137) of those that did not. We have divided long-term services into four categories: home-based, community-based, clinical and care-based (see Chapter 7 for more detail). Seventy-five per cent (n=38) of the cases that reached a conference were provided with a long-term home-based treatment/support service, most typically from social workers, but also from family support workers and community child care workers. Some 24 per cent (n=12) were provided with a community-based service, such as family support, or youth services. A clinical service, such as child psychology or psychiatry, was provided for 61 per cent (n=31) while 33 per cent (n=17) were provided with a care-based service, statutory or voluntary.

A home-based service was provided for 45 per cent (n=106) of cases that did not reach a conference, 11 per cent (n=27) received a community-based service; 30 per cent (n=79) received a clinical service; and 14 per cent (n=32) a care-based service. It may appear from this that in 32 cases children entered care without a case conference or multi-disciplinary planning; however, 17 of these cases were the subject of a conference either prior to the referral included in the sample or during the follow-up period, and were in fact planned at the multi-disciplinary level, although this did not occur during the sampling period. In a further 15 cases where children entered care, to the best of our knowledge, a case conference was not held. In six cases the reason was because the 'level of severity or concern did not justify it', in five it was 'intervention plan already formulated' obviously on an informal, or 'network meeting' basis.[8] These findings suggest that case conferences play a significant role in long-term service provision. Eighty-five per cent of cases that reached a case conference were provided with a long term service, compared with 58 per cent of those that did not receive a conference. Only six cases that reached a conference did not receive a long-term service. This disparity illustrates the important decision-making and filtering role of the conference in service provision. It has huge implications for substantiated low-risk cases which, in the absence of a conferences, are less likely to receive a long-term service. Moreover, while significant numbers of high-risk substantiated cases received long-term services (see Chapter 7) some did not, and their exclusion from case conferences means that they are not assessed or worked with at the formal multi-disciplinary level. Cases assessed as low-risk should not be adversely affected in the allocation of scare resources by the absence of a case conference.

Responses to children and families should be driven by need rather than the decision-making process. Information management systems need to be devised to enable child care managers to track the progress of, and service response to, all substantiated referrals, irrespective of whether they have received a case conference.

Case management: key workers and case reviews

Dates were set in advance for only 62 per cent of the case conferences held. Fifty per cent were set for between 20 and 40 working days after the referral, and 50 per cent for 40 days plus. In 92 per cent (n=46) of cases a key worker was nominated at the conference, 91 per cent of whom were social workers. Health board social workers accounted for 61 per cent of key workers. In four case conferences a joint appointment was made, and in all but one of these a social worker was one of the professionals appointed. In only one case conference was the appointed key worker(s) not a social worker. This case (136) involved multiple child care problems including physical abuse, neglect, emotional abuse, children out of control, juvenile crime, alcohol abuse by both parents, parents under stress and financial problems. The referral was not directly investigated as the parents were seeking legal advice regarding 'alleged harassment' from social workers and were refusing to co-operate. In the absence of a direct social work investigation, a guard and speech therapist met with the family and were appointed the key workers at the case conference.

Social workers now play a key role in case management, co-ordinating a number of services to the child and family, often without working directly with them. 'Key worker', therefore, no longer implies, as it once did, that social workers are the 'key' professionals working directly with the child and family, although this does still happen in many cases (see Chapter 7). For example, recent research into residential care for children in Ireland shows that many care workers feel frustrated that children's area social workers do not work directly with the children as was clearly expected. The care workers themselves often do not feel sufficiently skilful or well-trained to work directly with these traumatised and often challenging children (Clarke, 1998). Thus, the changing role of social workers has huge implications for the understanding and planning of inter-agency interventions, and of the roles and responsibilities of professionals, and their mutual expectations.

Perceptions of case conferences

Social workers generally saw case conferences as supportive: 'a very useful tool'; 'you're sharing responsibility, you're getting feedback from others as well'; 'it takes the burden off you in trying to make a decision, you can't make a decision on your own really'; 'the beauty [is] you have all this information, so it dilutes the focus on the social worker, so it's a joint decision, in terms of involving all professions, so it covers your back'.

Problems identified included: 'people were inclined to go with the majority rather than stand up and be counted'; 'in case conferences they say great things, like draw up care plans and you're thinking what's a care plan and how do I actually sit down [and do it]?'.

Sharing responsibility can lead to diluted accountability. One team transferred a case; it called a case conference and the social worker was concerned about the 'formality of the whole thing. Sometimes you can get snowed under with a case conference and stuff . . . I was tickled at the idea that we'd get a case conference to transfer a case when we actually have a waiting list here at the time to get case conferences for a more serious issue. I suppose they're beneficial'. For another social worker 'I think their role is to say we had a case conference and this was decided so somebody can be pinned down for not doing what they were supposed to do. . . . A lot of social workers would use the case conference as a kind of support me, look at me, look after me sort of a session'. There was also concern about status: 'I often think that the higher status person gets a lot more say' and this is 'particularly true of the medical profession'. While the case conference spreads the responsibility 'at the end of the day it's all left to the social worker'. There is a perception that the case management role of social workers may spread the work but not the responsibility.

The crucial issue of the difference between a case conference and a network meeting was well captured by one social worker: 'a case conference, for example, the parents would always be invited, and a DCC has to be present to chair the meeting and would be making rather more serious decisions, like a care order or maybe also discharge from care, depending on the situation, and that is what case reviews or meetings would be: a measure to prevent things from really blowing up, like in a situation that you call everybody and discuss it and review it.'

Parental attendance was widely acknowledged as necessary. 'I think that they have a right to know, if a lot of professionals are gathering up to discuss their family situation, that they ought to know; however it is quite intimidating, for them'. One (minority) view was that parents should not attend the whole conference:

> 'No, I don't think so, no because you have to have some kind of opportunity to discuss things among professionals and confide and just to see what best solution there is and sharing information. I think it would jeopardise the working relationship with the family. For example, the PHN, they don't want to be seen, actually it's the same with us. It is a conflicting situation because we have the confidence of the person, nurses more than us, they have confidence and then they have to attend and share their information and they have responsibility like we have and I think it would jeopardise their working relationship with the family'.

While most social workers accepted that parents were 'entitled' to attend case conferences and that engaging them in the formal decision-making process can lead to more effective practice, there were some reservations. 'I'm all for democracy. I wouldn't like as a parent somebody discussing allegations against me. But that said I've been in situations when you might be working with a very difficult family, people including myself would not feel free to give, to speak because of the fear of a physical attack, but generally speaking I think it's a good exercise'. Guidelines for including parents in case conferences should allow for their exclusion where there is a threat to workers' safety.

Parental involvement in case conferences

Parental participation at case conferences is now recognised as good practice in child protection and there must be compelling grounds to exclude them (McGuinness, 1993). However, most health boards are only beginning to come to terms with this obligation and the findings suggest that much work has to be done to meet this new international standard of best practice. In interviews, parents expressed great anger at being excluded from such meetings or brought in at the end, saying they felt humiliated and powerless (see Chapter 9). Parents were invited to attend the conference in just over half of the conferences, 27 cases (9), 72 per cent (n=13) of the Limerick team's conferences, 58 per cent (n=7) in Clare, and 35 per cent of Tipperary (NR)/ East Limerick. Fifty-four per cent (n=14) of the parents invited actually attended for part of the conference. At least one parent attended in eight of the 13 conferences in Limerick, in four of Tipperary (NR)/East Limerick, and in two in Clare.

The invitation or attendance of parent(s) to a case conference is not a sufficient indicator of involvement, their actual participation level is crucial. In only one case did the parents attend the whole conference, in the remaining 13 they only attended part of the conference. In 30 per cent of cases where parents were invited to attend, the case was primarily concerned with child behaviour/control problems. Physical abuse, sexual abuse and neglect were each the main presenting problem in 19 per cent. The best attendance was in child sexual abuse cases, where four of the five invitations were followed up, three of which were extra-familial CSA cases. In one case the father was the suspect abuser, but he did not attend the conference, the child's mother did. Hence the conferences concerning CSA were not attended by abusers. The worst attendance record occurred in physical abuse cases, where only one out of five parents attended. In nine of the cases where parents attended, one or both parents were noted to be the abusers, in five they were considered not responsible for the child care/protection problem. Of the 27 cases where parents were invited to conferences, the vast majority, 89 per cent, were previously involved with the health board, either in the MWHB region or outside it. Of the 23 conferences where parents were not invited to attend 74 per cent were previously involved with the health board.

Ten of the fourteen families from which at least one parent was interviewed for this study, were the subjects of a case conference. In five cases the parent(s) were invited to and attended part of the conference, and in all the children were placed in care at some point in the case career. In four cases the parents were not invited and care proceedings did not feature. More generally, the decision to invite parents appeared to depend on whether they were viewed as co-operative/voluntary clients. Sixty-five per cent (n=17) of the parents invited were considered by their social worker to be co-operative, 23 per cent (n=6) displayed varying levels of co-operation and only 12 per cent (n=3) were considered to be unco-operative, hostile clients. Only 35 per cent (n=8) of parents not invited to attend were described as co-operative, 8 per cent (n=2) varied their co-operation, while 57 per cent (n=13) were considered to be unco-operative. The lack of an invitation to unco-operative parents may alienate them further and intensify their hostility. The challenge to professionals in developing a fully inclusive practice is to engage with hostile clients at case conferences, in a system which operates in a subjective, arbitrary manner which no longer accords to best practice.

Case planning and managing high risk: Case 138

In this section, Case 138 will be used as a focus for bringing together, and extending, the analysis of the themes of case management, the law, planning and decision-making explored in this and other chapters. The case involves substantiated physical abuse in a travelling family, here called Gates, with domestic violence a significant feature. It is of particular value here because it is one of the most highly managed of the sample, being the subject of five case conferences and four CPN forms within a two-year period. No fewer than nine child protection 'updates' were submitted by the social worker to the CPN meeting within this period. The children were also made the subject of a supervision order. All relevant professionals involved in the case were interviewed for this research: the area social worker, PHN, family support worker, counsellor, school principal and gardaí. The mother, father and two of the children, aged ten and nine, were also interviewed. The health board had previous involvement which centred on providing access for the family to their children who were in care for non-child protection reasons. There were seven children, aged between fifteen and two at the time of the referral in the sample. The case was open for child protection concerns at the time of referral. Another child was born during the follow-up period.

The referral, and responses to it.

The referral came from a school principal to whose home the mother had arrived one night stating that she was in fear of her husband who was threatening to 'burn all the family in the caravan'. The principal wrote to the social work department: 'They were very distressed. The mother was crying, trembling and very frightened. She said the father has hit and beaten her and was very violent. . . . . Daughter also referred to her black eye incident and said that her father kicked her to the face and gave it to her and that she didn't get it from a bicycle fall as previously stated.'

The incident in which the daughter acquired a black eye had been investigated by the social worker and the gardaí six months earlier. The referral had been anonymous and the allegations were subsequently denied by the daughter, then aged ten, and the abuse was not substantiated. In relation to the new referral, the mother withdrew the allegations of violence by her husband and denied that he hit her or the children and the father denied ever hitting his children. A CPN form was subsequently submitted, and the social worker substantiated the physical abuse on the children. 'It had been confirmed [abuse] in the sense that [Mrs Gates] had left the family home with the children because of marital violence . . . and the children said it did happen, even though it was denied when I spoke to them'. The case was re-referred twice during the follow-up research period by the school who were concerned with the hygiene and care of a six-year-old child. Five case conferences were held on the family within a period of eighteen months and a supervision order was granted in relation to the children (five months after the initial referral in this study) which was renewed the following year. The children were deemed to be at 'high risk' at the time of the referral and 'very high risk' a year after the case had been referred.

The father's violence recurs in this case. According to Mrs Gates her husband's violence caused her to have 48 stitches to her face. 'I was bleeding all night. The face is the worst one everyone can see it . . . . I got a big stove on top of me. He threw a fireplace on top of me, four or five months after I was pregnant'. The father also acted in a violent and threatening manner towards professionals who called to see the family. He 'lunged towards' the public health nurse on one occasion when she called to the caravan. 'He was extremely aggressive. Only I was on the side of the public road, and I felt that I could shout or run'. According to the gardaí, 'there is no reasoning with him; he is a very violent individual'.

Strategies employed to ensure personal safety

This book has already shown that men/fathers are not worked with nearly as much as women/mothers, while other research has suggested that referrals involving violent men are 'filtered out of the system by social workers fairly readily' (Buckley,1998, p. 7; see also Farmer and Owen 1995, 1998; Mullender, 1996; Humphrey, 1999; Parton et al, 1997; and Edwards, 1998). In this case, workers did attempt to work with the father which meant having to adopt strategies that ensured both their own personal safety and access to the family. For the school principal, 'If I was making a visit to the van, I'd always have a man come with me'. For the (female) social worker, 'On two occasions I was accompanied by two male social workers. He can be quite verbally aggressive, quite threatening, "Have you ever been hit?", you know things like that'. The family support worker employs a different tactic when visiting the caravan. 'If he is really angry. I will physically remove myself towards the door and I will say, "Will we have a fag, lad?" and my lighter is in the car. I won't go back where I was sitting; I will stand at the door or sit nearer the door'. The mother also made professionals aware when she suspected that the father was going to try and intimidate them by winking or nodding, so that the health care worker would know to leave the caravan.

Gender and responsibility for domestic violence

The scrutiny of mothers, but not fathers, in their role as parent in cases of domestic violence means that the mothers may not get support or protection from the violence while being held responsible both for it and the children's protection, while themselves being abused. In this example, one case conference recommended that a stipulation be added to the renewed supervision order that the mother take all of the children with her when she left home because of the violence. Little consideration was given, however, to how the father might assume some responsibility for the care and welfare of his children, despite the fact that, although putting them at high risk, they were deemed to be safe enough in his custody. An effective response to the violence in this case depended on whether the mother was willing to make a statement against her husband and stand by it. When this did not happen, professionals became disillusioned, which limited their ability to secure her and the children's safety and to provide effective support. The gardaí said: 'The mother has done it [made a formal complaint] on one or two occasions. You go and investigate . . . in relation to going to court, which invariably you would, because of his history and past convictions and in the meantime they have made up. These two seem to stick together like glue . . . [and it] leads to total apathy with the members of the gardaí, particularly so with this couple.'

For the school principal, 'I mean it [making allegations and retracting them] could lead you to a situation of not reporting, like crying wolf . . . the mother and children could live very capably on their own. She's a good mother, but she's not willing to do it'. The family support worker asked rhetorically, 'What can you do? She has been offered a caravan someplace else, a barring order, and she won't take any of it on board'. The counsellor's view was that work needed to be done with the mother because: 'It's not just with [the father] that work needs to be done. [Mrs Gates] has an acceptance for violence as well, which is not acceptable'. Attention is given to the perceived 'shortcomings' of the mother instead of finding out why she finds it difficult to follow through with a barring order and then providing supports which will facilitate that process. The provision of support for the mother was made all the more difficult because the father was always present when professionals called to see her. The PHN 'got very little opportunity to talk to her, because as I say, I seldom got them separate'. The family support worker's role was to support the mother but she could not do this and eventually pulled out: 'There is no way I could offer the support to the mother, that I have offered to other women. It is very seldom that I would get her on her own because the father is a permanence there, he is the man, this is it. The mother is not available to me. [The father] has a serious problem, he is controlling.'

Separate counselling facilities for the parents were set up but the mother did not keep her appointment to meet with a psychologist. However, reasons for this were not explored and would have required an examination of possible structural, financial and emotional reasons. But again this was difficult because of the profoundly controlling behaviour of her husband. The first case conference recommended that a barring order be sought against the father, but the social worker did not want to pursue it at this time. 'Basically I didn't think it was appropriate at the time [The mother] isn't strong enough yet to do it, she'd have to be strong to cope with the children, to cope with the demands of getting a place to live, she'd have to be strong to do all that after the order and I don't think the mother is at present. She says that a barring order will not protect her from [the father] and when she does leave, she always comes back.'

The counsellor said 'I would be reluctant to take that action myself and I think that if the health board was to take out a barring order, there would be the safety for [the mother] herself and how [the father] would react with that'. The school principal said 'It won't do any good, because he mightn't honour it and he'll get all his family [involved]'. Evidently, the repurcussions of a barring order on the mother, and whether her protection could be ensured, affected the decision to take out a barring order. This nuanced form of assessment is to be welcomed but must be balanced with the potential for such orders to provide safety for the abused woman and children. While there is a risk of further violence after the barring order, it is the gardaí's role to ensure that breaches of the order are met with due process of the law; our findings suggest that service users and some professionals do not believe that an adequate protective response will always follow such breaches.

Intervention strategies

A primary prevention strategy in this case was to create change by teaching alternatives to violence. Counselling was seen as vital to this process, and the father was mandated by the court via the supervision order to attend a counsellor for his problem with violence and alcohol. According to the father, this was also part of a probation order which arose because 'I lost my temper, over a garda'. The counsellor was clear that the aim of the work with the father was 'To look at what is causing, what is underlying the violence and what has built up to the violence and what is happening for the individual . . .[I] try to understand what is happening for him and then try to reflect that back to him, so that he is more aware when he is more likely to be violent, so that he can counteract his build-up process'. The counsellor also believed that conjoint counselling in some domestic violence situations is good practice: 'A lot of the time, I will do couple counselling' but believed that this is only legitimate for the perpetrator when, 'accountability, responsibility and a desire to change have taken place'. He believed it was desirable in some cases for a female counsellor to be present to provide gender balance in such work, to help 'challenge' the man by letting him know the full impact of his abusive behaviour on women. The counsellor emphasised that abused women's rights to personal safety should be paramount, which can include helping them 'to be aware of when [perpetrators] are liable to become violent, likely to be aggressive and what are the causing factors'. The danger with premature couple counselling is that professionals can unwittingly end up implicitly reinforcing the perpetrator's attempts to direct attention away from their own choices to behave non-violently (Ferguson, 1997b, p. 11).

Thus, as the counsellor was aware, couple counselling could not be considered safe practice in Case 138, not least because the perpetrator had not accepted responsibility for his abuse. While the woman might be safe from abuse while actually in this type of counselling environment, she would be at risk of further abuse when she left the counselling session. In effect, the woman is placed in a 'double bind' where to talk of the abuse could put her in very grave danger (Adams, 1988, p.187). The counsellor was aware of this: 'I think a lot of the time, when I meet other couples, there are a lot of feelings of insecurity, and I feel that after I leave, that they are going to be exposed to violence'. The key point is that unless and until the offender has taken responsibility for his violence all interactions and incoming information will be filtered through a mindset that blames the partner and denies that he has a problem (Ferguson and Synott, 1995). A focus on anger management without an even more strategic attempt to challenge the offender's belief system and issues of power and control can actually increase the danger to the vicitm. Gondolf (1993, p. 247) argues that couple counselling is best introduced only after successful completion of a batterer's programme and after six to twelve months of known non-violent behaviour.

The abuser's responsibility for the violence can also be limited through a process of mitigation, which serves to minimise the violence (Milner, 1993, 1996). Thus the father's violence is assessed in relation to his consumption of alcohol. For the school principal, 'he's grandest when he's not drinking', and for the gardaí, 'This man when he has drink taken, has absolutely no control whatsoever'. The counsellor said that '[the father] felt that if he dealt with alcohol, he was dealing with the violence. And I would say to some extent, he was right'—not by way of an excuse or cause of violence but because of how alcohol heightens anxiety, tension and the potential to violence.

The PHN felt that the father's abusiveness to her could be at least partially explained as 'to do with the pressure of the day with the teacher calling and the gardaí calling'. This seems to suggest that the violence was not under the man's control, but brought on by incidents that annoyed him. It ties in with Milner's (1993) notion of 'operation of emotional control' whereby violent men are not seen as responsible for emotional control within the home because women are responsible for it. Moreover, the father was seen by the social worker to be gaining control over violent behaviour, for instance, when he chose to follow due process of law instead of fighting with a man who destroyed his caravan. 'He actually responded by not going down and killing [the man], which he probably would have done previously. He seems to be dealing with his anger a bit better outside of the home.' However, viewing the progress of the father in this manner is only appropriate if it includes assessments of how or if his behaviour has changed at home. There is no necessary correspondence between better anger management outside the home and within it; this is of fundamental importance precisely because it is the father's violence at home that has put the children at 'very high risk'.

Attention can also be deflected away from fathers in physical abuse cases through a process Farmer and Owen (1998, p. 50) term lack of evidence or denial: 'Where either, because the man denied causing the child's injury or because, in the absence of any direct evidence. . . . the worker focused on some other area of family difficulty'. For example, in this case, many of the recommendations from the case conferences were focused on trying to find a suitable Traveller site for the family to live. Implicit in this was the belief that the risk would be reduced if and when the family had more space and amenities. For the counsellor, 'I know their home is one of the problems they have at the moment, getting residence, so that they can live in some more acceptable harmony'. The public health nurse believed that, 'If they had a halting site it would take all the pressure and stress off the family'. Without doubt, better housing would have helped this family and was a legitimate focus for intervention. This shows how the cultural context of the family was taken into consideration. According to the social worker, parenting issues were hard to address because of their lack of resources. 'How can you clean the kids when you don't have anywhere to wash them and parenting at that level was difficult [to address] until they are based in a place where they do have facilities.' In this regard, this traveller family did get very beneficial material support to help them cope with their social exclusion and lack of resources. But the danger is that too concerted a focus on secondary problems such as alcohol abuse and poor housing, at the expense of making the father accountable for his violence, distracts attention away from the child abuse and domestic violence.

Inadequacies of the supervision order

The father's control over the family members was such that the allegations of physical child abuse were denied, often after actual disclosures from the children and mother. These retractions made it difficult for the social worker to substantiate the abuse. The social worker completed no fewer than nine CPN update forms on the family within a two-year period, all of which were noted to be 'unconfirmed abuse with case open for child protection concerns' (case file). Moreover, the father continued to hit the children—and the mother—even though there was a supervision order in place and the social worker was working directly with the children. For example, the mother went to the gardaí to make a statement about her husband allegedly assaulting her while pregnant but later withdrew the allegations. The ten-year-old girl informed the social worker and teachers that her father had hit her and her siblings with his fist on which he wore rings. The case file notes that there were visible marks on one child consistent with ring marks. In response, the social worker increased the number of visits to the caravan and challenged the father about the abuse, which he denied. The social worker was aware of the limitations of the supervision order: 'It's handy if he becomes unco-operative, in the sense that they've no choice, that I have to be involved, but it doesn't really offer any protection for kids, very little'. Nor was further protection in the form of care orders regarded as a solution, as account was again taken by the social worker of the children's cultural background: 'I just don't feel it's the right step for them. And we're talking about a whole new culture of people and houses. The son, if in care, would run away. There's no way you could ever move him'. For the school principal, 'They're not at risk from the mother and it [care order] would take them away from their mother'. Another factor influencing the decision not to obtain a care order may have been the family's suffering over the children already in care.

Implications for 'safe' practice

Because the risk in this case is directly related to physical abuse, we need to examine how the woman and children could be protected from the father's violence. Since the father was physically abusive to the mother and children, and reluctant to meet the specifics of the supervision order, other legal interventions might have been appropriate in this case. The Domestic Violence Act, 1996 gives new powers to both health boards and gardaí to pursue civil protection orders on behalf of women who are not in a position to do so on their own behalf. Yet neither the health board nor the gardaí saw fit to enforce their obligations under the Act. Nor is there any mention of the health board applying for a safety order—which is a non-molestation order—on behalf of the mother. This kind of case raises the issue of the degree of responsibility placed on women to take out civil orders for protection on their own and their children's behalf, and highlights the need for increased training about domestic violence and for policy guidelines which would outline the responsibility of health boards in those cases that warrant intervention under the Domestic Violence Act.

More inter-agency liaison could have taken place between the health board and the gardaí to ensure that: 1) the mother was supported if and when a barring order was implemented; and 2) the father was prosecuted for breaches of the barring order. The gardaí had arrested the father when 'drunk and disorderly'. For example, on the night of the referral he spent the night in the station. 'You go up and arrest him, bring him into the station, put him in a cell and generally wait until he sobers up'. This garda felt it was still a question of 'scratching for powers really in a sense to bring him in'. It is essential that the gardaí use the legislation to its fullest extent, so that such fathers are made accountable for their actions. The use of mandated counselling for the father, therefore, is to be welcomed. Yet, overcoming denial and creating a sense of responsibility is a vital first step when working with violent offenders (Dobash and Dobash, 1992, p. 245; Mullender 1996, p. 225). This process is best carried out in mandated group work based on a model of accountability, similar to the work carried out by the Cork Domestic Violence Project or MOVE (Ferguson and Synott, 1995; O'Connor, 1996).

The child protection plan in this case was facilitated by five case conferences, and many of their recommendations carried out. Despite this, the children were still regarded as at high risk at the end of the study period. Direct work with the children by the social worker consisted of getting them to talk about their feelings about home life. As the ten-year-old girl told the researcher, 'We go in [to see the social worker] and out every couple of months. We used to go in every couple of weeks. She'd say, "How are you today and how's mammy and daddy?" I think its [talking to the social worker] all right, you go away for a while and come back'. The older boy did not like being asked questions about his home life. 'I hate it, disgusting. They hold you up for too long, too much stupid questions that's what I hate. I don't like going in on my own because you won't be able to answer all [the questions]. You need your sister to answer some, you have to be safe like'. This is the boy who, it was felt, would run away if placed in care and there are already worrying signs in his resistant attitude that he is copying his father's hostility to authorities. On the other hand, the children were unanimous about what they wanted the social worker to do for them. 'Talk to daddy and mammy like they do when people fight they help them. That's what they do with daddy and mammy'.

The hugely difficult task of the social worker in this case, then, was to support the mother and children while at the same time engaging with involuntary clients. The social worker attempted to manage conflict in the relationship by negotiating with the family. Workers had to do this in a climate of intimidation from the father, which raises the question of how much work frontline professionals can be expected to do with violent and/or intimidating clients? The gender dynamic of this is all the more acute given that 85 per cent of the health board's social workers are women (Doherty, 1996) who have to deal in cases such as this with men who are controlling and abusive to women. This does not mean that there are no safety issues for male staff. On the contrary, not only do they have to deal with their own violent clients but, too often, the clients of others as well. This case exemplifies the trend identified in Chapter 3 of men being much more frequently asked to accompany female colleagues on visits to potentially violent clients. There are serious staff safety issues at stake here. Health board policy should spell out clearly what procedures to follow in such situations so that workers feel protected.

There is also the problem of balancing the care and control aspects of social work, for if professionals intervene in a manner which the family sees as coercive they could retaliate and pull back. This family moved away from the area for a short period while the supervision order was in place. The father referred to this in the research interview: 'She [the social worker] was telling me she'd put the kids in care. I didn't really like it. I moved away. I thought I was going to get rid of them [social workers], but they still kept coming round off me'. What seemed to happen in the interaction between the family and professional systems is what Reder et al (1983, p. 106) term 'disguised compliance'. When the family did not comply with the supervision order by permitting access to the home, the social worker adopted a more controlling stance and brought in male social workers to support her in confronting the father. By the father's own account, the social worker also challenged his authority by informing him that if things got worse, 'We'd go to court for a caring order'. What defused this tension was the father's assurance that he would co-operate and go to counselling, and that social workers could see the children when they wanted to. This translated to a form of 'disguised compliance' because there was little systematic evidence that the father was in fact changing or becoming any 'safer'. Thus the effect was to neutralise the authority of the social worker and return the relationship to the previous status quo. One year on, however, with the renewal of the supervision order, it seemed that the father was becoming resigned to social work intervention. '[Social workers] will probably see me for another three or four years, but I don't mind that's their job like'. Regardless of this, the 'closure' of a family system by seeking to avoid professionals must be viewed as a significant risk factor in child protection work.

By any standards, this was a very difficult high risk case and the level of work that went into it was impressive. It occurred in the one community care area in the region that had a coherent follow-up procedure for monitoring notified cases and was tightly managed in terms of those procedures by the CPN committee and case conferences. Again, however, when assessing safe practice, it is the direction of the work that it at issue rather than the sincerity with which it was carried out. It exemplifies the 'lose-lose' options that professionals often face, when bringing the children into care involves losses and risks, as does leaving them at home. Overall, the level of support offered in this case was found wanting because it failed ultimately to provide immediate protection for the mother and children. The failure was due to the controlling stance of the father and the inability of the professionals to get enough access to support the mother and empower her to leave with the children, or have him barred, in a way that would be safe for her and the children. In mandating the man to attend counselling, and in the real efforts that were made to engage directly with the mother and children, the practice in many ways extended to the outer limits of what could be achieved, even under a supervision order. The deficits in safe practice are essentially systemic in origin, rooted in the underlying theoretical understanding of the problem of physical abuse of children and women and the inability to have the father engaged with in a batterers programme. The case shows the importance not only of case conferences and a co-ordinated strategy for intervention—the level of which was indeed impressive—but also of a clearly articulated and shared conception of the correct way to work with abusers and their victims; one based on a deep, shared understanding of the control and power issues at the core of such cases and what is required to change them, and which should not involve premature couples counselling or family therapy. Thus it is not sufficient for inter-agency training to simply work to advance good inter-agency communication and decision making. Professionals need to have a clear corporate vision of what they are seeking to protect children (and adult victims) from and clearly negotiated and well-understood intervention strategies worked out in response.

Conclusion

This chapter has identified the factors influencing decisions to hold case conferences and illuminated the role that such conferences now play in decision making. A key finding is the relatively minor role played by case conferences in managing new cases and referrals, being largely concerned with cases with a history of health board involvement. The adverse consequences of filtering out cases which do not then receive long-term services have been shown. The filters exclude some identified cases of need, that is substantiated high-risk cases, from multi-disciplinary decisions and planning. Meanwhile, Case 138 has shown the danger in which children, abused parents, and professionals may be placed when cases are not managed by the multi-disciplinary system, and the challenges that face childcare professionals in managing high risk cases. The central role of formal inter-agency work in devising clearly negotiated and well-understood intervention strategies to achieve the safest response for all concerned was demonstrated.

Notes

[1] These five cases were primarily concerned with: physical abuse in one case, sexual abuse in two, parental difficulties in one and financial/housing problems in one. In the latter, the referrer was concerned about very poor and basic living conditions and the physical care of the children.

[2] Social workers did not substantiate 26 cases.

[3] Substantiated low-risk cases include cases where the risk to child(ren) was assessed as low or very low, while substantiated high-risk cases include those where the risk was assessed as high or very high.

[4] These figures add to more that 100 per cent as some social workers cited more than one reason.

[5] Some cases were known for more that one child care problem.

[6] The information was not provided to us in three cases.

[7] In five of these cases a case conference was planned but was not held during April–June 1996.

[8] 'Case being monitored', 'good informal inter-professional work took place' and 'insufficient personnel involved in case' were mentioned by the social workers in three cases.

[9] This includes an invitation to foster parents in one case, to grandparents in one, and a case where the child named in the referral was the alleged abuser and where the parents of the victim were invited to the case conference, not the parents of the alleged child perpetrator.

7 Promoting Safety, Welfare and Healing? Long-term Responses to Child Protection and Welfare Cases

When establishing how child protection and welfare systems work, and how safe they are, it is important to consider the provision of long-term services to those children and families who have been assessed as at risk or in need. This chapter provides a detailed analysis of the MWHB's provision of social work and other child care services in such cases. All the referrals in the initial 319 sample were followed up one year on, to establish what had happened up to July 1997. This method of analysis highlights the filtering process between the investigation/assessment of a referral and the input of longer term treatment/support services. As Figure 1.1 shows, 41 per cent of the 286 referrals to the social work teams were still open one year later, meaning that 59 per cent were filtered out. This chapter considers the work that went on with those cases that did and did not get longer-term services. The key research questions explored are: What services were offered to which children and families? To what extent are identified risks being worked with and needs met? What are the reasons that needs are unmet and how might they be resolved? A key distinction is made between investigative and treatment/support work. In essence, this chapter is concerned with post-investigative involvement and the 'intensity' of that involvement. Previous work (Parton, Thorpe and Wattam, 1997; Thorpe, 1994, 1997) has tended to consider whether social work services were provided to children and families, but not the broader nature of service provision. This book breaks new ground in establishing the multi-disciplinary nature of service provision, and shows the considerable impact that service development is having under the Child Care Act.

Promoting child safety, welfare and healing: An exemplary case (140)

Having examined the various stages of the child care and protection process, it is now appropriate to focus in greater detail on one case from referral to long-term outcome. This will help to draw out the key issues in the provision of long-term services to children and families. Case 140 involves substantiated emotional abuse and neglect in relation to four children. The eldest—here called Joanne (not her real name)—was aged ten at the time of the referral and her three brothers seven, five and two. The family were first involved with the health board two years earlier due to allegations of physical abuse and neglect by the parents, here called Mr and Mrs Smith. The case was closed for child protection concerns at the time of the referral in this study. It is a prime example of how particular combinations of services are put into substantiated cases, in this instance home-based (social work and family support worker), clinical (child psychologist) and care-based (respite care for the children). The case was worked with extremely effectively, with very positive outcomes for the children and parents, and provides an example of best practice, a baseline of exemplary practice against which to measure the degree to which intervention generally manages to promote child safety, welfare and healing. This case study is based on interviews with Mr and Mrs Smith (separately), Joanne, the social worker, family support worker and the school principal.

The referral and responses to it

The initial referral to the social work department was made by a school and centred on Joanne whose behaviour at school was alleged to be 'disruptive and aggressive' (case file). According to the principal it was: 'Very aggressive and very cheeky and very unusual behaviour. It was beyond what any teacher had to deal with. She would have kicked children in the stomach. I had children that ran away from school because of her . . . She was hijacking the whole class and the teacher in her class said to me at the end of this summer, "I blame her for my breakdown in health".' The principal asked to meet with Mrs Smith to discuss these concerns and suggested that the school seek further help, with Mrs Smith's consent. At this stage, the principal wanted to get psychological support for Joanne—'It was not just a problem for [the girl], it was a family problem'—and informed the social worker about the alleged behavioural problems with the request for psychological support. The social worker investigated the case and completed a CPN form and substantiated neglect and emotional abuse as: 'Mother shouting, critical and sarcastic with child, to the extent, child visibly upset. Mother unaware of child's discomfort and continued laughing at the child. Child got angry and accused of lying by mother. This appears to be a daily occurrence' (case file). There was also concern about home conditions, possible domestic violence and the parents' general capacity to cope.

The children were deemed to be at 'high risk' at the time of referral. It was noted in the case file that the mother 'does not like social workers, health board employees'. During the twelve-month research follow-up period the case was re-referred alleging that the mother had hit the child. The social worker completed seven CPN update forms within twelve months. The outcome was confirmed emotional abuse. A health board child psychologist was introduced to develop a behaviour modification programme with Joanne at school and she was assessed as 'depressive and suicidal' (case file). Respite care was also provided for Joanne and her eldest brother. One case conference took place a year after the initial referral followed by two review case conferences within a six-month period, at the second of which the case was closed for child protection concerns but left open for child care concerns. Joanne moved to a new school and was deemed to be doing well and was due to be re-assessed by a psychologist.

The social worker saw the emotional abuse as at the forefront of the child care issues: 'There is definite emotional abuse and it's very severe. There would be a lot of shouting and roaring between the parents. When they have an argument, the father's bags might be packed and they'd say, "Who are you going to live with?" . . . The children told me "Stop asking me who I'm going to live with". You could see the mother in front of you and the three kids and she would set them all off, they'd all have temper tantrums.' Both parents were aware of the impact that this type of behaviour has on the children. The father said, 'The kids used to start crying saying, "We don't want Daddy to go or we don't want Mammy to go". I suppose it was having a bad effect on the kids.' The mother said, 'They used to cry a lot. They would be afraid of me and the father fighting'. Mrs Smith explained her behaviour as 'Just losing my temper for nothing. Shouting, screaming, break things, kick doors and stamp upstairs and slam doors, smash cups and literally for nothing. It'd be the least little thing, like the ashtray in the wrong position.'

Dealing with 'hostile' clients

Initially, both Mr and Mrs Smith were adamant that they didn't want social work or any other kind of intervention. They felt this way, in part, because of past experience with a social worker. That social worker, as Mrs Smith put it, 'never gave me a chance to explain myself. If I tried to say something, she thought I was hiding things and if I didn't say enough, I was still hiding things.' For Mr Smith, 'She was coming down asking questions, questions, but there was nothing coming back.' They felt that that social worker did not explore with the family how she could help them to resolve some of their difficulties. Things got worse when one of the children was allegedly examined for sexual abuse while undergoing a medical examination. The parents both 'reared up' on the health board. The father said, 'I would not have gone near a social worker again and that is being straight and honest with you. I was very, very, wary and wanted nothing to do with a social worker.' Not feeling able to trust social workers meant that the mother could not actively engage with any formal support system, despite recognising the need for some help: 'I knew my little girl needed a psychologist. I couldn't come in here and say I think she might need someone to talk to. I thought if I do, they'll say I'm not looking after her and then bring me into a social worker.' Thus the parents developed an 'operational perspective' (Cleaver and Freeman, 1995) to child protection which, while it protected them from undue interference from an oppressive form of social work practice, left them isolated and bereft of the kinds of support they really needed.

The process of engagement

As this book has already shown, there are many voluntary clients in child care and protection who accept, and often initiate, professional involvement. However, as the analysis in this chapter will show, client resistance to intervention is such that it constitutes the main reason why long-term services are not provided in substantiated cases. Intervention with involuntary clients presents distinct challenges that we are only beginning to understand and theorise fully (Barber, 1991). The Smith case typifies how resistance can arise in some cases from problems with how the service is structured and delivered—the parents' dislike of the previous social worker's intrusive, forensic, uncaring protectionist approach. But it also reveals a patterned response, which has hitherto been neglected in the literature of child protection, where the clients' psychological and developmental problems block them from forming meaningful relationships and attachments, with professionals as much as with family and friends (Howe, et al 1999). Thus, we need to learn from successful cases about the process of engagement of resistant clients.

Social workers and other professionals have the difficult task in such cases of assessing the needs of the children while at the same time trying to engage a mother and father who do not want intervention. The social worker recognised that Mrs Smith was 'quite hostile you know, a lot of the time. With the mother very frightened of social work involvement and not trusting, the issues had to be explored very sensitively.' The family support worker found Mrs Smith 'extremely hostile and she used foul language. She did not want to know about social workers'. When the social worker made her first home visit, even though she was expected because of the negotiations with the school, Mrs Smith started 'crying' and asked, 'What did I do now?' The social worker did not push the issues too far and arranged to call again the following day. Facilitating this process meant 'trying to understand where the mother is coming from, and the issues she has gone through. You can actually work when you know where it's all coming from, you're going from what their issue is as well.' This strategy worked well to win over the mother, who was adamant that 'You need someone that is going to sit down, listen to you and not judge you, if you have a problem'. To get to the stage of addressing parenting issues, the family support worker worked hard to build a rapport with Mrs Smith which took some time: 'Maybe two visits a week for about a month until I drank her coffee, smoked her fags and she was quite comfortable with that. She gave me a load of personal stuff which was not really relevant to our work but it gave a bigger insight on her as a woman and as a mother and partner to the father and that was the way we worked it to try and help the mother help the children.'

The client's demeanour also affected how the social worker conducted her work. The mother's past experience with social workers is taken into account when considering her lack of engagement with professionals. This is quite different to an approach which sees her inability to focus on the problems as a consequence of her unwillingness to engage with social workers; this could lead to a non-responsive attitude from the social worker. As the social worker expressed it: 'When you go in to address an issue, she will try and dismiss it or keep talking about something else, then if you say something the wrong way with her you can get the door. I know her now and know how to say something. She's getting there, you know. Before, she used to see me and she was so petrified that her mind was racing. She might hear the first sentence and that was it.'

The family support worker was also very aware of how Mrs Smith struggled to listen, and worked to ensure that child protection issues were addressed while at the same time trying to *understand* where the mother was coming from. For example, she told Mrs Smith, '"When I am talking you are way ahead of me, you are thinking of answers plus another question at the end, so could we just talk today about [this problem]" and that would bring her back to parenting.' Helping the mother to help the children also meant focusing on Mrs Smith to make her feel better about herself. 'I felt she needed to like herself more, because she did not like herself' (family support worker). Building Mrs Smith's esteem was done by encouraging her to take care of her appearance. 'She did little things like get her hair cut. She had no teeth and then she went and had her teeth done. She began to look after herself a little more . . . it was much more positive stuff'. At first Mrs Smith found it easier to talk to the family support worker than to the social worker. Both professionals were aware of this and used it strategically to their advantage. As the social worker recounted, 'Sometimes it can be easier for the mother to hear things reinforced from the family support worker. She's less of a threat, so in the beginning she was able to focus in with the mother regarding parenting and stuff'. The mother was aware of this: 'I was lucky, because the social worker really did work with me, but she sent in the family support worker first and she softened me up, to be honest.'

Improving parenting skills and the practice of intimacy

Thus a main focus of the work was to promote personal development as well as improving parenting skills. As the social worker said: 'Their parenting is so disastrous that they really don't know how to start or what good parenting is. So it has to be done at a very slow level. It may take up to a year to discuss issues, even the most important issues. One step at a time.' The family support worker used small sections of a parenting book. She also showed how to physically care for a child, feeling that the mother 'was not really aware of the emotional stuff her children needed. She found it difficult to touch her daughter. . . . I could talk till I was blue in the face about nurturing and until the mother saw me nurturing it was no good until I left her to think about it.' The family support worker would give the daughter a 'hug' when she met her, in the presence of the mother.

Another example of teaching the practice of intimacy by 'modelling' nurturing is apparent in the principal's observation that 'There'd be very little affection shown to the daughter by the mother, you know even how her hair looked'. The family support worker agreed with this: 'Her mother was not taking care of the daughter's hair and it took maybe a month and then I went in one day and did the hair' and then told Mrs Smith to 'go down to the pound shop and get a bottle of oil and treat her hair and you can use half of it yourself.' This was, as the family support worker said, 'turning a negative into a positive in a very simple example'. Another such example was: 'The mother would focus on the daughter "got seven spellings wrong out of ten" and I'd say, "Brilliant—you got three right, get four right next week".'

Direct work with the child

A key role for the social worker was in doing direct work with the child. She met with Joanne every week for five months, and after that every two weeks. Joanne was allowed to set the agenda about when they would meet and what they would talk about. The child's mother or father were strategically not told what the social worker and their daughter talked about, unless it was a child protection concern that demanded limited confidentiality. As shown in Chapter 8, in common with other children (see also Butler and Williamson, 1994), Joanne really appreciated this: 'I knew that what I said there was no way it was going to get out, that helped me express my feelings more.' Part of the social worker's aim was to improve parental functioning from Joanne's viewpoint, who, for instance, told the social worker she was embarrassed because her mother was 'always roaring and shouting at her in front of her friends'. The social worker discussed this with the mother and daughter and 'a compromise was come to. Mum wouldn't do it, but she expected something from the daughter, that she would respond to the mother, fairly reasonably rather than ignoring her'. A key task for the social worker in her direct work with Joanne was to help her get her message across to her mother. As Joanne said, 'She said she was a social worker to help me in things I couldn't say to my mam, she'd help me to say them to her'.

Anger management

The social worker felt that it was Mrs Smith's 'behaviour that causes the problems and if the kids are to remain at home, it's her behaviour that has to change'. Mrs Smith had the same perception: 'The issue was me and my moods and my temper and how that was affecting the kids and how it was affecting my daughter in school'. Intervention also focused, then, on how Mrs Smith could control her 'temper', as she explained:'The family support worker was there to help me with losing my temper and how to cope with what if my daughter came in with a problem. Rather than say "Go away and leave me alone", I'd try dealing with it and if I couldn't, rather than shout at her, I'd say, "Listen, give me five, I'll have a cup of coffee". Whereas before if she came in, I would have said,"'If you don't go away, I'm going to murder you". I would have slapped her. I would've lost my head.'

Mrs Smith also recognised how the family support worker worked to increase her self esteem while at the same time teaching anger management skills, by 'just words of encouragement, you know, [for example], nobody's perfect. I always thought everything was my fault, I was stupid and silly, the family support worker showed me that I'm a person for meself'. Joanne spoke of how her mother had changed because of this work. 'If she was going to say something, she stops. In her mind I'd say she says, "No, I'm not going to shout, the family support worker told me not to do it" and she'd walk out of the room before she'd explode.' Moreover, Joanne conceded that she also 'exploded' against her mother and that the social worker helped her overcome this problem. 'She told me, it just wasn't worth it, put your foot down and say, "you're not going to explode" and just keep your head and think what you're saying even if she's exploding. I'm [now] able to keep control. I'm not as bossy as I used to be.' This is intervention work at its very best: through the therapeutic process the child not only receives support to deal with being poorly parented and is rendered safer, but herself is helped to learn anger management and emotional literacy.

Addressing the underlying trauma

A powerful part of Mrs Smith's narrative was an experience she had had ten years previously when at seventeen years of age she was raped and became pregnant with Joanne. She did not tell anyone at the time, including her partner, who had not known until recently who the father was. The mother carried around this 'secret' for over ten years and considered it to be part of the reason why she acted abusively. 'The father didn't know I'd been raped. He didn't know what was making me carry on like this. It was breaking me up, so I contacted the social worker, explained the whole lot to her and said will you work on it with me, yourself and the family support worker. That took so much off my head. I was able [then] to work on other issues that I needed to sort out.'

For the mother, the social worker's totally non-judgemental approach when she told her about the rape made all the difference and 'that made everything seem as if, God, why hadn't I been able to meet this woman ten years ago and tell her this and then it wouldn't have been so bad'. For the social worker, 'because the daughter is a product of rape, that is underlying a lot of how the mother sees her daughter. Because the mother can love the two boys so easily, so as those issues are addressed, that relationship will improve'. The school principal also mentioned that she saw Joanne's problems at school as being linked to the family structure. 'In the daughter's case, it's definitely the whole family thing . . . the father—he's not the daughter's father. And the daughter would talk about that in school.' The social worker and family support worker gave a lot of support to the parents around this time. As the social worker explained: 'That took, I'd say, about three months from start to finish, between father and mother coping and preparing. He finding out the first time who the daughter's father was and coping with that and moving on to the daughter, to tell the daughter.' In order to facilitate the father in coming to terms with the issues, the social worker and family support worker would call to the house later in the evening when he came in from work, something he very much appreciated: 'Most of the time it's nine to five and if you're not in, good luck! But the social worker and family support worker had never kind of done that, you know. If you needed a later time, they'd arrange it. There is very few people who have done that.'

The family support worker believes it is important to get the men/fathers involved: 'If you get the male on board it takes away the threat. It saves the woman from having to say what we talked about or what we can do or what we intend to do.' Getting the father involved in this instance, then, was seen as reinforcing the work being done with other family members. There was a worthy attempt here to develop a father-centred practice which was based on a recognition of the man's positive capacities to care for his children and partner, an inclusive approach he—like other men—greatly appreciate (Dienhart and Dollahite, 1997; Hawkins et al, 1995; Hogan, 1998). However, the man's role is, to some extent still minimized, because he is seen as a supplementary parent to the mother (Daniel and Taylor, 1999; McKeown et al, 1998). The intervention doesn't focus enough on how he should or could assume greater responsibility for the care and emotional management of the family (Milner, 1993, 1996; Edwards, 1998).

Dealing with an abusive mother

The work done in this case very effectively balanced authoritative child protection, negotiated family support work and informed risk taking. A year after the initial referral included in this study, Joanne called to the social worker and made a self-report to the effect that her mother had hit her, and Joanne showed the social worker her bruises: 'There was quite serious bruising. This is what she alleged, so I could have gone to the doctor with her and she could have been out of the home.' The social worker did not take this approach: 'I think you just take a risk, I know it's not good enough for the kid to have that sort of beating. Mum spoke about what she did and we all sat down together and the mother apologised and there was hugs and kisses.'

The social worker also took into account that the family had huge financial problems and faced eviction. To help relieve the stress, after the abusive incident respite care was provided for ten days for Joanne and her six-year-old brother. The social worker analyses abuse by mothers in a context which takes account of the adversity of mothering; this is done within a theoretical framework for understanding based on gender as a social construct, combined with an individual biography (Featherstone, 1996, 1997a; Kelly, 1996a, p.36). 'She has the main responsibility with the kids all day, so that's why it makes it more understandable'. However, the social worker was also clear that the mother was culpable and because of the female abuse the social worker was concerned that 'The kids are with her all day.' The social worker made it clear that 'the issue is you can't hit your children'. To reinforce this, although the social worker decided not to submit a CPN form on that occasion, she explained to Mrs Smith what would happen if and when she did complete one. 'So she is aware that the next incident will [result in] a case conference. I think it worked out okay'. She did, however, notify the gardaí of this incident but asked them to hold off their investigation because she and the family support worker were working 'intensively' with the family. Thus, despite—or perhaps even because of—the openness and trust in the relationship, the social worker was not afraid to take risks and to confront the parents with the consequences of child abuse. This is the kind of truthfulness in practice which is essential for promoting child safety and which shows how child protection can be done honestly in the context of support and healing work.

Inter-agency work

The one area of real difficulty in the case concerned effective inter-agency work. There was confusion between the school, social worker and family support worker due to a lack of understanding about the difficulties of implementing Joanne's behaviour modification programme, coupled with a difference of opinion about the nature of Joanne's disruptive behaviour. Teachers could not implement the behaviour modification programme which involved monitoring Joanne's behaviour at regular intervals. 'We felt that what [the psychologist] was recommending was fine for a one to one situation, but we have children in a thirty to one situation'. In addition, the principal expressed concern that the school was not asked, as part of the on-going social assessment of Joanne, how they were experiencing her behaviour at school, where she 'was still very demanding'. This raises the question why the social worker did not make some effort to find out the school's experience. The social worker felt that the teachers may not have liked Joanne because of their feelings toward her mother; this seems to suggest that the conduct of the teachers exacerbated the child's behaviour. On the other hand, according to the principal, 'behaviour was accepted from the daughter that wouldn't be expected from anyone else, we'd be trying to reach out to her, she had a very hard upbringing'.

There was some attempt to formally co-ordinate the effort in the case, through one case conference, followed by two review case conferences within a six-month period. It was recommended that both the mother and daughter have more regular appointments with the psychologist, which never happened because her parents moved Joanne to another school, after which her school behaviour and academic results improved. Conflict and tension is endemic in inter-agency work because of poor communication between members of the professional network (Reder et al, 1993, p. 68). Lack of respect for each other's roles and of feedback between the two systems resulted in conflict and tension, which only served to hinder inter-agency co-operation. This demonstrates how important it is for each member of the expert system to share a particular practice goal and to make explicit assumptions about what is being attempted, through what practice model, and how realistic, given the resources and philosophy of each agency, are such goals.

Outcome of the case: recovery and healing

At the core of the work with the mother was assistance in the construction of a new narrative of the self (Giddens, 1991). She herself is clear about why she found it hard to care for her children: 'I couldn't help my daughter because I needed help first'. Being able to shed the burden of the rape felt 'great . . . things got better with the kids, because it was all off my mind, I can talk to them now; before I shouted at them, because I didn't trust myself. I had all those emotional problems for ten years back.' Mr Smith saw how his partner 'is a lot better in herself, because a lot of the pressure that was on her, over that, [rape] was taken off'. Increasing her level of confidence has enabled Mrs Smith to become more intimate with her daughter, becoming more tactile with her, as she is with her sons, as the social worker observed, and 'there'd be a lot more laughs and fun'. According to Mrs Smith, this transformation extends to the practicalities of everyday living: 'We go shopping as a family now. I can do the shopping without screaming.'

Joanne said that before the work with the social worker, she herself 'was a really grouchy person and angry always, annoying my ma and just getting in the way. The social worker has just taught me better ways to deal with my problems and that made me feel better. If I was going home, I'd feel happier.' Here we see child care practice at its best, enabling parents and children to practice what Giddens (1992) calls the 'new intimacy'—emotional communication and negotiation in the context of equal relationships. The family are being assisted to move beyond traditional hierarchical forms of patriarchal relationships towards a 'democratic family' form (Giddens, 1998), where children are heard as well as seen and feel safe, women as well as men are treated with respect, and men as well as women are enabled to have expressive emotional lives and relationships. Promoting such self-actualisation and equality for all family members is central to the achievement of effective child protection, welfare and healing and constitutes what child care policy and practice needs to be all about.

Implications for theory and practice

Case 140 has been used here as an example of the 'best practice' going on in Irish child care and protection. Best practice in any case or system is always open to debate and arguably there are always ways in which improvements can be made and different approaches suggested. For instance, some may not agree with the 'informal' way the social worker managed the re-referral concerning the physical abuse of the child, whereas others will agree with her supportive authoritative approach. The practice in this case can in most respects be regarded as exemplary because of the different levels of intervention, and the ways in which the child care and protection process was managed including the careful way the referral was negotiated by the school with the social worker and the mother, the sensitive way the process of engagement with resistant parents was managed and the authoritative and supportive therapeutic work which promoted the child's safety, welfare and healing and enabled the parents to confront their difficulties and underlying trauma and ultimately find some healing.

We can see from this case that family support in the context of child protection has a number of dimensions including: *practical* supports: enhancing parental capacities and the competencies of both parents; modelling good care with children; mobilising resources—respite care; day care; family/community networks. Then there are distinct *therapeutic* supports which surround 'emotion' work/personal development, with children and carers which include: building self-esteem, care of the self; anger/emotion management/literacy; addressing the underlying trauma; mediating parent-child relationships; and promoting individualisation and self-actualisation in terms of the distinct needs and life plans of women, men and children (Ferguson, 2001c). Taken together, these dimensions of family support in the context of child protection as mapped out here can provide a necessary framework for promoting child safety, welfare and healing and the creation of democratic families, a goal which is how the essential overall purpose of child care intervention today needs to be understood.

While this kind of best practice was only achieved in some cases in this study, it has been used here to go beyond the dominant form of critique of child care practice which is based on a 'deficit approach', showing up what practitioners and child care systems allegedly do *not* do; what service users do *not* like, and so on. This is done in the belief that if practice competencies and policy are to develop effectively, students, academics/trainers, practitioners and policymakers need to have models of good practice available to them from which to learn and develop. In short, best practice needs to be set out so that it can be recognised and developed.

The work in this case went on in the context of increased accountability and bureaucratisation of child welfare—just the sort of social conditions which some argue have led to professionals working in legalistic, forensic ways which deliver a 'relatively restricted practice repertoire' (Parton, Thorpe and Wattam, 1997, p.183). Nonetheless, a form of creative intervention occurred that was tailor-made to the needs of the mother, daughter and even, to some extent, the father. The mother was extremely grateful for the help and support she received which, she insisted, prevented the children from going into statutory care: 'Without the family support worker's help, I wouldn't be here'. The social worker refused to engage solely in defensive practice, saying 'I try, if at all possible, for that child to be reared with its own family [and] when it's possible I really would be willing to go the hard slog with it'. In addition, while Parton et al (1997, p. 185) argue that childcare professionals don't accede to the 'negotiated demands of clients', here we see just how much the reflexive action of clients helps to construct the practice (see Ferguson, 1997a). For example, it was the mother who initiated social work support concerning the rape as she was determined to come to terms with it. In every sense, the practice was co-constructed by professionals and the service users.

While there were distinct inter-agency struggles between the school and the social work department, the case shows how social workers can work directly with children and parents while managing cases effectively, in this case the social worker supported the child and assessed child protection concerns and the family support worker concentrated on parenting and other therapeutic issues. The clarification of their roles is spelt out by the family support worker: 'I report to the social worker, she has the responsibility of the case'. According to the family support worker, attaining this type of relationship, 'has taken a long time and it depends on the social worker, they all have their own personalities'. These workers managed the inter-professional status struggles well; despite the rhetoric of partnership surrounding family support, these struggles permeate child care practice where some professions are more powerful than others (Jordan, 1997); in this case social work was more powerful than family support work.

This case-study also shows the positive impact of anti-oppressive approaches to child and family work. It has been argued that mother-blame is rife as social workers employ what they view as 'normal behaviour' as a benchmark when assessing risk and that this results in the scrutiny of the 'moral character' of the parent, predominantly mothers, rather than an assessment of the parent's social conditions (Parton et al, 1997, p.153; Hanmer and Statham, 1988). Arguably, more could have been done to challenge the father about the burden of responsibility shouldered by the mother for child care and family problems. Yet the professionals showed a good deal of respect for the way the couple had negotiated child care responsibilities and it is questionable whether it is ethical to tell families that their negotiated realities are unacceptable (McKeown, Ferguson and Rooney, 1998, Chapter 4). The mother, who was abusive to her children and initially hostile to the social worker, was not assessed solely on her presenting behaviour. Rather, due consideration was also given to the social and psychological factors which contributed to her makeup and behaviour. This is evident in the fact that despite the case being assessed as 'high risk', after her initial fear of intervention, the mother never felt at risk *herself* by virtue of being involved with social workers, 'No, they never gave me that impression'. These positive feelings towards social workers are quite different from the parents' initial feelings. This had as much, if not more, to do with how the previous social worker actually *conducted* herself as with the inherently 'stigmatising' and punitive nature of the child protection social work. As the father said: 'The first social worker was all talk and no action. But with this social worker and family support worker it tends to be listen and act. Previously I thought it was all against me and now there's somebody with me. It's more support than what I had previously.'

In many respects the practice was also refreshingly child-centred. According to the social worker, 'My job is that child. I work with the child with every case', which she duly did, meeting Joanne regularly over the twelve months of working with the case. However, the boys in the family were not engaged in any form of direct work, despite the fact that the social worker said 'they're probably getting it [abuse] as well'. In many respects the casework did not follow the tendency to treat children and mothers as one unit, as distinct from treating children as individuals in case work (Wise, 1995). In addition to helping Joanne with her immediate problems, the long-term child protection agenda was secured through this work. As the family support worker noted, 'the daughter has been empowered and if something does happen or she is very unhappy, she, as a child, knows where to go [to get help]'. Not only was Joanne treated as an individual separate from her mother, Mrs Smith was also treated as an individual in her own right and was strategically helped to feel better about herself. This confirms Featherstone's (1999) argument that it is in the interests of good *child* protection for professionals to help women to develop their own sense of self outside the lives of their children.

The mother's ability to care for her daughter was seen as directly connected to the past sexual violence perpetrated against her (see also Kelly, 1996b, p.130). Intensive effort went into supporting her in relation to this issue, so that she would be able to parent her children more effectively. Dealing with the underlying trauma is essential to healing and recovery (Herman, 1992). Moreover, as this case so vividly shows, therapeutic/healing work needs to go on with the children, as well as with the traumatised carer(s), to help them to gain the emotional literacy which will equip them to grow into adults who are able to practice intimacy in a respectful, healthy way.

Long-term treatment/support services: an overview

This case study can now be used as a background against which to evaluate the general provision of long-term services. The provision of services can be measured in terms of responses to all *referrals*, and, more specifically, to *substantiated cases*. The latter provides for the most meaningful analysis of the key issue of met and unmet needs given that, by definition, some need or risk has been judged to exist in the case. It is still useful to consider the longer-term career paths of all referrals, whether substantiated or not, to gain a picture of overall responses. Moreover, although some cases could not be substantiated, they still gave rise to concern for the children and families involved. Hence, there is a grey area of identified risk/need that needs to be taken into account in unsubstantiated cases. Long-term treatment/support services fall into four categories: home-based, community-based, clinical and care-based services. Sixty-four per cent (n=183) of referrals received long-term services.

Home-based services

Some 50 per cent (n=144) of referrals received a post-investigative home-based service. As would be expected, community care social workers are by far the most common service providers, being involved with 87 per cent of these 144 cases. A family support worker was involved in 17 per cent (n=25), a community child care worker in 13 per cent (n=19), a home help in 3 per cent (n=4) and a community psychiatric nurse in 4 per cent (n=5). Taken together, family support workers and community child care workers became involved in 30 per cent (n=44) of these cases. This constitutes the most significant type of family support work going on under the Child Care Act, far outstripping community-based services. When public health nurses (PHN), who were involved in 15 per cent (n=42) of home-based services, are included the proportion of home based services increases further.

Neglect is the most common problem in cases receiving home-based services, accounting for 21 per cent (n=31) of all such cases, 10 per cent were sexual abuse, 10 per cent physical abuse, 6 per cent domestic violence and 4 per cent emotional abuse. Some 19 per cent were defined as child behaviour/control problems, another 19 per cent as parental difficulties,

Table 7.1 Long-term community-based services

Service	%	No. of cases
Parenting course	8	3
Teenage support group	3	1
Refuge	15	6
Youth services	33	13
Rape Crisis Centre	10	4
Women's group	5	2
Victim support	3	1
Community mothers	3	1
Social services centre	3	1
Office visits to social worker	5	2
REHAB	3	1
Adoption society social worker	5	2
Probation	8	3
After school club	5	2
Family support service	10	4

Note: Some cases received more than one of the above services. The % total adds to more than 100 due to multiple responses.

Table 7.2 Long-term clinical services

Service	%	No. of cases
Medical social worker	3	3
GP	4	4
Family therapist	4	4
Adult psychologist	3	3
Child psychologist	31	31
Adult psychiatrist	8	8
Child psychiatrist	15	15
Alcohol /addiction	21	21
Psychiatric day hospital	2	2
Health board counsellors	17	17
Misc. counsellors	12	12
Educational psychologist	1	1
CSA service	2	2
Psychiatric social worker	1	1
Mental health services	1	1

Note: The % total adds to more than 100 due to multiple response

while parental addiction accounted for 5 per cent, financial/housing 4 per cent and miscellaneous difficulties 3 per cent. Together, neglect, parental difficulties and child behaviour/control problems accounted for 59 per cent of all the home-based services provided. This shows the significance of parenting/relationship problems in long-term work and the Smith case study (140) helps us to see what can and needs to be done.

Community-based services

Fourteen per cent (n=39) of referrals received a long-term community-based service (see Table 7.1). The key finding here is the predominance of youth services, reflecting the need for services with distressed and challenging teenagers. One-third (n=13) received youth services, including youth workers, youth groups, Youthreach and youth development projects. A community-based family support service featured in four cases. Although this may seem a small contribution, it is very significant when viewed within the local community. Within the region as a whole, most family support work is done by community childcare workers and family support workers in people's own homes. Neglect again predominated here, accounting for 23 per cent (n=9); 10 per cent were physical abuse, 10 per cent emotional abuse, 10 per cent sexual abuse, 10 per cent parental difficulties, while just 3 per cent were domestic violence. In over a quarter of all cases (26 per cent) receiving community services the primary problem was child behaviour/control which correlates with the high provision of youth services[1].

Clinical services

Thirty-five per cent (n=101) of referrals received treatment/support from a clinical service, child psychological services being the most significant, provided in 31 per cent of cases (see Table 7.2). This does not include child psychologists who were involved in the investigative/assessment phase of a case, but refers solely to treatment and support. Child psychiatry also features strongly, provided in 15 per cent of these cases. Counselling is also significant, provided in 12 per cent (n=12) of cases, including ten school counsellors. Counsellors, whether employed by the health board or not, accounted for 29 per cent of the clinical services, not including counselling specifically for alcohol/addiction which accounted for 21 per cent, including alcohol counselling, addiction treatment in the community and treatment in a residential centre.[2]

Once again, neglect and child behaviour/control problems predominated, accounting for 21 per cent (n=21) and 30 per cent (n=30) respectively of the referrals receiving a clinical service, while 9 per cent were physical abuse, 8 per cent sexual abuse, 4 per cent domestic violence and 2 per cent emotional abuse. Meanwhile, 14 per cent were parental difficulties, 5 per cent financial/housing, and 3 per cent parental addiction. The relatively high percentage of behavioural/control problem shows the extensive work done by clinical child care services, particularly with teenagers at risk.

Care-based services

In 17 per cent (n=49) of referrals the family received a care-based service. Foster care was provided to 83 per cent of these 49 families and included voluntary foster care, relative foster care (four cases) and statutory foster care. Residential care, both voluntary and statutory, was provided to 17 per cent. Neglect was the main problem in 25 per cent (n=12) of these referrals, physical abuse in 10 per cent, sexual abuse in 8 per cent, emotional abuse in 2 per cent, domestic violence in 2 per cent, behaviour/control in 16 per cent, parental difficulties in 16 per cent, and parental addiction in 10 per cent. The numbers of referrals involving physical and sexual abuse which ended in children entering care were comparatively low. Parenting difficulties, control and behaviour problems in children, neglect and addiction problems

Table 7.3 Combinations of long-term services

Services	No. of cases
Home-based only	43
Community-based only	5
Clinical only	24
Care-based only	6
Home- and community-based	8
Home-based and clinical	38
Home- and care-based	16
Home- and community-based and clinical	12
Home-, community- and care-based	4
Home-, clinical and care-based	17
Community-based and clinical	4
All four services	6

Note: Combinations of abuse were substantiated in some cases.

dominate, accounting together for 67 per cent of referrals ending in care. These are the problems to which the bulk of preventative work needs to be directed.

Combinations of services

Children and families received a single home-, community-, clinical or care-based service or several services in different combinations. Of the 144 cases that received a home-based service, for 30 per cent (n=43) it was the only service (see Table 7.3). For thirteen per cent (n=5) of the cases provided with a community-based service this was the only long-term service provided, as was the case for the 24 per cent (n=24) receiving a clinical service, and for 12 per cent (n=6) of cases in receipt of a care-based service.

The most frequent combination of treatment/support services was home-based and clinical (to 38 families), while 17 cases received a home-based, clinical and care-based service—the combination featured in the Smith case-study (140). The most frequent child care problem in referrals provided with a home-based service only, was parental difficulties accounting for 28 per cent (n=12). Neglect was the next highest, at 19 per cent. This demonstrates the importance of family support workers and community child care workers —as well as social workers—to cases involving borderline parenting and struggles to cope. Child sexual abuse and domestic violence accounted for 14 per cent (n=6) each where a home service only was provided. Notably, child behaviour/control problems accounted for only 5 per cent (n=2) of cases provided with a home based service only, which again shows the importance of the long-term work with troubled children and adolescents by clinical and community services. Moreover, 42 per cent (n=10) of the referrals provided with a clinical service only were defined as behaviour/control problems, and sexual abuse accounted for 17 per cent. The most frequent category of referral provided with both a home and clinical service was behavioural/control difficulties, present in 26 per cent (n=10) of these referrals. Neglect accounted for 24 per cent of these referrals. Sixteen referrals were provided with a home and a care treatment/support service, 25 per cent of which were behaviour/control problems, 19 per cent neglect, with a further 19 per cent concerned with parental difficulties. Sexual abuse and parental addiction accounted for 13 per cent of cases provided with care and home services in each instance. Physical abuse was the primary problem in one case and emotional abuse in one case.

Six cases from the sample received all four services, all of which, strikingly, were previously known to the social work department prior to the initial referral in the study, and five were open at the time of the new referral (Cases 22, 121, 255, 171, 180, 224). All six were processed through the CPN system and were the subject of a case conference at least once during the study period. Each case was still open one year after the referral. Hence, cases in receipt of all four services are invariably ongoing long-term cases with chronic problems which have been known to the social work department over several years.

'Intensive' social work intervention

The analysis so far has provided an overview of the provision of long-term services to all referrals. It is now necessary to examine the extent of social work intervention irrespective of the provision of specialist services and to deconstruct it into layers of involvement and meaningful work with children and families. Social workers are the first point of contact with families, the gatekeepers for other specialist services, and, as seen in Chapter 6, the nominated key workers in the majority of cases. Thus we need to examine the nature of social work involvement in the 286 referrals and what we shall call the 'intensity' of contact with families. While the provision of community, clinical and care services constitute discernible levels of intervention, it was beyond the scope of the research to establish the intensity of this work, although the case studies illuminate the form and meanings of these services.

Measuring the level of long-term social work raises a number of questions. What constitutes a social work treatment/support intervention? At what point does it change from investigative to treating/supportive? To quantify what constitutes meaningful long-term social work as opposed to investigation, layers of post-investigation involvement must be identified. Social work activity can be analysed in terms of: (a) no investigation; (b) investigation only, that is case closed upon investigation; (c) investigation followed by irregular social work visits which could be classified as either further 'monitoring' or support on an irregular basis; (d) investigation followed by regular long-term social work. The *intensity* of social work intervention emerges as a more useful measurement than simply the actual length of 'long-term' social work involvement. Duration is not a sufficient measure as it does not capture those cases that were open for a shorter term but received 'intensive' post-investigative social work. These cases, although not open on a long-term basis, did in fact receive significant social work inputs. Hence, 'long term' social work will now be framed as 'intensive' social work intervention, as the intensity of involvement paints a clearer picture in terms of meaningful social work activity.

To measure the intensity of social work involvement standardised criteria were applied. As part of the follow-up social workers were requested to record the frequency of their direct face-to-face contact with children, parents and significant others whether weekly, fortnightly, monthly, three-monthly or irregular. Irregular contact refers to sporadic on-going intervention. For example, social work involvement was minimal and irregular for Case 259. The case was open and was monitored by a PHN. It was decided that, for cases open for over six months, a monthly visit from social workers was the minimum involvement constituting a meaningful social work service.

Table 7.4 Case careers and long-term service provision

	Clare	Tipperary/ East Limerick	Limerick	MWHB
Referrals (n)	86	96	104	286
Of which	%	%	%	%
Intensive social work service	50	48	33	44
Other long-term services	21	23	18	20
Investigation only	17	19	32	23
Irregular long-term service work	8	7	8	8
Not investigated	4	3	7	5

However, different criteria were applied to cases open for under six months. For example, Case 61 was only open for six weeks, but the family were seen almost daily by the social worker: this clearly constitutes a highly significant service. The intensity of social work in cases open for under six months was measured by the number of contacts with the family during the lifespan of the case. Although this measure could be regarded as arbitrary, in order to evaluate practice a clear distinction has to be made between short-term and intensive post-investigation social work involvement.

Thus, of the 86 referrals received by the Clare team, 4 per cent were not directly investigated, 17 per cent were closed directly after the investigation, while 8 per cent received minimal, irregular social work contact. Meanwhile, 21 per cent (n=18) received a treatment/support service from other professional(s) but not from the social worker, and in 50 per cent (n=43) of referrals the family received intensive social work (see Table 7.4). It is important to note that other professionals may also have provided services in the 43 cases receiving intensive social work; 21 per cent (18 cases) were referred to other professionals in the absence of intensive social work support. Of the referrals made to the Tipperary (NR)/East Limerick team, 3 per cent were not directly investigated, 19 per cent were closed on investigation, 7 per cent received minimal social work and 23 per cent (n=24) received treatment/support from a child care professional other than a social worker. Meanwhile, 48 per cent (n=50) received intensive social work (see Table 7.4). Seven per cent of the referrals to the Limerick community care team were not investigated, 32 per cent were closed on investigation, 10 per cent received minimal social work, while 18 per cent (n=16) were referred to other specialist child care professionals and had no intensive social work. Thirty-three per cent (n=32) received intensive social work (see Table 7.4). Clearly, the Limerick team provides considerably less intensive social work than Clare or Tipperary/East Limerick, which provide about the same amount. Limerick also has slightly less engagement by other specialist child care services at 18 per cent of cases, compared to 23 per cent in Tipperary/East Limerick, and 21 per cent in Clare.

Taken together, at the regional level, one year after the initial referral, 44 per cent (n=126) of all referrals to the three community care teams received intensive social work, while 20 per cent were provided with treatment/support from a non-social work source. Hence, 36 per cent of referrals did not survive the filtering process and were not engaged with on a long-term basis by a child care professional or on an intensive basis by a social worker. This 36 per cent includes 5 per cent that were never investigated, 23 per cent that were closed on investigation and 8 per cent that received irregular social work contact which could not be classified as intensive (see Table 7.4). Again, it is important to emphasise that the classification of 20 per cent as being provided with services from a non-social work source includes only cases where a social worker was not involved on an *intensive* basis. The 44 per cent of cases with intensive involvement by a social worker may also have received specialist child care services (see Table 7.3 for these combinations of services).

Cases *not* engaged with post-investigation

A relatively high level of long-term services is provided in the MWHB region: 23 per cent of referrals across the region receive only an investigation, 64 per cent receive either intensive social work support or other long-term services (see Table 7.4). The proportion of referrals filtered out without a service is considerably lower than found in other research, especially into UK practice (Gibbons, 1995; Dept. of Health, 1995). Having identified the broad characteristics of cases that received long-term support services, we must now ask what are the characteristics of cases that did not survive the investigative process and were filtered out of the system without long-term services? Thirty-six per cent (n=103) of referrals did not receive a long-term home, community, clinical or care service. Were families offered such services but declined? How long were these cases open and what were the outcomes? Did these cases concern identifiable children in need of services which were not provided, and if so what were the reasons? Was the lack of a long-term service justified, for instance, where no problem was identified? The underlying reason why a long-term service was not provided is the key issue.

These questions are most relevant to substantiated cases. Thus far, the analysis has focused on services provided to all referrals, whether substantiated or not. It provides a useful long-term measure of the levels of social work and other professional activity, filtering processes and patterns of case careers. A critical issue is the input of post-investigative services into the 160 *substantiated* cases. The substantiation of a case implies the existence of a child welfare or protection problem and it is important to establish whether or not the identified needs for a service were actually met.

It should be emphasised that there may be difficulties for children in some unsubstantiated cases, but if there is no co-operation professionals are left with no choice but to withdraw. Moreover, the opportunity to substantiate such cases is severely compromised precisely because client co-operation is limited. Case 40 is a typical example. It was referred by a PHN expressing concern for a ten-year-old boy: 'child nervous, fears he will be left alone, fears being bullied, cries a lot and wants to know whereabouts of his mother at all times' (case file). The referral was defined as 'behaviour problems in child'. There were three other children, aged six, twelve and sixteen. The mother was seen eight days after the referral. The concern expressed in the referral was not substantiated, although in the opinion of the social worker it had some foundation. Two appointments were offered to both the mother and the child which they did not attend. The child was classed as very low risk. The social worker met with the mother on one occasion while the child refused to be interviewed. According to the social worker, services were offered to the family but they were 'not interested . . . it's like they haven't got the energy to do something about the problem'. The case was closed three weeks after the referral due to 'non-co-operation of the child' (see also Case 231).

The most significant reason for non-provision of long-term service, applying to a quarter (n=28) of cases, was lack of co-operation—services were offered but were declined. The child, parents or other family were not willing to co-operate. Child behaviour problems and alleged sexual abuse were the most frequent problem in referrals where services were refused, featuring in ten and nine cases respectively. Nor were all referrals that received post-investigative services substantiated. Of the 144 referrals that received a home-based service, 72 per cent (n=39) were substantiated. Crucially, however, 31 of these unsubstantiated referrals involved families who were the subject of substantiated referrals in the *past*, and 23 of these cases were open at the time of the new referral. Consequently, the majority of unsubstantiated *referrals* provided with a long term service had been involved with the health board for a considerable time prior to the referral included in the study and were ongoing *cases* which had been substantiated in the past.

Of the 160 substantiated cases, 63 per cent received a long-term home-based service, 16 per cent a community service, 39 per cent a clinical service, and 21 per cent a care service. Of the 101 substantiated cases provided with a home-based service, 96 were serviced by a social worker. Thus 40 per cent (n=64) of the substantiated cases did not receive an intensive social work service, but five cases were provided with a home-based service from other sources. Thus, 59 substantiated cases were not provided with a home-based service of any kind, of which 17 (29 per cent) received other specialist child care services; another 11 per cent were referred to a specific child care service and social work involvement was reduced to a minimum or even discontinued. In ten of these 17 cases the service was clinical, in three it was care-based, in two it was community based and in two both community and clinical services were provided. The main power and responsibility for the provision of long-term child care and protection services still lies with social work as 60 per cent of substantiated cases received an intensive social work service. Yet significant needs were met by specialist child care services in the remaining 40 per cent of substantiated cases where social workers maintained only a nominal involvement. As we have seen, the role of social workers under the Child Care Act now combines case-worker and case-manager—a challenging mix.

In a total of 42 cases—26 per cent of substantiated cases—no long-term service of any sort was delivered. At first sight, a service gap of over a quarter of all substantiated cases seems very broad. However, in 16 of these 42 cases a long-term service was offered but the family either refused to co-operate or did not deem the service necessary (Cases 45, 79, 112, 120, 122, 159, 161, 189, 190, 239, 247, 275,297, 291, 298, 305). In one case the social worker noted that psychological services, although necessary, were not available (Case 308). Of the remaining 25 cases (16 per cent of substantiated cases), two were transferred out of the MWHB region (Cases 25, 192) and in another two the family left the area without the cases being transferred on (Cases 73, 127). In ten cases the family was seen on a short-term basis on more than one home visit by the social worker and seven of the cases were closed as the 'identified problems were solved'—the need was perceived to have been met (Cases 78, 151, 168, 251, 248, 294, 317). Case 168, for example, was referred by gardaí as 'mother [aged 21] presented herself at Garda station with broken jaw, her father had beaten her up badly during the night and she was hospitalised . . . girl has seven-month-old baby boy, she needed protection for herself and baby'. Both domestic violence and emotional abuse were substantiated. The case was closed after eight weeks as the mother was referred to the county council housing office and was subsequently re-housed. The social worker met with the mother on three occasions and closed the case. Three further such cases were still open and were being monitored by a PHN (Cases 259, 268, 318). In a further two cases the family was met on a once off basis by the social worker and the case was then closed with monitoring by another professional (Cases 223, 237). In two substantiated cases the child was met on a once off basis and seen by another professional in an investigative capacity (Cases 282, 286). In one case the mother was met on a once off basis and 'given advice' (Case 289), and another was closed after one social work contact as the seventeen-year-old was in prison (Case 319). Two cases (Cases 111, 177) were still open one year on, although the child and/or parents were only seen in an investigative context, and another three cases (Cases 280, 28, 281) were closed with only one social work contact. Thus, lack of client engagement, as opposed to lack of services, is generally the main reason for non-provision of services. This is typified by Case 189 which was referred by a school expressing concern for the 'overall level of care at home' of fourteen- and fifteen-year-old children. It was also suspected that the children were left unattended while the parents went out drinking. Problems identified included neglect, alcohol abuse by both parents, failure to thrive and housing difficulties. The case was open at the end of the research period with monitoring by the school and PHN. Both parents refused to co-operate with the social worker and were considered to be 'very antagonistic towards MWHB involvement'. According to the social worker attempts were made to engage with the family but these were unsuccessful.

The second main area of concern is where there is a problem and client co-operation, but the services don't meet it, perhaps because of other pressures and demands. Case 248 concerned a nine-year-old child 'not attending school, running around the town unattended and unsupervised, parents recently separated, mother and child spent some time in [women's refuge]', and was closed after one year with no long-term services. Neglect, emotional abuse and domestic violence were substantiated. The social worker met with the child on one occasion, the father twice and the mother five times. The mother was considered to be a 'co-operative client' but was not worked with beyond the initial referral. It appears that the case remained open for one year in the administrative sense but drifted with little direct work done with the family.

The processing of a case through the CPN system affects the provision of a long term service, with a 7 per cent deviation between cases that were

Table 7.5 Types of post-investigative service provided to substantiated abuse cases

Abuse	Service type supplied							
	Home-based		Community		Clinical		Care-based	
	%	No.	%	No.	%	No.	%	No.
Neglect	52	52	46	12	46	29	65	22
Emotional abuse	33	33	42	11	33	21	21	7
Domestic violence	27	27	27	7	24	15	18	6
Physical abuse	15	15	12	3	10	6	24	8
Sexual abuse	7	7	12	3	13	8	6	2

notified and cases that were not. Differing notification patterns are evident in each type of long-term service. Sixty-seven per cent (n=94) of cases that received a home-based service were notified to the DCC, compared with 74 per cent (n=28) of those in receipt of a community based service, 68 per cent (n=68) of a clinical service, and 75 per cent (n=35) of a care-based service.

The problems that do or do not receive post-investigative services

The pattern of service provision for different kinds of child abuse or child care problem is another crucial issue. Home based services were provided in 52 per cent of cases where neglect was the most prevalent form of substantiated abuse, in 33 per cent it was emotional abuse, in 27 per cent it was domestic violence, in 15 per cent it was physical abuse, and in 7 per cent sexual abuse (see Table 7.5). Clinical services were provided for 29 per cent of neglect and 21 per cent of emotional abuse referrals with lower rates of provision for physical and sexual abuse. The numbers of cases receiving community-based services are considerably lower, with neglect and emotional abuse again predominating. A significant finding is the number of cases receiving long-term services where domestic violence has been substantiated, even though other forms of child abuse are also present. A significant 65 per cent of care based services (22 cases) were for neglect cases (see Table 7.5).

Table 7.6 Long-term service provision to children in cases with substantiated sexual abuse

Nature of abuse	Long term treatment/support service to children			
	Yes		No	
	%	No.	%	No.
Non- contact sexual abuse	75	3	25	1
Contact non-penetrative sex	66	4	34	2
Penetrative sex	75	3	25	1
Suspect non-contact sexual abuse	0	0	100	1
Penetrative/possible finger or object	0	0	100	1
Suspect non-penetrative sex	100	5	0	0
Child was perpetrator of sexual abuse	100	3	0	0
Child suffering now from previous sexual abuse	100	1	0	0
Penetrative sex with a minor	0	0	100	1

Table 7.7 Long-term service provision to children in cases with
substantiated domestic violence

Nature of domestic violence	Long term treatment/support service to children			
	Yes		No	
	%	No.	%	No.
Physical violence by male to female	60	35	40	23
Evidence of injuries to female caused by violence by male	71	20	29	8
Verbal/psychological violence by male to female	69	42	31	19
Physical violence by female to male	100	3	0	0
Verbal/psychological, by female to male	100	12	0	0
Violence by male to female through control of money and her movements	63	20	37	12
Evidence of depression/mental ill-health of female caused by violence by male	83	20	17	4
Evidence of depression/mental ill-health of male caused by violence by female	0	0	100	3
Evidence of adversity/distress for children caused by domestic violence	74	25	26	9
Suspect verbal/psychological violence by female to male	0	0	100	2
Suspect physical violence by female to male	73	8	27	3
Suspect evidence of adversity/distress for children caused by domestic violence	52	13	48	12
Suspect physical violence by male to female	83	19	17	4
Suspect verbal/psychological violence by male to female	62	8	38	5
Evidence of domestic violence—unspecified domestic violence	83	5	17	1
Suspect violence by male to female through control of money and her movements	33	1	67	2
Suspect evidence of depression/mental ill-health of female caused by violence by male	71	5	29	2
Suspect evidence of physical injuries to female caused by violence by male	0	0	100	9

The clear implication is that neglect is the area of greatest need in child care and protection work, with the more high-profile problems of physical and sexual abuse demanding relatively limited long-term service provision. Having identified the broad parameters of service provision to particular types of problem, it is now possible to consider the kinds of difficulties within each of the categories that did or did not get services.

Substantiated sexual abuse cases: Sexual abuse was substantiated in 19 cases for 25 children, 12 of which, involving 17 children, received a long-term service (see Table 7.6). As Table 7.6 shows, the nature of the sexual abuse in the seven substantiated cases that did not receive services was significant. In one case where penetrative sex was substantiated a long-term service was not provided—the family was offered a service but declined. In five such cases, the family were unco-operative and did not want a service. In two, the family received investigative services only with no offer of long-term support. As the sexual abuse case-studies in Chapter 5 showed, the main reasons for this service gap is lack of parental co-operation, allied to a passive social work response partly due to the ambiguous the role of community care social work in highly legalistic assessment procedures.

Substantiated physical abuse: Physical abuse was substantiated in 16 cases (21 children), 15 of which, involving 20 children, received a long-term treatment/support service. In only one substantiated physical abuse case was a post-investigative service not provided. This case (192), which involved current bruises to the child's body, was transferred out of the area shortly after the investigation. Thus, in the remaining 15 cases services were provided and accepted. Interestingly, parental resistance or ambiguity about the social work or therapeutic role was not such a barrier to service provision in physical abuse cases.

Substantiated domestic violence: Domestic violence was substantiated in 42 cases for 105 children, 31 of which cases, involving 85 children, received a treatment/support service. In 60 per cent of cases (n=35) where 'physical violence by male towards female' was substantiated, a long-term service was provided, leaving 23 cases without a service. In 20 of those cases (71 per cent) where physical injuries to the woman were substantiated, a long-term service was provided, thus eight such cases were left without a service. In all three cases where physical violence to a male by a female was involved a long term service was provided (see Table 7.7). Services were provided in a relatively high 83 per cent (n=19) of cases where physical violence against the woman was suspected, as opposed to known about, leaving four such cases without services. In 42 cases (69 per cent) involving verbal/psychological violence by the man against the woman, services were provided, and in 19 cases they

Table 7.8 Long-term service provision to children in cases of substantiated
neglect

Nature of abuse	No. of children	Long term services Yes	No
Poor parenting skills	94	70	24
Children left unattended	58	39	19
Very poor home standards due to poor parenting capacity	44	41	3
Children unkempt and poor hygiene	25	25	0
Children poorly fed and hungry	14	12	2
Suspect poor parenting capacity	14	9	5
Underage baby-sitter	12	12	0
Children under weight	11	9	2
Wilful withdrawal of care	9	9	0
Children inadequately clothed	9	9	0
Non-attendance at school	7	7	0
Suspect poorly fed and hungry	6	5	1
Very poor academic skills	6	6	0
Parents unable to care for children	5	5	0
Suspect children unkempt/poor hygiene	5	4	1
Untreated head lice	4	3	1
Suspect wilful withdrawal of care	3	3	0
Failure to control behaviour	2	2	0
Suspect children left unattended	2	1	1
Children taken to pub/parents under the influence	2	2	0
Parents did not visit GP as requested	2	2	0
Suspect inadequately clothed	2	2	0
Severe skin problems/not receiving medical attention	2	2	0
Untreated scabies	2	2	0
Children taken out late at night	2	2	0
Non attendance at medical appointments	2	1	1
Non-organic failure to thrive	1	0	1
Child brought to UK without health board consent	1	1	0
Overcrowding at home	1	0	1
Child not allowed to develop emotionally	1	1	0
Parent did not place emphasis on education	1	1	0
Mother is neglectful	1	1	0
Child bullied and intimated	1	1	0
Inconsistent parenting skills	1	1	0
Child left to fend for herself	1	1	0
Child doing what he likes	1	0	1
Child shown where people commit suicide	1	1	0
Child left caring for three siblings	1	1	0
Child has very poor speech	1	0	1
Child's medical needs neglected	1	0	1
Child at high risk of neglect	1	1	0
Child left in care of other family	1	0	1
Suspect mother is a prostitute	1	0	1
Child put to bed at 5pm/no food after 3pm	1	1	0

were not. While services are being provided in a considerable number of domestic violence cases, many do not receive services following the investigation, including high risk cases involving known injuries to women and harm to children. The reasons for this service gap, as the analysis in this book has already indicated, include failure to focus on the perpetrator, women's failure to follow-through on civil actions such as barring orders, and lack of support from professionals in enabling them to do so, and lack of attention to the therapeutic needs of children in domestic violence cases.

Substantiated neglect: Neglect was substantiated in 71 cases (164 children) of which 56, involving 123 children, received a long-term service. Thus, 15 substantiated cases did not receive a treatment/support service. Some 74 per cent of cases, involving 70 children, where 'poor parenting skills' was substantiated received a long term service, while 24 such children did not (see Table 7.8). Some 67 per cent of cases, involving 39 children, where children left unattended was substantiated received a long-term service, leaving 19 such children without. This can be partly explained by the more 'episodic' type of response demanded in 'home alone' situations, where parents are warned or advised about their behaviour and no follow-up is deemed necessary or possible. In 93 per cent of cases, involving 41 children, where the problem was 'very poor home standards due to poor parenting capacity', a long-term service was provided, leaving just three children without. Services were also provided in 100 per cent of cases, involving 25 children, where the substantiated concern was that the children were unkempt and there was poor hygiene. Hence the major service gap here lies in cases of poor parenting skills.

Substantiated emotional abuse: Emotional abuse was substantiated in 51 cases for 110 children, 39 of which, involving 86 children, received a long term service. 'Witness to violence' was the most commonly substantiated form of emotional abuse, affecting 29 children, 66 per cent of whom were provided with a long-term service, while 19 such children were not. 'Witness to alcohol abuse' was the next most common type, affecting ten children, six of whom were provided with a long-term service (see Table 7.9). The provision and apparent acceptance of post-investigation services in cases where emotional abuse was substantiated was comparatively high. This may be because domestic violence features strongly and mothers accept the need for intervention.

In summary, a long-term service was provided in 63 per cent (n=12) of cases where sexual abuse was substantiated, in 94 per cent of substantiated physical abuse cases, 74 per cent of substantiated domestic violence cases, 79 per cent (n=56) of substantiated neglect and 76 per cent (n=31) of substantiated emotional abuse cases.

Table 7.9 Long-term service provision to children in cases of substantiated
        emotional abuse

Nature of abuse	No. of children	Long term services	
		Yes	No
Witness to violence	29	19	10
Witness to alcohol abuse	10	6	4
Parent(s) verbally abusive	9	7	2
Child not knowing mother's plans	6	6	0
Caught between parents access dispute	7	6	1
Reaction to marital breakdown	5	5	0
Conflict between mother and boyfriend	4	4	0
Parent(s) mental health	4	4	0
Witness to arguing between parents	3	2	1
Children used by father to get at mother	3	3	0
Child exposed to drugs and adult behaviour	3	3	0
Inappropriate discipline	2	1	1
Father comes and goes—upsets child	2	2	0
Separation from siblings	2	0	2
Mother emotionally distant from child	2	1	1
Let down by father re-access arrangements	2	2	0
Not allowed to have any friends or outside interests	2	2	0
Relationship between mother and child volatile	2	2	0
Child suffers form depression	2	2	0
Child hyperactive/poor parental control	2	2	0
Mother does not want child	2	2	0
Very poor emotional environment	2	2	0
Trauma as a result of CSA	2	2	0
Poor parental skills	1	1	0
Mother refuses to see daughter	1	1	0
Father has blocked access to mother	1	0	1
Child acting out	1	1	0
Given too much responsibility for younger siblings	1	1	0
Affected by parents separation	1	1	0
Name calling/manipulation/threatening behaviour	1	1	0
Not allowed to express own opinion	1	1	0
Mother places blame on child	1	1	0
Overcrowding in home/rows with grandmother	1	1	0
Emotional abuse from brother venting anger	1	1	0
Over dosed/said parents did not care	1	1	0
Prevents daughter from leaving home	1	1	0
Name calling	1	1	0
Mother exhausted/unable to cope	1	1	0
Child rejected by father/homelessness	1	1	0
Inconsistent parenting	1	1	0
Child taken on long walks, 5-6 miles	1	1	0
Copies father/treats mother abusively	1	0	1
Parents absent from home	1	0	1
Concern for child CSA abuser	1	1	0
Child overeating for comfort	1	1	0
Child scapegoated by father/prefers male siblings	1	0	1
Forced to eat food that child didn't want	1	0	1
Emotional trauma	1	0	1

Conclusion

In this chapter we examined the service response to cases, with particular emphasis on long-term outcomes. Twenty-six per cent of substantiated cases did not receive services. A number of reasons for this gap have been identified of which by far the most important is that the families themselves did not want a service. Some parents of children who had been sexually abused outside the family did not want the matter to be taken any further with their children and withdrew co-operation. Other, usually neglectful, parents did not regard themselves as having a problem. They were involuntary clients and wanted to see the back of the health board as soon as possible. Some cases were lost because of other professional pressures and priorities: they were closed or lay dormant and no meaningful work was done to promote the children's welfare. Such a shortfall between referrals and the provision of services leaves parents who have received little more than an investigation feeling alienated. It occurs largely because of the absence of resources for long-term co-ordinated treatment, counselling and preventative services.

For the most part, however, significant services *are* being offered and this chapter has shown the variety of ways in which they are provided by different disciplines, either alone or in combination. A profile has emerged of how the child protection and family support aspects of the Child Care Act are working in practice. The benefits arising from the development of the system since 1993 are apparent, especially in the provision of clinical services such as psychiatry and psychology to young people suffering distress and manifesting serious behaviour and control problems. It goes without saying that these services, which are already overstretched, need to be developed. A complex division of labour now exists in the provision of long-term services, with social work having a core co-ordinating function. In 40 per cent of substantiated cases social workers do not engage in active casework, or simply manage the case, while the primary therapeutic and support work is done by other professionals. Although social workers are incleasingly engaged in case-management, the degree of their involvement depends on the circumstances of the case and whether more formal inter-agency co-ordination has taken place. Nevertheless, social workers continue to provide an intensive long-term service in 60 per cent of cases, often in combination with other services. This sheds important new light on the totality of work that is going on in child care and protection and the role of social work and its links to other roles and services.

The image of the harassed social worker rushing about doing nothing but investigating child abuse, upsetting parents and having little of substance to offer children in need, at the expense of meaningful therapeutic work with children and families, is now almost a cliché of child protection. Without doubt, many social workers have a sense of relentless demands on their time and energy and of things being out of control. 'Prioritise' is the message that social workers are constantly getting from management, and this in itself brings added pressure. While the demands of case management are increasing, social workers are doing considerably more supportive work with children and families than is conventionally understood. Services are however underdeveloped and struggling to keep pace with growing demands. It is worth emphasising again that neglect is the most common form of problem and there are simply not enough community-based services available to promote the welfare of such disadvantaged children and keep them in their families.

As the Smith case study, an example of best practice, showed, the best outcomes involve well co-ordinated therapeutic and practical support work with parents and children. Despite the good work and significant contribution that these professionals are making many feel undervalued. Interviews with family support and childcare workers, for instance, indicate that they feel 'non-specialised'. One family support worker described her role as 'a yellow pack worker', while another felt she was 'taking the donkey work from the social worker'. The invaluable work being done by clinical and family support services has gone largely unacknowledged in previous research and writing on child protection which has focused only on social work practice and failed to examine the multi-disciplinary context within which services are delivered (see Thorpe, 1994; 1997; Parton, Thorpe and Wattam, 1997). It has been assumed that if social workers aren't involved no work is being done. As this chapter has shown, this view ignores 40 per cent of post-investigative work by a variety of services. Moreover, it fails to do justice to the various combined work being done by social workers and other professionals in 60 per cent of substantiated cases. This overview may boost the morale and sense of purpose of professionals who do not have access to the big picture while going about their daily work and may not fully appreciate the outcome of their labours.

Hence the importance of the case study approach and documenting exemplary work such as Case study 140 from which much may be learned about practice and system development. As that case illustrated so well, the objective of intervention is not simply 'safety' or even the promotion of 'welfare' in some simple sense, but the promotion of healing and the capacities of children, parents and other carers to practice intimacy. The importance of this becomes even clearer in light of the fact that the most important single factor affecting whether services are provided is the willingness of the child and family to accept them. It is important not to see the refusal of services as simply a product of some deficiency in the client and to consider what it is about the system itself and practitioner approaches that leads clients to reject services. Thus, training and system development needs to focus on providing professionals with the skills to work with client resistance, whatever its sources.

Notes

[1] A further 14 per cent (n=39) of cases engaged with other 'community' services not included in Table 7.1. These were: school liaison officer, three cases; money advice and budgeting service, three; legal advice, five; gardaí, seven; community welfare officer, 13; JLO, three; St Vincent de Paul, five; special school, three. The reason for their exclusion is that they provide a generic service, are not linked to child protection intervention per se and contact with them was generally on a once-off basis.

[2] The CSA service, which carries out assessments in suspected CSA cases, is included in long-term clinical support as in these two cases it was explicitly stated that its role was therapeutic as opposed to assessment.

8 Beyond Protection: Child Care Problems and the Promotion of Welfare

Achieving the correct balance of child protection and family support, safety and prevention is now generally regarded as critically important in the design and delivery of child care services. Many international studies have shown the failure of child care systems to achieve this balance due to the dominance of child protection and have recommended that systems refocus on family support (DoH, 1995; Gibbons et al, 1995; Parton, 1997). Remarkably little research attention has been given, however, to the needs of children and families in 'welfare' scenarios, the kinds of child welfare practice engaged in or the ways in which systems could move beyond protection (see, however, Farmer, 1997; Gibbons, et al, 1990). In this chapter, we contribute to filling this gap by developing the analysis of definitions and long-term outcomes in child care and protection. We focus specifically on the service response in cases defined as child welfare, that is those which fall outside an 'abuse' categorisation, and compare and contrast them with outcomes in abuse cases.

While we have already shown that the notion of a 'child protection concern' has come to dominate the way the system frames child care, the prevalence of child welfare concerns referred to health boards reveals a broader definition of child care than simple child 'protection', one which significantly affects social work case loads and has implications for policy and practice in terms of how the system categorises, responds to and monitors such cases. In line with the remit of this research to evaluate the extent to which the elements of a safe, good quality child *protection* service are in place, we have concentrated in previous chapters, when considering the balance of protection and welfare, on the response to abuse cases. In Chapter 7, we presented a case-study exemplifying how effective family support can be provided in the context of child protection, and welfare and healing promoted as well as child safety. In this chapter we focus on the effectiveness of intervention from the perspective of child welfare. The extent and nature of welfare referrals in the child care system must be examined if only because there are a substantial number of such cases, and health boards now have a statutory duty to go beyond protection and to promote the welfare of children in their areas by providing family support services. This chapter questions the degree to which these obligations are being met by presenting a profile of child welfare cases, needs and problems, and exploring to what extent the welfare of such children is being promoted through long term service provision.

Child welfare cases: key patterns

Child welfare problems were identified as the main presenting problem in 47 per cent (137) of referrals. In 41 per cent (56) of these welfare referrals a child protection concern was also cited, although this concern was considered secondary to the main presenting problem. Neglect was a protection concern in 40 per cent (27) of the welfare referrals, emotional abuse in 30 per cent, domestic violence in 25 per cent, sexual abuse in 18 per cent and physical abuse in 5 per cent[1]. This demonstrates the close links between child welfare and neglect, emotional abuse and domestic violence cases. Three main categories of referrals are apparent in practice: those involving both protection and welfare concerns—48 per cent of cases (n=138); those with protection concerns only—23 per cent of cases (n=67); and those with welfare concerns only—28 per cent of cases (81 cases). In the latter category, behaviour/control problems were the most prevalent concern, with 43 cases involving one or a combination of the following problems: child out of parental control; child behaviour problems; parent/child relationship problems; self-harming behaviour; or substance abuse. The typical behaviour/control referral involves out-of-control children, invariably adolescents, behaving anti-socially and sometimes criminally, sometimes harming themselves and engaging in substance abuse. The prevalence of such problems places significant demands on the system especially on social workers working with adolescents in great need, who are often distressed and challenging. These 43 'behaviour/control' referrals account for 15 per cent of all referrals.

The general category of 'parental difficulties' was the main problem in 22 welfare referrals, 7 per cent of the entire sample. The concerns related to either one or a combination of the following problems: parents under stress/general coping difficulties; mental health; or access/custody disputes. Referrals with child behaviour/control and parental difficulties as the *primary* cause of concern with *no* protection concerns accounted for 22 per cent (n=81) of all referrals. The figure does not include referrals defined as protection which included behaviour/control and parental problems, or referrals defined as welfare but also concerned with protection. A child behaviour and/or control problem was cited in over one third of all referrals (see Chapter 2 for combinations of child care/abuse problems). We will now consider how the system responds to this high number of non-abuse welfare cases in terms of resources and available family support and therapeutic services.

Child welfare: risk, needs and case careers

When account is taken of case careers and health board involvement *before* the initial referral in the study a still more complex picture of the 81 welfare referrals emerges. Protection concerns had been expressed in just under one-third (n=26) of the cases leaving 55 cases, 19 per cent of the total sample, as welfare-only cases with no history of physical, sexual or emotional abuse or domestic violence or neglect. Nineteen of the 81 welfare referrals had previous health board involvement unrelated to child protection. Thus 54 per cent (45) of the welfare referrals had a health board history. Thirty-six per cent of the 45 cases had been involved with the health board for under one year prior to the present referral, 43 per cent for between one and six years, and 21 per cent for over six years (two families were known for sixteen and one for seventeen years). Forty-one per cent of the 45 previously known cases were still open at the end of the research period. These figures highlight the long-term nature of the work done in a substantial proportion of child welfare cases. Some 61 per cent of the cases with health board histories were open at the time of the referral included in the study. A significant number of child welfare *referrals* concerned already established child welfare or child protection *cases*[2].

The extensive health board involvement reflects high levels of adversity for children, as does the current risk assessment. Where risk was assessed for child welfare cases, 60 per cent were considered to be at low or very low risk, while 40 per cent were deemed to be at high or very high risk. By comparison, 46 per cent of children in substantiated child protection cases were assessed to be at low or very low risk and 54 per cent at high or very high risk (see Chapter 3)[3]. Thus substantiated child protection cases are more often viewed as high-risk, but the proportion of child welfare cases viewed as high-risk is still significant.

Child welfare scenarios

This argument can be developed by examining the four types of child welfare cases which emerge from this data: behaviour/control problems without protection concerns; behaviour/control problems with protection concerns; parental difficulties categorised as welfare; and parental difficulties categorised as both welfare and protection.

Behaviour/control problems: substance abuse

Case 294 is typical of the cases referred to the health board for the sole concern of child behaviour problems and of cases concerned with adolescents abusing alcohol/drugs/solvents. The case was referred by a hospital paediatric department as 'thirteen-year-old girl along with six other girls took excessive amount of cider, collapsed in heap . . . two other admissions separate referrals. Two young men in their twenties purchased drink for girls. This information also alarming, one of girls reported to be in a relationship with twenty-year-old' (research forms). Both the parents and the child were interviewed by the investigating social worker and a frontline social worker colleague. Substance abuse was substantiated. The case was not notified to gardaí as 'could not be categorised as per guidelines'. Recommended interventions included child psychiatric team for assessment and support for both parents in coping with the child. The child attended child psychiatry and a family support worker and a social worker engaged with the family on a supportive basis. The case was still open at the end of the research period and was re-referred as the mother was finding it difficult to cope with her daughter who continued to drink and abuse substances.

Another typical example of this kind of concern for children is Case 251 which was referred by gardaí who 'stated that child [twelve years] is going missing from home and parents unaware of his whereabouts also child is glue sniffing and petrol sniffing' (research forms). Behaviour problems, substance abuse and juvenile crime were cited as the child care concerns. The child and her mother were interviewed one day after the referral and the child went on to attend child psychiatry. The case was closed two months after the referral as 'identified problems solved', in that the school and gardaí gave good reports on the child's progress.

Self-harming behaviour

A typical example of children harming themselves is Case 282. It was referred by a school as a 'teacher observed child trying to cut his hands with a piece of broken glass. Also observed existing cuts on both hands' (research forms). The nine-year-old child was not seen by the investigating social worker, but the parent(s) were interviewed ten days after the referral. The child was medically examined by a GP; the social worker had advised the parents to take the child to the GP to request that a referral be made to the child psychiatric services. The case was not referred to the gardaí as 'child abuse not in existence in this case at this time'. Although the provision of child psychiatric services was recommended the social worker concluded that 'long waiting lists will undoubtedly cause delay, there is a need for extra resources for psychological and psychiatric services to be readily available to situations of need' (research forms). This case was closed after one month and required 'minimal social work involvement' as the key need was for clinical services. Clearly, then, although clinical services were widely used, there was a perception that they were not sufficiently available to meet the needs identified.[4]

Juvenile crime

Case 267 is an example of issues arising in cases of adolescents engaging in criminal activity, where there was also concern about drug abuse. A mother referred her concerns about her sixteen-year-old son abusing drugs; he 'sometimes has knife in his possession'. Child out of control, behavioural problems and abuse of drugs were noted in the referral. The youth was interviewed by the investigating social worker, the substance abuse was substantiated and it was deemed a high-risk case. The gardaí were notified of the referral before the social work investigation and it was discovered that the youth was known to them for previous offences, had been in the Juvenile Liaison Officer (JLO) scheme and the 'sergeant [is] still involved with the child'. The youth was referred to and attended psychiatric services for drug addiction treatment and was offered a hostel placement, which was refused. The social worker made monthly or two-monthly home visits and the case was closed after one year.

Parental difficulties

Case 271 provides a typical example of the 'parental difficulties' strand of child welfare in the absence of child protection concerns. A social worker made the referral as 'child [five years] in hospital due to mother's inability to cope at this time, no abuse of child occurred'. Following a network check with the GP and a psychiatrist, the social worker noted that 'mother not suffering from depression but requiring a break and support'. The mother and child were seen within one day of the referral and 'parents under stress' was substantiated. Although the protection of the child was not a concern, the case was notified to the DCC. The child was placed in voluntary foster care. The case remained open on a family support basis for the duration of the research period and the social worker emphasised that 'no abuse of child occurred, mother sought help, facts straightforward' (research forms).

Case 82 provides another good example of typical child welfare work. It involved four children, a fifteen-year-old male, and his three sisters aged sixteen, thirteen and four, and was referred by their father who informed the social worker 'that his wife left home last week. He has four children—father needs help in looking after the children as he works full time' (this quote and the following quotes are from the research forms). Both the father and children were seen on the day the father made the referral. 'Parents under stress' was substantiated as 'father needed help in day to day looking after of children'. The case was not notified to the gardaí as 'degree of concern did not warrant garda involvement'. The home help service was organised for the family for five days a week. The case was closed after four months as 'identified problems were solved'. While the 'possibility of direct work with children around the issues of their parents separating' was considered by the social worker at the outset, social work involvement was minimal as 'there was never concerns of abuse, father came looking for home help, this was introduced and worked well'. The social worker felt reassured that a constructive supportive relationship had been established such that 'dad knows that if he requires further help to contact us'. This intervention, then, was very much in the mould of classic child welfare/family support work. No attempt was made to involve the children's mother in this case, and the services stepped in to compensate for the loss of the traditional carer in the home.

Behaviour/control coupled with child protection

Case 249 provides a good example of a child behaviour/control referral with child protection concerns; the sixteen-year-old boy's protection was of concern as well as his out of control behaviour. The referral was made by a MWHB social worker involved with the siblings of the child who was the subject of the new referral. His siblings were in foster care at the time of the referral. Referral information included 'this boy attends the youth service by day, he has caused thousands of pounds worth of damage to YS property during angry outbursts. Parents are separated, some siblings in care. Boy was previously in care for short periods but could not be contained. Now living in a derelict flat with father who is an alcoholic. The boy joins his father with the winos and takes drugs'. The family had a long history of involvement with the health board and the boy had only recently been referred to child psychology regarding his destructive behaviour. Neglect, child out of parental control, child homeless, loss of parent through family breakdown, alcohol abuse by father, parents experiencing mental health problems, and housing problems were all cited as child care concerns. The main presenting problem was defined as neglect. Domestic violence was also substantiated following the investigation.

A case conference recommended that the youth reside in a youth hostel. He went on to attend an alcohol treatment programme and was provided with hostel accommodation. However, he soon withdrew from both. The father was regarded by the social worker as an abusive parent because he provided 'no food or nothing like that, he is a complete alcoholic'. But case definition and culpability had become ambiguous because of the boy's age and danger to himself. The dilemma was whether to 'label it as abuse, is it abuse by the father or the child himself?' The challenges in providing services to help this young man were set out: 'effectively the youth service are putting up with him because they have invested in staff and have taken a personal interest in him . . . but we have nothing to offer him. I don't think so, we tried the adolescent boys' hostel, they have an outreach programme but he didn't avail of it, he wasn't interested, he broke eight or nine appointments'. The benefits such services could offer to this child were viewed as 'nothing, at this age. If he doesn't want to be helped I don't think you can help him, he's just a law unto himself, he's been in care, the outreach service is available but he doesn't want it and the alcohol treatment centre is available to him but he doesn't want it. What do you do? It isn't a question of no services it's a question of he doesn't want to avail of it'. Children's reluctance to take up services is a recurring theme in behaviour/control cases, which reflects the challenges in working with neglected and out of control adolescents and their parents. This kind of case also reveals the absence, nationally, of secure facilities in which to place such high-risk, out of control young people. There was a national debate, and outcry at times, during the study period over the absence of secure facilities. Following a series of judgements by the High Court in such cases the Department of Health and health boards are now obliged to provide secure accommodation for such young people in 'high support units' (for a useful summary of how the High Court has ruled that the State has a constitutional obligation to provide care for 'unruly' children with very special needs see O'Morain, 2000).

Parental difficulties coupled with child protection

Case 15 illustrates the difficulties of striking a balance between child welfare and child protection work in terms of adopting the most appropriate response in the investigation of the referral and delivery of services. It also shows the complexities involved in the cohort of cases where child welfare *referrals* are made in well known *cases*, and how the response to (re)referrals can only be fully understood in the context of the complete case-history. The case was referred by a neighbour expressing concern for an eight-year-old girl and thirteen-year-old boy because of their single mother's drink problem. It was noted in the referral that the 'mother is a good housekeeper and good at taking care of the children but goes on drinking binges'. The neighbour was concerned as the mother was allegedly taking her daughter to the pub with her and exposing her to 'inappropriate behaviour'. Loss of parent through family breakdown, parents under stress/general coping difficulties were the child care concerns defined in the referral. Despite the inference of moral danger, child protection concerns were not identified as an issue by the social worker and the referral was framed in the context of the mother's coping abilities.

The family had long been involved with the health board as a result of older siblings' behaviour problems and financial/housing issues. More recent concerns centred on the thirteen-year-old's behaviour and a referral regarding his father 'interfering with him'. There had also been prior referrals concerned with the mother's drinking and her sexual behaviour in pubs in the presence of her children, all leading social workers to question the mothers 'ability to care and protect' the children. On one home visit prior to the referral in this study, the mother was informed that 'serious action will be taken by the health board' if the situation didn't improve. Despite such threats, which reflected a high level of assessed risk, the case was viewed in the main in terms of the mother's inability to cope. The social worker interviewed for the research considered the mother to be vulnerable, 'fighting the odds' in a one parent family. In response to the (new) referral in this study the social worker 'very specifically' approached the mother about the alleged risk to the child in the pub. Further referrals were made in relation to poor housing conditions and the mother's drinking. The gardaí also informed the social worker that the eight-year-old girl had been missing from school for a three-week period. Regular social work home visits were made which according to the social worker focused on the mother's drinking (the father had ceased to be resident in the home for some time prior to this phase of referrals) and some material support was given to the family.

The social worker saw her main role as supporting the mother. Discussing whether such cases should be defined as protection or welfare she said that in her opinion, the mother could drink and cope with her life and responsibilities quite normally, 'it's just every now and then it gets totally put of hand'. In responding to sporadic drinking binges the social worker felt 'there is nothing more I can do except to give her support and meet her again'. The mother's 'behaviour' was central to framing the response as child welfare: 'this poor women, its' really tough, she's [isolated], she does a bit of drinking at the weekends and normally it doesn't interfere with her housework'. The social worker's view was that the children were generally well looked after. The mother was offered addiction counselling and home help services, but she refused them. Her reluctance to engage in any real way with support services was the reason for the case's lack of long-term services, apart from regular social work home visits. This echoes a key finding of this research on the prevalence of parental resistance in those substantiated cases not provided with long-term services (see Chapter 7). Very often, in the absence of sufficient grounds to pursue a statutory order, social workers (or any other professional who is able to gain entry) are left with little option but to try to persist with the case themselves. The social worker worked with the mother by supporting her or by 'warning' her about her behaviour. Supporting the mother allowed the children to remain at home by helping their mother to stabilise her drinking for a time. In adopting a largely child welfare approach, the social worker noted that 'you have to kind of support her and encourage her. No matter what family I'm working with, I feel it's important that I'm someone who is there to help this family get out of the crisis they're in and that I'm not there as someone to threaten them and tell them you did this, that and the other'.

This case typifies the kind of unglamorous, longhaul, routine work that is at the core of family support work with vulnerable children and parents, especially where the aim of intervention is the basic one of trying to ensure that the children are safe enough and thrive sufficiently to stay within their family of origin. In Harris's (1993) terms, what is needed is 'milk van support', as opposed to 'fire-brigade' support (see also Gilligan, 1995). It also shows up very well the ambiguity in a significant proportion of cases where the boundary between suspected abuse and known adversity in terms of children and parents in need can be very difficult to determine. In this instance, the tension arose from a clash between alleged incidents of 'abusive' behaviour which placed the children in moral danger, along with excessive drinking which jeopardised a woman's capacity to care for her children, and the vulnerability of a single parent struggling to cope. Here again we see that the categorisation of the case is less important than the way the child and family situation is conceptualised, the nature of the services offered, whether they are taken up, and how they are delivered to meet identified need in the case.

Long-term outcomes and system responses to child welfare

These typical child welfare case scenarios are good examples of definitional issues, and the concerns being worked with, whether rooted in the child's or the parent's experience or behaviour. It is now necessary to analyse the long-term outcomes and child welfare responses on a more systematic basis. While in child welfare terms, the kinds of behaviour cited in these cases is not considered to be *abusive*, it is regarded as having detrimental effects on the child/family. As with child protection cases, needs were identified in substantiated child welfare cases; the question of how (well) the system ultimately responds to these needs and whether welfare is promoted is more important than how the system defines and categorises cases.

In terms of outcomes, cases concerned solely with welfare generally fared less well than those with child protection concerns. Thirty-five per cent of the pure welfare cases were closed by the end of the three-month sampling period, 46 per cent were still open and active and 19 per cent were open but inactive, with the remainder either transferred or never investigated. At the end of the twelve-month follow-up period, 78 per cent were closed. Half of the open cases remained open due to the re-referral of a child welfare concern during the follow-up period. By contrast, just 8 per cent of the 26 welfare referrals that included protection concerns were closed by the end of the three-month sampling period, with the remainder open and either active or inactive. Just 43 per cent of these (26) cases with known child protection concerns were closed by the end of the follow-up period in the study, compared to 78 per cent of pure child welfare cases[5]. This shows that although welfare referrals were open for considerable periods of time, welfare referrals with a protection history were more likely to remain open than those without.

In analysing what actual services these cases received, it is necessary to consider responses to all the referrals and specifically to those that were substantiated. This is because although some *referrals* were unsubstantiated the *cases* still received services because they were already open and active at the time when the referral in this study was made. Sixty-two per cent (n=50) of the 81 child welfare referrals received a long-term service. Of these, 72 per cent (36) received a home-based service, mostly social work. Seven cases received a service from a family support worker and five from a child care worker. Another 18 per cent of the child welfare referrals received a long-term community service (including a parenting course, teenage support group, youth services, after-school club), while 76 per cent were provided with a clinically based service (22 per cent counselling, 12 per cent addiction treatment, 22 per cent child psychiatry and 20 per cent child psychology). Twenty-eight per cent received a care-based service, both statutory and voluntary.

Child welfare referrals with protection concerns at some point in the case career received more services than 'pure' welfare referrals. Fifty–five per cent (n=30) of the 55 'pure' welfare referrals were provided with a long term service compared with 79 per cent (n=44) of the welfare referrals with a protection concern. Of the 55 'pure' welfare referrals, 55 per cent (n=30) were provided with a long-term service, 33 per cent received a home-based service, mainly from social workers and child care workers. However, a child care worker provided a service for only three cases and a family support worker for one, indicating that the bulk of child care and family support services are provided to cases with a protection concern. Forty-two per-cent were provided with a clinical service (18 per cent with alcohol/addition treatment, 21 per cent a school or health board counsellor, and 32 per cent child psychiatry or psychology.) Meanwhile 9 per cent of pure welfare referrals received a care-based service (voluntary residential, foster or hostel care), and 6 per cent a community-based service (teenage support group and youth worker)[6]. These patterns confirm the pattern of interventions in child welfare cases shown earlier in the chapter in terms of the division of services between particular professionals with clinical services being offered to many distressed teenagers.

A similar kind of division of professional labour is apparent for substantiated cases; it is also clear that welfare cases with a protection concern are over-represented in the provision of services for substantiated welfare cases. While 64 per cent of substantiated pure welfare cases were provided with a long-term service, 95 per cent of substantiated welfare cases with a protection concern received a service. Of the 137 referrals defined as child welfare, 55 per cent were substantiated, 80 per cent (n=61) of which were provided with a long-term service. Of the 56 welfare referrals where a protection concern was also raised, 64 per cent (n=36) were substantiated and 95 per cent of these received a long term service. Thirty-two of these cases received a home based service, provided to 29 by a social worker, to five by a family support worker and to three by a child care worker. Sixteen cases received a clinical service, of which seven received counselling, four addiction treatment, six child psychiatry and one child psychology. In seven cases a community-based service was provided (parenting course, youth worker, women's group and youth-reach), and in nine cases a care-based service (two residential care, six foster care and one hostel). Of the 26 welfare referrals with a previous history of protection, twelve were substantiated. Nine of these received a service, for eight of which it was a home based service provided by social workers, for one a family support worker and for two by child care workers. For seven cases a clinical service was provided (child psychiatry in four, child psychology in two and counselling in two). Meanwhile, five cases received a community-based service (parenting course, youth worker and after-school club) and four cases received a care-based service (four foster care and one residential care).

Of the 55 'pure' welfare cases, 51 per cent were substantiated, 64 per cent (n=18) of which received a service. Thirteen cases received a home-based service, eleven from a social worker and two from a child care worker.

Eleven cases received a clinical service (child psychiatry in three, child psychology in four, alcohol addiction treatment in three and day psychiatric hospital in one). Four pure welfare cases received a care-based service, three entered foster care and one was provided with hostel accommodation. One case received a service from a community-based youth worker.

The main reason why long-term services, or what in Chapter 7 we called 'intensive' social work intervention, were not provided in substantiated welfare cases was the child or family's refusal to co-operate or view that the service was unnecessary; these essentially involuntary clients accounted for five of the thirteen cases where a service was not provided. In four cases the family was seen on a short-term basis by a social worker on more than one home visit and the case was closed as the identified problems were solved, that is the concern in the referral was addressed. For example, Case 78 was referred due to financial/ housing problems and the local community welfare officer and county council facilitated short term accommodation and financial aid. In two cases the child was seen once by the social worker and in an investigative capacity by another professional. One case was closed after one social visit investigating an underage pregnancy and one case was still open one year on with the child and mother seen by a social worker in an investigative capacity only.

Conclusion

In this chapter we analysed the nature of child welfare cases and the kinds of responses to them by health boards and the wider expert system. We have shown the great needs of the children and their carers in such cases and the very real work that is being done with them; however, this effort is given little formal recognition as it falls outside the official child protection system. The absence of a protection concern appears to affect the provision of treatment/ support services. Referrals concerned with both protection and welfare problems are most likely to receive a service, with substantiated welfare cases with a protection concern the most likely of the welfare cases to receive a service. It might be argued that these results reflect a lower level of need or risk in welfare cases, compared with child protection cases. Clearly the level of risk and need in many (60 per cent) substantiated child welfare cases is low but significant levels of need and child and family adversity are routinely identified in as many as 40 per cent of child welfare referrals. Thus, in an important sense, what is being shown here are the different constructions of need and risk and divisions of professional labour operating in the system in relation to different child care scenarios. This is apparent in the relatively high level of clinical services provision to adolescents in distress and the relatively low level of family support services provided to pure child welfare cases compared to those with protection concerns. While this is an entirely appropriate division of professional labour in some instances, it suggests a need to (re)balance child protection and family support services to ensure that each welfare case receives the most appropriate response.

This also raises the important question of what constitutes a 'family support' service. Are secure high support units for distressed and out of control adolescents family support or child protection services? Or does it really matter what they are called as long as the assessed safety and welfare needs of the child are provided for? The chapter has shown that in many respects the protection/ welfare categorisation oversimplifies a more complex reality, given that so many referrals have elements of both. The evidence suggests that the child care literature needs to be much clearer about matching the particular needs of children and their carers with particular services and provide a conceptual language that will do justice to the complex realities of practice. The official status of child welfare cases with no child protection concerns in the Irish system needs to be clarified. There is no structure in the current system for codifying and accounting for the child welfare work being done. There is no child welfare or family support equivalent of the Child Protection Notification (CPN) system. Given that child welfare referrals constitute 28 per cent of all referrals and 'pure' child welfare cases 19 per cent, their official status needs to be clarified in a system dominated by protection. What is at issue is not only how these cases should be defined, and organisational categories developed for them, but also how cases are responded to and services provided for vulnerable children and carers, irrespective of case definition.

Notes

[1] This adds up to more than 100 per cent as more than one child protection concern was cited in some referrals.

[2] The ambiguous status of cases is also apparent in that 38 per cent (n=31) of child welfare referrals were notified to the CPN system, in spite of the fact that no protection concern was cited in 14 of the 31 referrals notified. Notification led to these ostensibly welfare cases entering the protection system. These cases may have been notified by social workers whose practice is to notify all referrals (see Chapter 4).

[3] In 24 cases, 30 per cent of the welfare sample, the social worker considered risk assessment to be 'not applicable', while in a further 21 per cent the risk to the child was not assessed or not recorded. So data on risk assessment was provided by social workers for just under half, 49 per cent, of these cases. This is an indication of the difficulty of using child protection risk assessment for child welfare cases.

[4] It was beyond the scope of the research to examine the intensity of the clinical services provided in every case as it would have required detailed interviews with every clinical

practitioner.

5 This also compares with the 205 child protection referrals left in the sample when the 81 welfare referrals are taken out (including 149 defined as protection and the 56 defined as welfare but also citing a protection concern *in* the referral), of which 19 per cent were closed after the initial sampling period and 48 per cent were closed at the end of the follow-up period.

6 Some cases received treatment/support services from one or more service providers (see Chapter 7 for a discussion on combinations of services).

9 The Consumer View: Children's and Parents' Perspectives on the Child Care and Protection System

The views of professionals are crucial to understanding the nature of child care and protection systems. It is now broadly accepted, however, that adequate evaluations of services need to include the voice of the consumer (Butler and Williamson, 1994; Cleaver and Freeman, 1995; Farmer and Owen, 1995; Thoburn, Lewis and Shemmings, 1995). The value of this should already be clear from this book, as case-studies in earlier chapters included the voices of children and parents. In this chapter their views are the main focus of attention. While Irish research into child protection has begun to include parental perspectives (Buckley, Skehill and O'Sullivan, 1997), the voices of children are still completely absent from published accounts. This, then, is the first study of its kind in Ireland to include interviews with children, as well as their parents. Thirteen children were interviewed, seven girls and six boys ranging in age from eight to eighteen years. Access to them was facilitated through their parent(s)/carers, at least one of whom was interviewed in each case for the study. All the children were interviewed separately from their parents, nine at their home, three in health board offices and one in a residential unit. Each child was paid £10 for their time.

The children's perspectives: the denial of information

The children's views contained a range of feelings and opinions, from deep gratitude for professional intervention to anger and confusion as to why the State had become involved with them and their families. One of the main criticisms, voiced by many children, was they felt they were denied information. The children in care were especially critical of a lack of information from social workers as to why they were being placed in care. As one ten-year-old boy commented 'I didn't know what was wrong, I didn't know why we were up there [residential care] or anything, I didn't know why, what, what it means or anything' (Case 283). This family had been involved with the health board for over six years with a history of physical abuse, domestic violence and neglect. Both parents were considered to be abusive, although their 'ability to cope' in terms of family support intervention was addressed. The children's mother was also critical of her children being placed in care.

In Case 311, concerned with neglect, alcohol abuse and domestic violence, a thirteen-year-old boy expressed dissatisfaction with social workers' communication because he had been informed that he would be away from home for six to seven weeks but remained in care for six months. He felt that 'it [foster care] just kept on going on, they should have told me . . . drove me mad that did'. The children were placed in statutory foster care and returned home on a supervision order. His twelve-year-old brother was also critical of social workers' poor communication, which left him 'just confused . . . I didn't really know what was happening until it was totally explained to me . . . we were there [foster care] for about a month, that's when I got kind of clear in my mind' (Case 311). He felt that he was in care for 'no reason. They sent us . . . they kept us away from our family for six months for no reason'. Although the children in this case clearly viewed foster care in negative terms the mother voiced her 'appreciation', and felt that her children being in statutory care resulted in many positive changes in her life. However, she too was critical of the level of information provided and the explanation of the legal process.

In a child sexual abuse case the children were told by social workers that they were going into foster care for two to three weeks, but the fourteen-year-old commented: 'after a while it came to like a month being away and thinking it's been longer than two weeks . . . were we ever leaving?' (Case 224). The two children were placed in foster care for the duration of a CSA assessment, following which the board applied for and was granted full care orders. Another fourteen-year-old girl complained that she was not informed by social workers either that she was going into care 'they just took me . . . my mother had washed all of my clothes so the clothes I had were wet so I didn't take them, they took me though'. According to this child's ten-year-old brother '[we] just went into the care and mother told us to go into the car, she didn't tell nothing else. We got brought up to [residential unit] . . . nothing [no information], they never said nothing, I don't know why I was in there or nothing'. He did not feel able to ask social workers why he was in care because he feared they might prevent him from participating in recreational activities: 'because I think they would not let me go anywhere then, the good part was when they were letting me go swimming and everything and that's why I didn't ask them, I didn't ask them anything . . . and that's how we get outside the door' (Case 283).

Understandings of professional roles

The children displayed varying levels of comprehension of the social work role. One ten-year-old boy confused social and residential care workers and did not perceive any differences between them (Case 283). Another thirteen-year-old boy commented that no one ever explained to him what a social worker's job entailed: 'I think they should do that [explain] . . . I'd know who I'm talking to and who they are and what they are about' (Case 311). Several of the children commented that they did not know 'anything' about social workers prior to becoming involved with them, while others stated that they were quite clear, 'I know straight away like' (Case 283). An eleven-year-old girl explained she 'hadn't a clue [about social workers] but she [social worker] had explained it to me, she explained that she was a social worker to help me with my problems and things that I couldn't say to my mam, that she'd help me to say them to her, all that stuff' (Case 140). Another child, aged thirteen, considered the social worker's job to be 'like when people fight they probably help them, that's what they does with mammy and daddy' (Case 138). She viewed the social worker role 'as to help people . . . they helped us a bit like'. A twelve-year-old boy said, 'I don't know nothing about them', but 'the first time I met [social workers] I knew there were bad people' (Case 283).

(Not) listening to children

Social workers' listening skills were identified as poor by some of the children who felt that social workers did not hear them or take their concerns on board. A thirteen-year-old boy considered social workers to be strangers, and not people he felt able to confide in: 'they were strangers and I didn't really know them so I thought why tell strangers your problems'. He felt 'they don't listen to me . . . I don't like them that much, I wouldn't tell them everything, I don't trust them that much I don't know [why I dislike them], I just do' (Case 311). His twelve-year-old brother would not 'tell' social workers 'anything' and insisted he could 'never talk' to them about his problems. A fourteen-year-old girl was of the opinion that social workers asked too many questions. She was 'more able' to discuss her problems with a psychologist than the social worker as the psychologist 'spent more time with us [social worker] only comes in and then she leaves' (Case 224). A twelve-year-old child felt that social workers 'won't be listening, they'll just say yeah and all that and they'll be driving away when you're talking to them' (Case 283). Having the radio on in their car was, for him, the big giveaway: 'say if they were bringing you for a spin and they had the radio on and you were talking, that's not a good listener'. Another child felt that social workers didn't listen 'because they're probably too busy and they can't' (Case 138). An eleven-year-old boy could tell when social workers were poor listeners, 'when you're talking they're like dummies, say I'm talking like and they are there like a dummy, with their mouth flopped and their ears up' (Case 138). A fourteen-year-child felt not listened to when he was having difficulties in his care placement: 'I wasn't getting on very well there myself . . . and they [social workers] said they'd try to do something, talk to them but nothing ever changed'. He felt that social workers did not listen to him because he was young and that if he was five years older they might have, and 'if they had they might have done something about it but they didn't' (Case 311).

On the other hand, several children considered their social workers to be very good listeners. As one eleven-year-old girl summed it up: 'they'll be looking at you, nodding their head an odd time and when you're finished talking they'd explain what was wrong, because if she wasn't listening she wouldn't know what I said . . . I like the way she just can answer the question, she knows the answers, she's been listening during the question and she's been listening to the questions and she was answering them as well! So you know she has got the skill of listening while trying to answer a question you know' (Case 140). For a fifteen-year-old girl 'they pick up on things very fast, and they get on it straight away, I think they do anyway, like if you told them that you wanted to visit your foster family you've been with before, they'll get on to it straight away if they can try to arrange it. . . . they sit down and concentrate they're good listeners as well about your problems, because they try to do the best they can like, to sort it out' (Case 283).

In addition to listening skills, the extent to which children discussed 'problems' with social workers emerged in interviews. A twelve-year-old considered some of the social workers he had met as 'nice' and easy to 'talk to', while others were 'snobby' (Case 311). Two children didn't talk to social workers without their mother being present as they didn't feel 'comfortable' with the social worker (Case 283), while a twelve-year-old in this family described social workers as 'very nice do you know, they listen to you, they talk to you, they know how you feel and stuff'. This child's fifteen-year old sibling, who was in foster care at the time of the interview, commented 'I usually get very agitated when people ask me questions, I just get very agitated, like my social worker, I hate sitting down with my social worker asking me this, that, that . . . they'd be asking you blah, blah what happened there'.

An eleven-year-old child described it as *'easy'* to discuss her problems with social workers (Case 140), while a twelve-year-old commented that he only ever liked one social worker and spoke with contempt about the others (Case 283). The social worker he liked 'was kind to me and all that when the other social workers were at me'. A twelve-year-old commented 'I didn't want social workers to come to my door, I didn't ask . . . don't like them . . . just don't like the cops or social workers . . . just don't like them, didn't like those sort of people'. He felt that social workers 'didn't talk to me that much' (Case 311). An eleven-year-old girl 'pops in' to see the social worker on a regular basis for 'a chat', and the social worker is quite open to these informal meetings (Case 140). An eleven-year-old boy commented 'if I had a problem like I'd tell a social worker, yeah someone that'd help me' (Case 138). Several children noted that they would discuss their 'problems' with parents or teachers rather than social workers. One felt that if social workers spent more time with him 'it would be easier to talk to them' (Case 311).

Changes of social workers were identified as confusing by some children. A thirteen-year-old commented 'well you see there was three different social workers while I was staying there [foster care] . . . you'd see one twice, next time there's another completely different person coming along then there could have been another different person, it didn't feel right. Say I went one week to talk to them, firstly I'd have to talk to somebody that I never, that I hadn't seen before, the next day there could be somebody different. The week after there could be somebody different, they change like the wind' (Case 311). His twelve-year-old brother voiced the same criticism, 'I had enough of them. You see what they are like . . . there's a lot of them. You'd get mixed up between them, I'd plenty of it to last a lifetime . . . I was just sick of them coming up and asking me questions'.

The impact of intervention on the children's lives

Some children viewed intervention as having effected positive changes in their lives while others considered the impact to be negative. In Case 224, an eighteen-year-old spoke of the positive effects foster care had had on her life, she felt 'happy' living in foster care, 'I was happy like because I wanted to get away from [home]'. She was of the opinion that she would be 'dead' had she remained at home. She recalled her reaction to being told by a social worker that she was being placed in foster care, 'I think I was sort of excited about it, I remember the first day that we left mum and dad . . . I was excited about it at first'. Her fourteen-year-old sister felt that social workers had 'changed my life . . . I mean changing my life in a good way'. She viewed social workers as 'someone who helps you', and described the social worker profession 'it's like the law, that's what I thought the minute that social workers ask all the questions, like you go to court and everything with a social worker and have like all those big bosses'.

An eleven-year-old girl felt that she had become 'something else' as a result of the work that had been done with her and her family. She has become a 'better person . . . I'm able to keep control, I'm not as bossy as I used to be . . . I just think that [social worker] and [FSW] have been a great help to my family' (Case 140). A fifteen-year-old girl felt that 'well now they did a lot for me, a lot for me, they got me in foster care, I got on very well there . . . I could be sleeping on the streets if it wasn't for the [social workers]'. In relation to being placed in care this child commented 'they took me out of home. That was the best thing because I'd say I'd be dead by now if I was still living at home, I would be dead, I would be just dead because I'd end up doing something stupid or something . . . they know when something's going on at home and the kids shouldn't be there, sure that is right to be taking them out when they shouldn't be at home, sure I think my brothers and sisters, they don't have a life at home, I know they don't, I didn't have one at home'. This child was able to reassure her sister about professionals: 'they do a lot of their things, I would say that I told my sister when she was coming into care they were just going to help her out, because she thought that they were something like the guards or something like that, because I knew what they were and what they were there for'. In relation to the experience of care this child commented: 'I'm doing grand at the moment, I'm never going home it's not home to me, I've been in care too long. Care is my home'. She still has reservations about professionals: 'I don't like going in [to social workers] on my own, because they ask too many questions and you won't be able to answer them all and you need your sister to answer some like, they help people . . . make people be friends' (case 283). An eleven-year-old boy felt that intervention 'changed [my life] a good bit like, when we were younger there was no social workers around like, we could do anything we want'.

Some children did not view social work intervention as having brought any positive changes to their lives (Case 311). A twelve-year-old and his thirteen-year-old brother were in relative foster care and felt there was nothing positive about it. As the twelve-year-old put it: 'all I wanted to do was come back home that's all I ever wanted to do'. And as the twelve-year-old boy in Case 283 commented about residential care: 'I hated it, you weren't left step outside the door or anything, had to stay in the house all day, you'd to stay in and if you go out, if you're allowed out, one of them has to go out with you and if you just step outside the little gate thing, a barrier'. He felt that all social workers had done was 'give us hell, hell that's all they are, hell'. His ten-year-old brother felt that 'they're after just tearing [the family] we're all turning bad over it'. He would 'never trust' social workers, as they tell you one thing and do another. His eight-year-old sister felt that all social workers took children away from their families and 'we don't like them'.

In summary, what clearly emerges from the interviews with children is the poor communication and quality of information given to children, especially in relation to plans for children in care. Poor communication was also evident in children's perception of social workers, that is, what a social worker is, what they actually do and why they are involved with their family. The findings are supported by other research which has shown that trust and confidentiality are key issues for children and young people in their dealings with child care professionals (Butler and Williamson, 1994). Children fear that professionals will act on whatever information is disclosed without giving the young person a choice, or seek their consent or input or negotiate with them. For Butler and Williamson (1994, p. 123) moving beyond this has to involve social workers and other professionals in child protection in 'a trade-off between confidentiality and risk'. They suggest that working contracts could be set up between young people and professionals to incorporate children's views as to what information will be used and in what manner.

With regard to the availability of staff, 'child abuse does not keep office hours' (Butler and Williamson, 1994, p. 125) and professionals need to find ways of hearing children when they need to speak. Helplines are one obvious possible solution to this. Children and adolescents are also acutely aware of the age of professionals who need to be aware of how the 'generation gap' can contribute to children not feeling understood and closing off (Butler and Williamson, 1994). The more trendy and child-friendly—the 'cooler' the service in the eyes of young people—the more they will be prepared to access it (Osborne, 1999). Working contracts incorporating children's perspectives need to take account of planning about their lives, processes in which they need to be fully included. Children's views as to what information will be used and in what manner also need to be respected.

The parent's perspectives: initial perceptions of intervention

Sixteen parents—twelve mothers and four fathers—were interviewed by the research team. Access was negotiated through social workers who gave each parent a standardised explanatory letter requesting their participation in the research. Parents who agreed to be interviewed then gave permission to be contacted directly by the research team. Interviews took place at a venue of the parent's choice. Each parent was paid £20 for their time.

Several parents described feelings of shock and anger when recounting their first meeting with social workers. A common initial perception was that social workers only became involved in families who 'abused' their children and that their main interest was the removal of children from the family home. As one father said: 'when they first arrived I was livid, you know a social worker, as soon as anyone hears of a social worker involved, it's all battered children you know like sexually abused children, so any time one hears of a social worker mentioned now that is what runs through everybody's mind, it was a bit of a shock to me because I never had any dealings like that before, when they came it was a bit of a shock, I really did not know what to expect' (Case 140). Some felt that if they knew the social worker was calling it wouldn't have been such a shock. Another father commented that when he first met a social worker 'she was telling me she'd put the kids into care and all this, more or less trying to frighten me . . . I didn't really like it, I moved away, I bought a car and we left. I thought I was going to get rid of them [social workers] but they still kept coming round. So I said what the devil, I might as well go back where they keep following me around, they've done more good for me than I thought they would like, I was trying to avoid them because I thought they were going to send away the kids' (Case 138).

Another mother described the initial social work visit as 'frightening' due to her fear of 'losing' her children, a fear of social workers she felt is present in the entire community (Case 311; See also case 157). This case was concerned with neglect, domestic violence and the mother's alcohol abuse. Her three children aged thirteen, twelve and three were placed in relative foster care as a temporary resource while she was recovering from alcohol addiction. In Case 51, concerned with neglect and domestic violence, the mother said: 'I felt it an awful wicked intrusion in my private life . . . you know which is all we have and I felt desperate'. She felt that the social workers made 'mountains out of molehills' and she felt 'ashamed' to be involved with them as people should be able to get on with their lives without outside support. For another mother 'there is a lot of people who don't like social workers, they think like with the social worker coming that there is something wrong'(Case 53). Another mother felt that as she herself was involved with social workers as a child she was viewed in a negative light: 'they never left me alone because I was involved with them, they presume that because I had problems when I was a child that [child] is going to have problems you know that kind of way . . . just because I'm involved with social workers since I'm fifteen does that mean I'm automatically a Mid-Western Health Board case?' Her own past had 'labelled' her as a poor parent (Case 265).

Positive accounts of intervention

Many of the parents described their experiences of intervention in a complimentary light and were positive about the impact it had had on their children. The mother in Case 172 felt that social workers had come to her 'aid' in helping her with her son who had behaviour/control problems, 'she did everything for me, and we've had great contact . . . .you know I could always ring her and she'd always call you know'. The boy was placed in a residential unit and 'they are very good to him down there, they are after changing him completely you know to what he was . . . I know there was help there and she [social worker] was going to do it. Well she knew more, I mean I wouldn't have known what to do'. Although, as we have seen, the mother in Case 311 was fearful of her children being placed in care, she felt that intervention 'is in the interest of the child . . . which I appreciate a lot, it's definitely all for the children, are they all right?, to know how they are doing, the whole lot'. She described her relationship with the health board as 'a very good relationship. I thank them today, I appreciate, I mean at this stage I feel they did the right thing [placing children in care] because I wouldn't have been, I would never have been right, I'd often be saying would I have given up the drink, would I still be put there, would I be dead?' She would not have achieved the progress to date without the intervention, 'my life has changed so much it's unbelievable'. She described her relationship with her social worker as 'a great relationship . . . it's great to have a bit of communication with them' (for similar positive comments, see Case 140, in Chapter 7).

Workers' flexibility in meeting with parents, especially (working) men, by arranging to call in the evenings was considered by a father to be 'good' practice. Another father initially 'didn't like' social workers as he felt 'they were going to do me a lot of damage or something' (Case 138). However, he now felt that 'they done me a lot of good . . . they'll probably see more for another three or four years . . . but I don't mind, that's their job like, well I'm more or less delighted that they are doing it because they're keeping me off the drink'. The father in Case 166 was provided with social work support and home help services following separation from his wife and considered social workers to be very 'helpful . . . I would have nothing bad to say really about them all, they did their best as far as I can see'. The mother in Case 53 described her social worker as 'a very understanding and caring man . . . [he] didn't want to separate nobody from nobody, just wanted to help. Very, very nice man you know that understood the situation. He was just very, very good'.

Negative accounts of intervention

Many parents did not view the system and how it operates in such a positive light. Exclusion from the decisions about the care of children in care was a key criticism. One mother felt that she was not provided with adequate support and was quite vocal in her dissatisfaction with access arrangements: 'they say their interest is in keeping families together . . . then when it comes to [child] coming in, when they can't bring her in, they just can't they should have somebody else to cover for them while they're on holidays' (Case 265). Her view was that social workers 'sometimes now they don't say directly what they mean . . . they kind of beat around the bush, they wouldn't come out and directly say something, they'd say it in a nice way rather than just come out with it, they put things in a nice way even when they mean something else'.

Some parents were critical of the demeanour of professionals. In a child sexual abuse case the father regarded the senior social worker who made a joint home visit with a garda as 'quite aggressive . . . and he also brought the police which was in my opinion to instil fear, to use the old heavy stick, use the big stick to instil fear' (Case 224). This father now had 'no confidence in the health board, I couldn't trust them'. This lack of trust was based on the social worker informing him that his children would be in voluntary foster care for a few weeks and they are now in long term statutory care. This father 'fought for my kids . . . I love those kids more than my own life. They were my whole life, but once they took them that was it, I had no trust in the Mid-western Health Board'. For him, 'if they actually help people I don't know but I also think that they they manage to drive people apart'. His wife, from whom he was separated, also felt that social workers 'are good at making threats, I've been co-operating which they say is a good idea, they say co-operate because if you don't co-operate you know I won't ever get my girls back, that type of thing, that sounds like a very strong demand'. This mother felt 'bullied' by social workers 'he [SSW] says he's going to fight me . . . and well he can be very over demanding'. She felt that social workers were 'watching' her, 'they're like a fly, they'll follow you around'. She felt that the health board did not listen to her. These two parents had two children in long-term statutory foster care.

Several of the parents divided social workers into 'good' and 'bad' categories. For the mother in Case 283 who had been involved with social workers for several years due to neglect, alleged physical abuse and domestic violence, 'some of them have been all right and some of them haven't'. She viewed social workers as 'goodies' and 'baddies', the difference being: 'the goodies will believe what you're saying [and] from the outside point of view that you're doing you're level best, the baddies no matter what you say to them, they presume otherwise'. [They] just want your life's blood and that's it'. She described a bad social worker as 'more interested in what colour your walls are painted in your house', feeling like they were passing judgement on her because of the material condition of her home. 'So I think they should see beyond, because I've often travelled in some of their cars and they've often been absolutely filthy, diabolical . . . I've gone into their offices and I've seen their mugs on the table and everything and I wouldn't pass judgement on that'. The difference between 'good' and 'bad' social workers for one father is 'I mean some social workers were ok they weren't bad some of them . . . you kind of like some of them better, their attitude you know. More of them are hard and they're afraid to go out for fresh air, they want to keep you inside, you know scared, but some of them are nice, they'll talk, passable enough' (Case 224).

As Chapter 5 has shown, in extra familial child sexual abuse cases parents' perceptions of social work and the wider child care and criminal justice system was generally very negative. Parents were critical of what they viewed as a slow response to their child's disclosure. They considered the level of social work contact and the support for their children and themselves as poor. A recurring complaint was a lack of feedback from social workers on the progress of the investigation. Parents felt ill-informed and excluded from decision-making and were generally disillusioned with the outcomes of CSA cases.

Perceptions of how social workers practiced

Several parents felt that the social worker directed all their attention to working with the children. As one mother put it, when social workers call they come to see the children 'not much about me, that's the way I see it'. She felt the social worker should call more often than the 'every month or six weeks' (Case 138). Some felt that more real support and help from social workers and others might have prevented children from being placed in foster care. As the mother of a toddler in care put it: 'they were just coming down to see how she was. They just called out and just looked around the house kind of, and see how [child] was and then go away, they'd never sit down and talk, like they'd never sit down, never ask me about me, how I was getting on or anything like that' (Case 265). By comparison, one mother felt that the social worker worked with her as well as her child, 'they don't just come in and say "well, right we're going to do this"', I mean they talk to you and explain it to you' (Case 172). For another mother her social worker 'would listen to you if you had a problem and not judge you on it . . . you need someone that is going to sit down and listen to you and not judge you' (Case 140).

Parents with children placed in care

Parents with children in statutory care were generally more critical of the 'care system'. One father whose two children were in voluntary care due to sexual abuse and were subsequently placed under long term care orders criticised social workers for not communicating to him the reason for the admission to care, 'they gave away very little information but apparently the girls were assessed and they said the best way of assessing the girls was to take them away from this environment' (Case 224). He agreed to allow his children to be placed in voluntary foster care and was informed by a senior social worker that it was 'completely voluntary they said they'd be back after four or five weeks . . . but that went down the river'. He admitted, however, that he was given 'plenty of notice' of care proceedings. He considered foster care to be a 'terrible punishment' for children and was unhappy with access arrangements.

One mother described the removal of her children to foster care: 'they called that morning. They had another report got like that I was drinking that I was out, and the three children were basically left on their own . . . pain I will never forget as long as I live, oh I'll never forget it, it was so sad like. It's an awful experience, a frightening experience'. She was aware that care was a possibility due to her continued drinking and this was explained to her, however she felt that the legal aspect of care was not adequately explained. She received letters from the health board requesting her to 'sign this and sign that, no explanation, not knowing what these were about, I read them and read them and read them and I still couldn't understand them. I didn't have no one to ask about them'. She too was critical of access visits in terms of times and venues, she 'begged and begged for the health board to give me access . . . I wanted more access because I knew that they were going through as well'. The access visits with her daughter took place in health board premises for an hour: 'there should be better places like for seeing kids. Inside in a room for an hour, I mean that is not great access . . . there's nothing in the room, it's a big room, what are you supposed to do with a child in there for an hour, I couldn't do anything with her in there. I felt locked up'. Overall this mother was 'grateful' that her children were placed in care as it effected many positive changes in her life; however improvements in the care system need to be made (Case 311).

The stigma attached to care influences parents' accessing it: 'if there was something else there without using the big fostering word' (Case 157). Just the word fostering 'frightens the life out of me and then this big stigma if they get into the social workers you will never get your kids back, all this goes round in your head like'. Another mother said the effect of her child being placed in care was, '[I was] crazy, I couldn't cope with it at all, that made me worse if anything like . . . .you know I couldn't handle the situation' (Case 51). On a positive note some found respite care a great resource but fears had to be allayed before it could be received favourably: 'until [social worker] sat down for one and a half hours one day and explained it to me, that it was respite, and that is an absolutely fantastic service, I availed of it last year but until then I wouldn't have dreamed of it' (Case 140). Another mother whose children were in voluntary foster care felt that her options and the whole process was explained very well to her (Case 138).

Parental views of case conferences and involvement in decision-making

A case conference was held for ten of the fourteen families where parents were interviewed for this study. In five cases the parent(s) were invited and attended part of the case conference, in four cases the parents were not invited. In all five cases where the parent(s) attended the conference, their child(ren) were placed in care at some point in the case career. By comparison, care proceedings were not a feature in any of the four cases where the parents were not invited. All of the parents who attended a case conference expressed feelings of fear, anxiety and/or nervousness. One said she felt degraded by the whole experience. Only one parent expressed positive sentiments regarding the case conference. This case was concerned with behaviour/control problems. The mother felt that the case conference included her in the decision on the best service for her son, even though she was not present for the entire conference. It was 'great, they talk, everyone listens to you. I came in, what was talked about and what ideas I had and had I anything to say about it, so I thought it was great, 'twas nice. I think it was great, their attitude, we talked about everything . . . improvements and what has to be improved' (Case 172). This mother had met all the case conference participants at various stages prior to the conference. She commented that this 'helped' as 'they weren't really strangers'.

Case study 265 provides compelling evidence of parent's views of case conferences and their overall sense of exclusion from decision making processes. A grandfather expressed concerns about his daughter's care of her fifteen-month-old child. He contacted a social worker based in a community centre who in turn referred the concerns to the community care social worker:

> mother spends much of her time with known alcoholics, leaving her child with anybody who cares to mind her, has bungalow, has not stayed there for a long period, huge arrears and bills, child dirty (case file).

The mother had been involved with the health board due to homelessness since she was fifteen years of age. Neglect was considered to be the main presenting problem. According to the social worker the child's physical appearance was extremely poor and there was concern about her emotional well-being in that she had no difficulty at all in going to strangers: 'she was a very affectionate child anyway, she would take to anybody' (case file). The mother and child were seen by the investigating social worker and a frontline social worker colleague two days after the referral. The home conditions were 'inspected' and were considered to be sub-standard. The bedroom 'was dirty, it was smelly'. The case was assessed as high risk due to the presenting condition of the child, the mother's lifestyle, that she was drinking, out all day with the child in the buggy, the child not being fed, except with crisps or chocolate but not wholesome food. The case was monitored by the social worker in the community centre 'until it came to a crisis point'. A case conference was called which confirmed the high level of risk and decided that the mother would bring the child to a crèche on a daily basis, that she would engage in a 'training group' on home-making skills and join a parent support group. However, the mother refused to engage with the services. She couldn't be found at home, by social workers or public health nurses (PHN); when traced, she refused to avail of 'an alcohol assessment'. She did attend the crèche; however, a check had to be made every day to make sure she attended. A review case conference was held in light of the mother's perceived lack of co-operation and it was agreed that the child would go to respite care for the weekends and attend the crèche during the week where she would be monitored. Following the respite care the child was returned to her mother's full-time care. However, on the day of the child's return her mother requested full-time care because 'she was unable to cope'. The mother had given up her corporation house and had financial problems. It was agreed that the child would be placed in voluntary foster care for a four-week period, during which the mother obtained temporary accommodation in a hostel but was 'thrown out of there because of her behaviour' (case file).

At the end of the four weeks the mother sought the return of her child but this was refused because her state of mind was so poor that she wasn't in tune with the child's needs. Evidence of neglect included the child attending the crèche in the clothes she had slept in, smelling of urine. Another case conference was held and the decision made to apply for a care order. The application for the care order was subsequently adjourned as the mother became pregnant and had 'stabilised' to some extent. Following the board's refusal to return the child to her mother's care the mother went to England for several weeks. She returned and was admitted to a psychiatric ward for a number of weeks. Following her discharge from hospital, according to the social worker the mother 'went downhill'. The social worker felt that a supervision order would not have been appropriate in this case because there already was contact with the child and mother, but the care of the child wasn't good enough for the child to be left at home, it had deteriorated so much along with the mother's mental health. The mother attended some of the case conferences, being invited in towards the end and told of the decisions and what was expected of her, 'she really didn't engage at all'. The social worker was clearly of the opinion that if the mother had co-operated with the initial case conference recommendations the placement of her child in foster care might have been avoided. By the end of the research period, with the mother pregnant and due to give birth soon, another case conference was planned to discuss the future of this child. There was a possibility of the new baby being taken into care at birth; however, the mother was more 'stable', had accommodation and there were hopes of linking her in with supports in the community.

Mother's perspective

The mother was interviewed prior to the board's application for a care order and the birth of her child. She recalled her first contact with social workers when she became homeless at the age of fifteen and lived in a girl's hostel until she was almost eighteen. Following the birth of her daughter she secured corporation housing. At this time she received a lot of support from her own father in rearing her daughter. However, after her father went to England 'I couldn't manage [child] any more and I went to the social worker and they helped me out'. She recalled contacting the social worker to seek assistance: 'well you see I went into them and said to them that I felt I couldn't look after [child] because too many things were getting on top of me'. Of her initial request for temporary foster care, she commented, 'they said they'd put her into voluntary care for four weeks and said to me sign the form, I just signed the form, but they knew I was upset . . . I didn't even read it, I just signed the form'. She was critical of the initial social work investigation because 'they just called out and see, just look around the house kind of and see how [child] was, and go away, they'd never sit down and talk, like they'd never sit down, never ask me about me, how I was getting on or anything like that'.

She felt that she was not provided with adequate support. She was encouraged by social workers to return to the hostel following her request for temporary foster care, when 'really I feel like they should have left me in my house and let me do it on my own, rather than put me in a hostel and get me looked after, if I'd had to do it on my own, I'd have had to do it. If I hadn't the offer of the hostel I wouldn't have been able to leave'. Had the social worker made more of an 'effort' to encourage her to stay in her home she might have been in a better position to care for her daughter. In response to the question of what support she needed it was 'just encouragement . . . to let me know I was doing ok and if I needed any help with the house I think they should have helped me more with keeping my house and get a job, a course or something'. She felt 'tricked' by the social worker: 'when I was in the hostel I just can't have her back because I've nowhere to bring her, which I know that if you haven't got a home for a child you can't look after her, it was kind of I couldn't win and I felt then that they had tricked me'.

With regard to her experiences of case conferences:

'I went to it but I stayed only about five minutes. I didn't want to stay in there. I was frightened, there was a big long table with loads of people there. I don't know who they were, my doctor was there and the health board was there and other social workers but I didn't know who any of them were. I just came in and they'd spoken before I went into the case conference, and when I went in they just said to me, well you need to do this now and you need to do that and you need to do this and they were throwing all these things at me and they were all strangers, so I got up and I said look I said I'm not listening to this and I walked out.'

She described feelings of 'fear': 'I was so, I was more afraid like because I didn't know any of them and they were telling me all these things to do'. She did not really speak at the case conference because 'I was afraid to open my mouth, I was afraid to say anything, suppose I said the wrong thing'. No one had explained to her prior to the conference who was going to be there and what was going to happen. She felt that she was not given a chance to explain her situation at the case conference, 'they had discussed it all anyway, they'd made their minds up, that's the way I felt so I just walked out'. She felt that what she had to say would not have made any difference to the case conference decisions. She feels excluded from decision-making about her own and her daughter's life: 'I felt like even though it was about me, it actually wasn't, because I knew nothing about it, and they were discussing me in the case conference and when I went in I feel like a stranger, even though it was about me, I knew nothing that was being said, I didn't feel like they were trying to help me, I felt like they were just telling me what to do'. In response to what could have been done to help her: 'well if they'd ask me what I'd like to do, they wouldn't tell me what to do. If they say to me what would you like to do, where would you like to be this time next year, don't say well you can be here this time next year. Why would I want to be where they want me to be . . . they never asked me, they told me'.

Another case conference was due to be held several weeks after the research interview and she was aware of a planning meeting that had taken place in preparation for it. 'I keep asking them to meet me and explain to me what was said at the planning meeting, so when I go into the case conference I won't be dumb, . . . I'll know what has been said and what's going on'. In her attempts to get feedback, 'I keep getting this series of appointments and we're busy and we're not available and we'll get in contact with you. She's my daughter and I'm entitled to know what's said about me and her'. In response to what parents need in terms of case conferences she felt:

> 'Well, I think, I know there needs to be people there, but if you could get people, I mean if you've your doctor there, a public health nurse there, why can't they give their views and write it down and just meet one or two or something because you see all those people and you get frightened, do you know what I mean? . . . explain to me their views, don't have them there like. It's very frightening to see loads of people, you feel like you're that small like and you don't know what to do. You're afraid to open your mouth, in case you say something wrong so I think really when they have a case conference, it should be more smaller. I know they need people's opinions, but they could do it in writing or something because it's very scary for anyone to go in there like that. You're under enough stress going into a case conference, besides seeing all these people.'

She had hopes of obtaining a flat which would enable her to care for her daughter, and to return to study and complete her Leaving Certificate. She had made the social worker aware of her plans and they were discussed at the planning meeting, to which she was not invited. She had asked to go but her request was declined. She felt she was being 'fobbed' off by social workers. The social worker had informed her that her daughter would not be returned to her until she 'has a plan' at the core of which is getting accommodation before the child can be returned which she says she has given to them and is anxiously awaiting their response. She was of the opinion that the board was not now pursuing a care order. Her overall perception of social workers is that: 'sometimes now they don't directly say what they mean. They kind of beat around the bush, they wouldn't come out and directly say something, they'd say it in a nice way rather than just come out with it, they put things in a nice way when they actually mean something else'. In relation to her overall relationship with social workers: 'I feel like with the social workers that even if I'm fed up I have to put on a mask and pretend I'm not, or if I was down or I was upset'. She does not trust social workers as 'they never keep their promises'.

Other parental views

Other parents expressed negative views of case conferences. Having attended one, one mother declined invitations to subsequent conferences because 'they all just listened to my views . . . I got no feedback on anything, do you know what I mean, whereas if you were told where you had gone wrong, where you stood . . . I didn't bother going to it because what good was it going to do me' (Case 311). Another mother felt that 'they just sat there and listened' and that the conference did not take on board any of her views. She felt excluded from all of the decisions for her daughter's care (Case 265). Mixed opinions were evident in relation to attending all or part of the conference. One mother would prefer to meet one or two people only as meeting with a room full of 'strangers' was 'nervewracking' (Case 311). Another wanted to attend all of the conference. This mother noted that she wanted to go to the conference with everyone present or not at all as it was 'wrong' for professionals to discuss her case in her absence (Case 283). She had been involved with the health board for several years due to neglect and had been at several case conferences. Her requests to attend the entire conference had always been refused. She had attended an entire network meeting, however. Initially she wasn't 'allowed' to join the meeting but she 'persisted'. The children were placed in foster care and she felt that she was not adequately informed of the legal proceedings, an experience that has led to a lack of 'trust ' in social workers and management. Her daughter was in long-term foster care at the time of the research interview and the mother felt excluded from a planning meeting that her daughter, foster parents, social worker and management were having. She was, however, invited to meet with the social worker to discuss the outcome of the meeting: 'I don't think them meeting the parents at one stage, the foster parents at one stage and the parents at another stage is any way good. I don't think it develops anything but absolute anger'. She felt that 'it's either they will work together with the parents or you don't do it at all'.

This mother also expressed dissatisfaction at being kept waiting outside the case conference, 'I've often waited three quarters of an hour to get into a case conference. I've complained about it. I've often knocked at the door and said well if you're not out in two minutes I'm going away and thank you very much'. She found the experience 'degrading . . . you wouldn't leave a dog outside the door would you?' There was a shortage of hospitality too: 'there was never any offer of even tea or coffee at the case conference, in which there should be . . . they might just have the facility for a kettle. No one's asking for a cream cake! you know it's a matter of principle isn't it? because when they come to my home I'd say well do you want tea or coffee and if they didn't they didn't and if they did they did'.

Going into the conference was 'very nerve racking and all the questions. It's like committing a crime and facing the judge, you're such a long time. It doesn't do anything for your confidence to be waiting that length of time'. Her recommendations were that 'there should be no waiting, I think all the parents involved have a right to be there and they [professionals] should all be there, if your child is going to a psychologist or whatever they should be present if it's going to be anything successful'. Information should be provided to parents prior to the conference: 'have everything written down, both sides, what the parents want to say, before the meeting and if possible write down what they're saying at the meeting'. If parental views were set down on paper before the case conference 'you'd have a better understanding of what you want'.

In four of the cases where parents were interviewed a case conference was held but they were not invited to attend. The impact on the mother in Case 138 was that 'it'd make you feel a bit low like, they [parents] should be invited in'. Another mother in an extra-familial child sexual abuse case commented that there was 'loads of case conferences', however 'it wouldn't have even dawned on me to be present at them to be quite honest with you . . . they said their hands were tied completely' (Case 167). Another mother in an extra-familial sexual abuse case (Case 293) was not invited to attend any of the case conferences. The garda informed her of a case conference: '[garda] said to me if you like you can go to them but [social worker] turned around and said to me there is no need for you to be there'. She felt that the social worker should not only have invited her but encouraged her to go to the conference. This mother made an attempt to go to another case conference even though she was not invited, but by the time she arrived the conference was over. This all 'annoyed her' as she felt excluded from the decision making, particularly in relation to any measure taken against the suspect abuser.

Conclusion

Two recurring grievances are evident from the parental interviews in relation to case conferences. The majority of parents who expressed a view did not feel included in decision-making processes or that the conference really took account of their views. Practical aspects such as over-long waiting times and inadequate waiting facilities also need to changed. Case-study 265 demonstrates again how the professional system gets locked into intense struggles with parents around care and control. The mother accepted some responsibility for not caring adequately for her child and that she needed support, but felt unable to receive it when the case reached a crisis because of the alienating manner in which it was offered. This mother might have been willing and able to acknowledge her problems and accept help regardless of how it was offered. But it seems likely that she would have been more prepared to accept support and avoided the reception of her child into care had she been included in decision-making in a meaningful way (see also Cleaver and Freeman, 1995).

The health board needs to prepare for the inclusion of children and parents in decision-making structures and processes in a systematic way. Training needs to be provided for all professionals on how to maximise meaningful parental participation at case conferences, and in other decision-making processes. Several practical measures could be taken to ease parent's feelings of anxiety, nervousness and even anger. The suggestion that parents should be provided with a list of professionals attending the case conference—ideally prior to the meeting—could easily be adopted. Other practical measures such as providing the parent with adequate facilities, such as a private waiting room, reading materials, tea/coffee facilities should be implemented. What clearly emerges from the interviews with both parents and children is the importance of good communication and the need for good quality information to be provided by professionals. While child care is always a co-construction between professionals and those using the services, the shape and spirit of casework is heavily determined by how inclusive professionals are prepared to be and the manner in which they wield the considerable power at their disposal.

10 Safety and Danger in the Child Protection System

A number of processes and criteria were used in this study to evaluate the 'safety' of health board child protection systems. This chapter presents another perspective on the 'safety' question by examining the incidence of further injury or harm to children in the 286 community care referrals; this is perhaps the single most crucial measure of how well the system protects children. To determine the incidence of further injury/harm to children already known to the board, each referral was tracked over the twelve-month follow-up period (July 1996–July 1997) and re-referrals identified. Particular attention was given to cases substantiated following the initial social work investigation in 1996, and to cases processed through the child protection notification (CPN) system, which were officially defined as child protection cases. A sample of re-referrals of re-substantiated cases of child abuse where attempts had been made after the initial referral to protect the children was identified. These cases provide key evidence of the limitations of the system for protecting known abused children and form the basis for the analysis in this chapter. The implications are then assessed in the light of the findings from the research.

Re-referrals: a general profile

Thirty-one per cent (n=88[1]) of the 286 community care referrals were re-referred during the follow-up period, a re-referral rate of just under one-third of all referrals, which by any standards is high. Neglect was the primary reason in 31 per cent of re-referred cases, 10 per cent were for physical abuse, 9 per cent for domestic violence and 6 per cent for sexual abuse. Child protection was the main concern in 60 per cent (n=53) of the re-referred cases, 40 per cent were primarily concerned with child welfare difficulties (see Table 10.1).

Of the 53 cases where a protection concern was re-referred, 72 per cent had been defined as protection at the *initial* referral stage, thus 28 per cent of the protection re-referrals were initially defined as welfare problems. Twenty-six per cent (n=6) of physical abuse referrals were re-referred[2], 40 per cent (n=24) of neglect referrals, 55 per cent (n=6) of emotional abuse referrals, 22 per cent

Table 10.1 Primary presenting problem in re-referred cases

Primary presenting problem	%	No.
Neglect	31	27
Physical abuse	10	9
Domestic violence	9	8
Sexual abuse	6	5
Emotional abuse	5	4
Child welfare problems	40	35
Total	100*	88

Note: The % total does not add to 100 due to rounding

(n=8) of sexual abuse referrals, and 37 per cent (n=7) of domestic violence referrals. Once again, the dominance of neglect as a recurring problem is striking.

A further striking finding is the recurring nature of child protection problems: these re-referred cases have histories of health board involvement prior to the initial referral included in this study. In total, 8 per cent (n=23) of the community care sample that were previously known to the health board for protection concerns were re-referred during the sampling period (April–June 1996) for protection and were re-referred during the subsequent year for protection. Thus, 8 per cent of cases can be regarded as multi-child protection referrals. Of the six re-referred cases initially defined as physical abuse, three were re-referred as physical abuse, two as neglect and one as domestic violence. Four of these cases had histories of health board involvement for child protection and/or domestic violence concerns. Of the eight re-referred cases initially defined as sexual abuse, five were re-referred for a welfare concern, two for neglect, and one as emotional abuse. Five of these cases were previously known. Of the seven initial referrals defined as domestic violence, four were re-referred as domestic violence, one as neglect and two as welfare problems. Of the four referrals defined as domestic violence and re-referred for the same concern, two had been known to the health board prior to the sampling period for domestic violence and protection concerns. Of the 24 referred neglect referrals, 13 were re-referred as neglect, two as domestic violence, three as physical abuse, one as emotional abuse, four as child welfare and one as sexual abuse. Half of these cases were previously known to the health board for child care and protection and/or domestic violence concerns. Of the six re-referred cases initially defined as emotional abuse, one was re-referred as sexual abuse, two as child welfare, two as domestic violence and one as sexual abuse and neglect. Five were previously known to the health board.

(Re)substantiated re-referred child abuse cases

While it is important to analyse the outcomes of all the referrals, the crucial factor used to evaluate the safety of the system is the re-substantiation of abuse in re-referred cases. Difficulties in providing protection clearly arose in such cases. Of the 160 referrals substantiated following the initial referral in 1996, 133 had protection concerns. It is important to note what a 'substantiated' case means and that the social worker did not necessarily 'confirm' abuse in all of these cases. As we have seen, substantiation does not necessarily mean proof: it means that on investigation social workers felt that the concerns expressed in the referrals were well-founded, but 'evidence' to confirm the case in definitive terms was not necessarily available. At its weakest, substantiation could be a 'gut reaction' by the social worker, but more usually there was at least some supporting evidence for the concerns outlined in the referral. Case substantiation rather than confirmation has been used to measure safety because of the need to capture cases where children were considered by the social worker to have experienced some form of abusive behaviour. A good illustration of this can be seen in Case 290. The social worker substantiated abuse and the board instituted legal proceedings to obtain a full care order, having earlier secured an emergency care order and an interim care order. However, while the child was categorically identified as in need of protection, the outcome of the case was 'unconfirmed abuse' as there was a lack of forensic medical evidence to 'confirm' the case in a more definitive sense. Had the research team chosen case confirmation as the organising variable for measuring safety, cases where abuse was clearly suspected to have (re-)occurred but was not 'confirmed' would not have been captured. Of the 133 substantiated child protection referrals, 31 (23 per cent) were re-referred during the follow-up period of which 21 abuse cases were re-referred for a protection concern and the re-referreed concern was substantiated[3] and ten subtantiated abuse cases were re-referred for a protection concern which was not substantiated.

Re-referrals, CPN notification and re-substantiation

While 'safety' issues arise for both substantiated and un-substantiated referrals, those cases substantiated *and* notified to the child protection notification (CPN) system have particular relevance when considering accountability and the effectiveness of the system to protect. Cases processed through the CPN system have been interpreted throughout this study as those *officially* defined as child protection/abuse. It is crucial to determine the rate of substantiation and re-referral in these cases as they are the ones which bring the full operation of the child protection system into view. A total of 177 cases were notified to the DCC following the initial referral, and abuse was substantiated in 92 of these. Twenty-four of these 92 originally notified and substantiated child protection cases were re-referred for a protection concern during the follow-up period. In 15 of these 24 cases the re-referred concern was substantiated. These 15 cases constitute the key sample of re-injury/harm in substantiated 'officially' recognised child protection cases where strategic attempts were made to protect the children yet 're-injury' or further harm occurred; they provide further key evidence of the limitations of the system in protecting known abused children.

These 15 notified and substantiated, re-referred and re-substantiated cases were initially referred as: neglect in seven cases; emotional abuse in two; physical abuse in three; parental difficulties in one; parental addiction in one and sexual abuse in one (all were substantiated as abuse), and they were re-referred as neglect in eight cases, physical abuse in four, domestic violence in one case, sexual abuse in one and emotional abuse in one case. Thus, once again, the predominance of neglect in substantiated high risk cases is clear, with physical abuse also having a significant presence. The relatively low rate of sexual abuse cases is also striking. In seven of these 15 cases legal/care proceedings were instituted to protect the children from further abuse. Substantiated child protection cases which were *not* notified to the DCC but were re-referred and re-substantiated are also an important cluster of cases in terms of measuring the effectiveness of the system. In 92 cases the concern expressed in the initial referral was not notified to the DCC and in 32 of these the concern was substantiated. Seven of the non-notified and substantiated cases were re-referred for a protection concern, six of which were re-substantiated.[4]

In summary, then, the 21 substantiated child abuse cases which were re-referred for a protection concern with this re-referred concern being sub-stantiated constitute 7 per cent of the entire community care sample and 15 per cent of all *substantiated* cases with protection concerns. Within this the fifteen cases which were notified to the DCC, substantiated upon investiga-tion, re-referred for a child protection concern and again substantiated, con-stitute 5 per cent of the entire community care sample and 11 per cent of *substantiated* cases involving child protection concerns. The findings suggest that in 11 per cent of cases the system was unable to prevent further child protection concerns being substantiated, given that child abuse was substan-tiated following the initial referral and was again substantiated. Furthermore, these 15 cases represent 16 per cent of the 'official' substantiated protection cases in that they were processed through the child protection notification (CPN) system. This means that in 16 per cent of officially defined and substantiated child protection cases the system is known to have been unable to prevent further child protection concern being substantiated within twelve months of initial case substantiation. In addition, the five cases[5] where the concern was substantiated although not notified to the DCC, re-referred and re-substantiated, are also cases in which children are known to have experienced further harm. The good news, however, is that in 85 per cent of *all* substantiated referrals involving child protection and in 84 per cent of *officially* defined child protection cases there is no evidence of re-harm to the children.

Long-term treatment/support services

Important questions arise concerning the provision of services, priorities set and the general careers of these re-substantiated re-referred cases. Re-referred cases are much more likely to be provided with a long-term treatment/support service than cases referred on only one occasion. Eighty-per cent of all re-referrals were provided with a long-term treatment/support service, moreover 83 per cent of the 23 multiple child protection referrals received a long term service. By comparison 58 per cent of the cases that were *not* re-referred received a long term service. Similarly, 80 per cent of the notified, substantiated and re-referred protection cases were provided with a long-term service. Hence services were put into the family where child protection concerns were substantiated, a re-referral was made and re-substantiated. Seventy-two per cent of these cases received a home based service, 20 per cent a community-based service and 44 per cent a clinical service. Some 36 per cent received a care-based service, as compared with 16 per cent of non-re-referred cases. Statutory action took place in a higher proportion of re-referred, re-substantiated cases, legal/care proceedings being instituted in almost 50 per cent.

These findings are encouraging in that the majority of re-referred cases received more than just a social work investigation and received long-term services. However, the question of how well these services actually protected children from further abuse and harm now needs to be addressed. Safety issues are immediately apparent in that 17 per cent of the multiple child protection referrals did not receive a long-term service, and social work and other involvement ceased after the investigation. This raises important questions concerning gaps and constraints in the system. Information management systems need to be put in place to track children in families that are being continually referred for child protection concerns and to record reasons why long term services are not provided, especially in those multi-substantiated protection cases that received a long term service, yet further harm to children was substantiated.

The unpredictability of child protection and an unsafe system: Case study 290

It is clear that safety in the child protection system can be analysed in relatively straightforward terms of outcomes of 're-abuse'. There is a major substantive issue here concerning the overall (in)ability of the system to protect known children at risk. Closer examination of the cases in question shows, however, the complexity of the 'safety' question and that it would be misguided, and indeed deeply unfair to the practitioners involved, to characterise these outcomes simply in terms of 'system failure' even though this is certainly relevant to some cases. The case studies presented in this book have already provided for an analysis of many of the critical issues in short- and long-term management of high-risk cases. These issues will now be further crystallised through Case study 290, which is based on analysis of the case records and interviews with the community care social worker, a student social worker, garda, family support worker (FSW), PHN, community family support service, a hospital consultant and another member of the hospital staff. The GP declined to be interviewed. The mother in the case, here called Anne, consented to be interviewed but did not keep the appointments, while the children were too young to be interviewed.

After the initial referral in the study, the case was re-referred no fewer than six times in the follow-up period and is an apposite case-study to use at the end of this book as it demonstrates a number of key themes: the difficulties involved in engaging resistant parents; the shift of social workers' role to case management while other disciplines do the 'therapeutic'/support work; the gaps in communication between professionals which resulted in (and arose from) a focus on the mother to the neglect of the children and a sharper risk assessment. Most of all, perhaps, it demonstrates vividly the difficulties of managing safety in child welfare/protection work when cases take (unpredictable?) new directions and low-risk cases become (redefined as) high-risk ones, in this instance, being redefined from borderline neglect to serious suspected NAI.

The first referral to the community care social work department that forms part of this study was made by a hospital paediatric department in

April 1996. Referral information included:

> Mother had left two children aged two and ten months in care of a babysitter. During the time that mother was out the ten month old baby . . . got sick and babysitter admitted him into . . . hospital. Mother did not show up until the next afternoon. Gardaí and social work department were notified (research forms).

There were two children, here called Shane (ten months) and Rachel (two years), both of whom had been left in the care of the babysitter whom their mother had approached on the street and was unknown to her. Shane became ill that night and the babysitter went to her own GP who admitted the child to hospital. The hospital had contacted gardaí the previous evening in order to locate the mother, and referred the case to community care, requesting that they attempt to locate the mother and inform her that her child was in hospital. Anne arrived at the hospital the day after Shane was admitted.

Response to referral

The social work case file contains an account of involvement with the family, but the details of events are disjointed and difficult to follow in terms of the chronology of the case. It appears that a second referral was made by the hospital in 1996, by telephone: 'child presented on frequent admissions to hospital . . . recurrent admissions for colds, chest infections, nasal infections, mum can't cope with him, child demanding, home help required, child discharged and due in six weeks for clinic' (case file). A hospital discharge slip was sent to the social worker requesting the social worker to 'assess family needs . . . home help?' There is no evidence in the case file of the referral outlined above from the hospital concerning Shane's admission whilst in the care of the babysitter.

Five days after the first referral came in, the hospital contacted the social work department and thanked them for looking into the 'home situation' and again requested social work involvement with the family. It is unclear from the case file what the social worker 'looked into' with no documented home visits between the first referral and this third request for social work support for the family. It would appear that two social workers from different health centres were involved with the case at the referral stage, in that concerns from the hospital were made known to one social worker and the case was then transferred to another social worker. Anne was initially spoken to at the hospital and 'challenged' by a social worker to explain her whereabouts on the night that Shane was admitted. According to the social worker a 'tougher investigation' was carried out in Anne's home when she was interviewed ten days after the referral—several home visits had been attempted but Anne was not available.

Anne 'acknowledged concern for the baby's health but excused her own behaviour of not returning to the family home at night'. The social worker established that the children had different fathers and 'in both relationships there was a level of domestic violence involved'. The issue of alcohol abuse was discussed with Anne. The main focus of the visit became an access dispute between Anne and Shane's father and she was advised to contact a solicitor. Anne also disclosed that she had been sexually abused as a child. Anne was felt to be under a lot of stress due to the relationship with her ex-partner and to be 'quite isolated as well'. Both children were resident with their mother, a lone parent, at the time of the referral, in local authority housing, living on social welfare. Attendance at a group in a women's refuge was offered as 'she experienced some level of domestic violence'. Alcohol counselling was recommended which she agreed to attend.

The social worker felt that Anne was 'fine' towards social work intervention. She had been in care as a result of confirmed child sexual abuse, and was 'used to social workers . . . she knew the system basically and she was open'. Neglect, domestic violence and parent under stress were identified as the child care problems at the referral stage and the investigation following Shane's admission to hospital resulted in the substantiation of neglect in the form of 'child underweight, child poorly-fed and hungry, child left with underage babysitter' (research forms). The assessment of the hospital staff concluded that the 'general care of the child was poor'. Neglect was also substantiated for two-year-old Rachel in the form of 'child neglected due to poor parenting capacity'. The level of risk to the children was assessed as low. Positive statements regarding the care of the children were made, in that Anne assured the social worker that she made adequate child care arrangements when she went out at night. The home was noted to be 'clean and well equipped' and the children 'well-cared for and clean'. Anne was not involved with any other professionals at this time.

Regarding neglect, the social worker stated, 'I think it is inappropriate to leave the children in the care of a stranger'. As to whether this meant 'abuse', the social worker replied 'no'. However, 'it is not open to interpretation, it is quite clear that this was neglect on her behalf'. Thus, although Anne's behaviour was considered to be 'neglectful', it was not deemed 'abusive' and the intervention was generally framed around a welfare type response, with the emphasis on the mother's vulnerability and need for support. While the gardaí were informed of the case by the hospital when Shane was admitted in order to locate Anne's whereabouts, no formal notification occurred. Nor was this referral from the hospital initially notified to the DCC. The social worker judged notifications unnecessary because of the mother's co-operative response: 'given that it was open and she acknowledged her problems, and she let us in the door . . . she was open for [Family Support Worker] to call and she did acknowledge, she arranged to make appointments, child care arrangements, she also followed up appointments with the PHN'.

Subsequent referrals

The case was re-referred three months after the initial referral, by a PHN following concerns from a local crèche attended by both children: 'mother was drinking, collecting children from crèche with alcohol taken. Query her ability to care for children, query her babysitting arrangements and financial status' (case file). The PHN knew Anne quite well, who she felt was quite lonely and isolated. 'I spent a lot of time talking and listening and things like that'. She had stepped up her involvement following the initial referral. Anne refused home help and was encouraged to get in touch when she needed help and advised that a social worker would be calling to her. The PHN 'wasn't happy'. As well as making a referral, the PHN submitted a CPN form in respect of both children listing 'physical neglect, emotional abuse and potential abuse' as the concerns. The PHN cited several incidents where Anne arrived to collect the children from the crèche whilst intoxicated. On one occasion a twelve-year-old girl arrived to collect the children but crèche staff did not permit her to take them. Prior to the submission of the CPN Anne arrived at the crèche with obvious physical injuries, bruising to the face and lips bleeding. She alleged to crèche staff that Shane's father had assaulted her, was encouraged to contact gardaí but refused to do so. The PHN noted on the CPN that she had informed the family's GP that Shane had not received any of his vaccinations. This referral was made in the context of these incidents and concern for the children as they had not attended the crèche for the previous five days and their whereabouts was unknown.

The whereabouts of the children was the PHN's biggest concern at the time of the referral. She sent a memo to the social worker: 'I wanted to find the whereabouts of this family and ensure the safety of the kids . . . that was my biggest thing, where was everyone'. The direction from the CPN committee advised the PHN to inform the gardaí of the situation, to liaise with social work in order to establish the whereabouts of the children, to advise crèche staff that children should not be released to parents who are intoxicated and to convene a case conference immediately. Both the social worker and PHN made several unsuccessful home visits. On investigation, both neglect and alcohol abuse by Anne were identified by the social worker as child care concerns, with neglect considered to be the main presenting problem. The social worker felt that if the alcohol problems were addressed neglect 'would probably right itself, however as a health board child protection service neglect is the most important category' (research forms). Neglect was again substantiated, with both children classed as low risk. Both the gardaí and DCC were notified of this referral. The investigating social worker never met with the father of Shane, but another social worker did meet him once. The PHN was informed by the social worker that the team leader felt a case conference was not necessary and that social work will 'keep a handle on what's happening'. The PHN requested this decision in writing, given that she had been directed by the CPN meeting to convene a case conference immediately. The PHN felt that things then stabilised in that the 'Family support worker was in there, they were happy, social work department was happy at the way things were going there wasn't a need'. Social work visits focused on Anne's drinking and its consequences for the children. Shane was now living with his father. The GP was informed by the social worker of the referral from the PHN.[6]

Although there was a good support system in place in terms of extended family, the PHN perceived Shane as 'so irritable . . . if you looked at him he'd scream, if you went near him he'd bawl', and arranged for the area medical officer (AMO) to see him. The PHN's only concern in relation to Rachel was that 'she was very advanced for her age, she was clued in, she used to protect her mum'. The social worker was clear that the PHN had most of the direct contact with the children while social work was focusing on Anne. At this stage a replacement PHN made several unsuccessful home visits and did not actually see Anne or the children for several months, until the original PHN took over the case again and resumed home visits in mid-1997.

Six months after the initial referral, the crèche made two further referrals, the first because Anne was arriving to collect the children whilst intoxicated, and the second because Shane was 'abandoned' in that he was not collected from the crèche until 9 pm. The social worker attempted unsuccessfully to locate Anne and asked the gardaí to do so, and followed this up on the advice of the team leader with a home visit to establish if the children are 'well cared for and enquire about future care arrangements and to get further involved into family business' (case file). The children were classed as low-risk as Anne was able to provide 'proper child care facilities' in the form of the crèche or her friend, who was visited by the social worker in order to confirm that she looked after Rachel. A further complaint was made alleging Anne was intoxicated and questioning her ability to care for Rachel. In response, the social worker and FSW made a joint home visit to Anne and 'she assures us that she is not drinking while having [Rachel] in her care . . . if she goes out she leaves her in the care of her aunt' (case file).

Shane's precise whereabouts was often unclear from information provided by various professionals. It appears that he was residing with his mother or his father on a sporadic basis. During the time that Shane was living with the father, the social worker was of the opinion that the PHN was involved as social work was not visiting the father's home. According to the social worker herself, 'we don't actually have a whole pile of information from the time when the child lived with the father . . . we were more focusing on [Anne] and her alcohol problems'. The case was not officially transferred to a social worker in the father's area as 'we hadn't really concerns in relation to the father'.

Family support and therapeutic work: the process of non-engagement

Huge efforts were put into providing Anne with help for her problems. The FSW from the community care team (as opposed to the community based service) first became involved following the referral when Anne admitted that she had a drink problem and disclosed to the social worker incidents of domestic violence. The FSW's involvement was 'basically to continue visiting mother to see what the possibility is of getting help for her drink problem . . . to ascertain whether [Anne] was prepared to go for help'. Anne agreed to intervention on a regular basis but the FSW 'had very little contact with the children because they were either in the crèche or she would have brought them up to her friend or whatever'. She met with Shane on only three or four occasions, but with Rachel on a regular basis. The FSW's approach to working with Anne was:

> 'Basically I have tried as woman to woman to listen to her concerns and her concerns are many and deep and one of the things I gradually came around to was getting [Anne] to name her issues and the issues she has gradually spoken about and come up with are these: one, that she was sexually abused if not raped by her father and her two sisters have been . . . it would look like [Anne] is carrying a lot of guilt about the girls being abused as well, she's saying if she had stayed at home, they wouldn't have been abused, she went to live with her grandmother . . . that whole issue of her family set up is continuous for her.'

Anne was also under stress because of her fear that her ex-partner would apply for custody of the child. She would not go for legal aid as she feared her drink problem would be used against her 'and she'd lose the two children'. The FSW had no contact with the father, but if he had been living with Anne her role would be to do direct work with him also. She believed all Anne's difficulties stemmed from alcohol: 'What I tried to do from very early on was face the drink problem with her'. But although Anne 'named' her issues, 'she really wasn't prepared to do much about them'. The FSW arranged alcohol counseling appointments for Anne, but the service was not available immediately. Anne attended only one counseling session and the counsellor recommended that she attend an addiction group in a psychiatric day centre. Anne met with the group facilitator on one occasion but did not engage further because, the FSW felt, of the stigma of psychiatric services. Residential addiction treatment was recommended, but again Anne did not take it up. The FSW felt 'frustrated' that Anne was being sent from agency to agency. Yet, despite her reluctance to engage with addiction services, for the FSW 'I would feel that it was important to believe in her, I continued visiting her and hoping . . . because I have worked a good bit with people with addiction and I think there comes a day when . . . I wondered would she decide to eventually get help'.

The FSW believed she had the most direct contact with Anne in order to work with her alcohol problem and she saw the monitoring of the children as the primary role of the PHN. She still felt that Anne 'was a good mother', but did have concerns for Rachel as she 'almost wanted to protect [Anne] from us, which would be typical of a child of an alcoholic mother . . . in some ways she was taking on the mother and didn't want [Anne] upset'. Although she felt the level of support quite good, 'I would always have concerns really'. The social worker viewed the PHN as having had the most direct contact with the children and that this had been agreed upon as part of the intervention as all social work intervention also focused on Anne. The social worker saw the FSW's role as paramount and the social work role as 'more in the background, more like arranging services' thus demonstrating the changed role of social workers to case managers, as shown in this research.

The social worker regarded Anne as a 'genuine' person, and felt that 'the relationship with her is OK, she is not defensive, she is kind of open although she pays lip service to a degree, she agrees to things but she doesn't do them . . . she plans to do it, she's just not ready'. The community family support service also conceded defeat, having made numerous attempts to make contact with Anne. They convened a meeting with the FSW and community care social worker to examine ways in which their service could engage with Anne on the issues of 'drink problem, stable relationships, her inability to be on her own'. Some months later, the family support service and social worker managed to meet with Anne who agreed to do some 'individual work' with her alcohol problems and to attend a parenting course and a woman's group. According to the family support service, 'the main focus of that was to give her an opportunity to meet other parents outside of the home . . . she was very isolated at the time'. Anne engaged on just two occasions—'she seemed to be very reluctant indeed'—and it was decided, after almost a year of trying, to pass the case back to the health board 'and only be involved if there were further concerns at that stage'.

Differing professional thresholds of concern

According to the hospital, staff had a consistently high level of concern for the children. Shane was admitted to hospital on six occasions during the twelve months following the initial referral and there was on-going concern about his 'not reaching his developmental milestones'. He was unable to chew food or eat by himself and, 'sat in the corner of his cot like a rabbit watching everybody'. Nor was he always brought to attend follow-up appointments. The hospital was also concerned when it estimated that in the first year of his life, the child had had five carers. According to the hospital, community care were informed of all hospital admissions; however there was no evidence of this in the social work case file nor did it emerge in interview with the social worker. The main medical concern was 'the care of the child and the failure to thrive', which was viewed as non-organic. However, no concerns had been expressed about the father's ability to care for Shane which is why, the social worker concluded, 'we basically didn't investigate'.

The PHN expressed dissatisfaction with the level of communication in relation to the hospital admissions. It appears that she was made aware of two of the six admissions, but felt it extremely important that she be informed of all hospital admissions. Such information is 'huge, absolutely huge' in co-ordinating concern and should have, at a minimum, led to a network meeting. There is no structured or formal system to ensure public health nurses receive information about all hospital admissions and discharges. The hospital was expressing concern to the social work department and she was unaware of such concerns. As far as the hospital was aware all social work involvement was with Anne and 'nobody seems to be involved with [father]', and as a consequence, 'somehow this child slipped through the net in many respects'. This happened because 'he [father], wasn't taking him to his clinic appointments, he wasn't getting the stuff he should have from the public heath nurse, he wasn't being seen in the community, so there was a long gap when nobody was seeing him'. The FSW also saw this as a 'drawback'. Thus, by all accounts, there was a breakdown in communication between the hospital and community care social work and public health nursing. Details of who was actually caring for the child and monitoring the care he received are very unclear.

From neglect to suspected NAI

Almost a year after the initial referral in this study, Shane, then aged two, was admitted to hospital with an arm injury. According to the hospital the child presented as 'unwell . . .irritable . . . depressed, cranky.' He was referred to various consultants and x-rayed on numerous occasions. There was no accident or injury or event that could explain the injury, but a congenital disorder might have caused it so it was not possible to confirm NAI. The consultant met with the father and found him to be straightforward and concerned. He did not, however, discuss the background to the injury with him. He saw his role purely as clinical, to try and establish medical facts and to offer an opinion on whether the injury was non-accidental. He felt there was a strong desire from other professionals for him to support a 'traumatic diagnosis' and concluded that there 'was a high suspicion' of NAI.

Within a week a case conference was called by the hospital. The FSW felt that Anne was 'blackened' at the case conference in that her drink problem was discussed yet she was not caring for Shane at the time of the injury and it was wrong for her to be implicated. 'I did say she was trying and she's a very open woman and she has admitted to a drink problem'. The FSW expressed concern at using information as 'evidence' against the father, 'it was given to pile more stuff on top of him. I found that appalling . . . that is overstepping a boundary'. According to the case conference minutes the ward sister stated that '[father] had been abusive and aggressive towards hospital staff' and according to parents of other children on the ward he was 'rough in his handling of [Shane]'. Both parents' visits to Shane were 'erratic'. The consultant was concerned at the large number of people attending the conference and the degree to which people were attempting to ascribe blame for the injury. The PHN was not initially invited to the case conference as the PHN in the father's area was invited. This was particularly ironic given that it was the original PHN who had been requested by the CPN meeting a year previously to convene a case conference. The original PHN insisted on attending the case conference as she had a lot of information to share and felt other professionals would still be unaware of if she had not heard about the case conference. She feared that people might use different addresses to 'beat the system', especially now that they were alert to the practice of network checks.

Evidence of the lack of accountability of the child protection system is apparent in the fact that the case conference did not have a copy of the direction the PHN had received from the CPN meeting the previous year, which led her to comment 'like nobody's checking, did you do your practice, did you do your work'. The social worker identified a lapse in professional contact while Shane was living with his father because they were focusing on the mother. The case was not officially transferred to the father's area as 'we hadn't really any concerns in relation to the father'. The PHN expressed concern about the quality of multi-disciplinary communication: she had not been informed that Shane was living with his father; and was not informed of Shane's injury by an area social worker or the hospital but heard about it from someone else. The PHN was unaware that the father had full-time care of Shane, believing that shared care was still in operation and home visits to the child were unsuccessful because he was not even resident there.

Decisions made at the case conference included: (1) emergency care order to be applied for in the event of the father removing the child from hospital; (2) the garda to inform the garda station covering the hospital of the situation and 'put them on alert'; (3) the area social worker nominated as the key worker; and (4) consultants to carry out further investigations of the injury (case file). The father removed Shane from hospital the day after the case conference and an application was immediately made for an emergency care order. However, when hospital staff contacted the gardaí they were unaware of the situation as the garda who attended the case conference appeared not to have carried out her part of the child protection plan. She, however, when interviewed as part of the research, said a report was completed and submitted to the relevant station sergeant. This would indicate a breakdown in internal garda communication. The garda who attended the case conference was not the initial garda assigned to the case, but attended as the initial garda was unavailable. She felt the reason a guard was requested to attend the case conference was 'in the event of the father coming to the hospital to take away the child and set up some procedures or some sort of system whereby we could get an emergency care order. I was really swung in at the deep end at the last minute and I went along so that there was a representative there you know, nothing more really'.

When Shane was initially admitted to hospital neither the extent of his injury nor the suspicions surrounding it were outlined to the father, but an explanation was given following the child's return under an emergency care order. An interim care order was granted with a full hearing pending. According to the social worker, the father claimed that the injury was an accident. He was then living with his partner and her three children. Hospital staff did not think this woman had a good relationship with Shane. The social worker consulted with the team leader and a network check was made with the PHN regarding the partner and she was not interviewed by the social work team. The PHN did, however, speak to some neighbours who had 'no concerns in relation to his partner [who] appears to be a pleasant woman, a well-liked person within the local community'. Clearly, the degree of concern should have been heightened when Shane was admitted to hospital with the injury. As to whether there would be concerns for the partner's children given the suspected NAI to Shane, the social worker said: 'well, basically we would have to prove first of all that he was the one who inflicted the injury. I suppose this is a matter for the gardaí to investigate, you know suspected NAI'. The hospital did, however, express concerns for these children, and a ward sister allegedly saw a 'black bruise' on the side of the father's partner's face.

According to the hospital when children are admitted they are the hospsital's responsibility and when discharged they are the responsibility of community care. The hospital informs community care of child protection concerns, but this can cause problems if the child is in hospital and viewed as safe and community care contact is 'kept at a minimum'. Shane was not high on area social work's list of priorities because, the hospital felt, prior to the injury 'we weren't looking at injuries, we were looking at neglect'.

Outcome of the case

The health board applied for a full care order which was not granted, largely because of lack of medical evidence to prove NAI. Hospital staff felt most unhappy with how the legal proceedings were conducted and one view was that a *guardian ad litem* should have been appointed. The judge apparently accepted the explanation that Shane must have injured himself accidentally. Social workers were alarmed that in court Anne made very positive statements about the father, 'she stood up there and said he was a great man, very caring father'. This represented a complete reversal of her former position where she had consistently told social workers the opposite, and expressed fears about the care of the child by the father. Anne had even informed the social worker that she was not in a position to care for Shane and would prefer the child to remain in the care of the board than be returned to his father. Anne, the social worker concluded, 'is not ready to care for the child'.

The upshot of the mother's statement and the uncertainty surrounding the medical evidence was that the judge ordered the health board to withdraw from the situation and close the case.

No fewer than seven referrals were made to the community care social work department during the sampling and one year follow-up periods of the research. Technically, the outcome of the case from the health board's perspective was 'unconfirmed abuse'. While a medical condition/injury occurred, its cause was never fully established and thus physical abuse was not confirmed. At the end of the follow-up stage of the research a garda investigation had not yet taken place as they were awaiting the findings of the hospital assessment. One year on from the initial referral, the social worker classed Shane as at high risk and Rachel as at low risk. The FSW was as committed as ever to Anne, envisaging working with her for another two years: 'well I would hope, this is my hope and with a drink problem you never know, but my hope is that [mother] will respond to treatment. I hope that I would support her, I would hate to drop her at this time'.

Conclusion

This case study usefully illustrates many of the key issues raised in this book, especially those concerning multi-referred child protection cases with resistant parents who have significant problems, the challenges of effective inter-agency work and definitions of safe practice. As the chapter has shown, problems in providing on-going safety for known at-risk children occurred in some 15 per cent of substantiated child protection cases. In this particular case, after the suspected NAI, all attention and social work intervention appears to have focused on Shane and his injury with little intervention for Anne and Rachel. It appears that Anne and Rachel, and Shane and his father were treated as completely separate cases with no social work involvement with the father prior to the injury, or much after it. The social worker was clear that she would not want to be the key worker in relation to both 'cases'. She envisaged continued involvement with Anne but felt that another social worker should take over the other part of the case 'I think I could not split myself between the two parties here'. She was not satisfied with the time available to work directly with children.

The hospital continued to view the case as high-risk and feared that the child is 'going to come back in here in a box'. The case highlights poor communication between hospital and community care and shows the need for a formal notification system between the hospital and community care in terms of a formal referral procedure, follow-up and feedback. Health boards need to put such a procedure in place to include the processing of on-going information from hospitals about children at risk. A system to facilitate the sharing of follow-up information and feedback to relevant professionals should also be put in place. The case study also illustrates the drawbacks of the CPN system shown earlier in this book. The professional who made the initial DCC notification and who was directed by the CPN meeting to take certain actions was not even invited to the conference which took place following renewed concern many months later. The initial actions—in particular the calling of a case conference—were not in fact taken, which underlines the lack of a CPN mechanism for checking up on whether its directions were followed. Without an adequate system for co-ordinating and managing information about children known to be at risk, such children, when they turn up in different ways and parts of the system, can be treated as entirely separate cases and the significance of their case *history* and what is known by various professionals gets lost. Such administrative gaps are also revealed in poor case recording and serious gaps in information in case files, including vagueness about the subjects of referrals. Health boards need to design an administrative system in the form of a register of information on known children at risk, including information on who made any child protection notifications the register should be open to all professionals who have concerns about children.

A striking characteristic of the case is how, prior to the suspected NAI, different professionals had different knowledge and perceptions of risk. While the hospital had concerns about frequent hospital admissions and failure to thrive, the PHN was concerned about Anne's inability to cope. Yet something broke down in the communication of these concerns, in the sense both of how they were conveyed and how they were heard. The FSW was enlisted to help Anne with her drink problem and became an important ally. Anne was offered family support services from the community and residential addiction treatment but took up neither. Area social work, meanwhile, regarded it as a low-risk case, barely worthy of ongoing intervention, with a vulnerable, borderline neglectful mother resistant to intervention. While area social work maintained a nominal case-management role, the support and therapeutic work was attempted by other professionals. The FSW appears to have formed some kind of a relationship with Anne, but most of the work done had little success as Anne failed to attempt in any meaningful sense to change herself or her problems. This again confirms that professionals need to become more skilled at working with involuntary clients and much more aware of their defences and manipulations and the impact of their behaviour on children and the professional system itself.

Similar efforts were made to engage this mother as were used in Case 140 (see Chapter 7). But it is the complexity of the process of *non*-engagement that is apparent here in the way the mother was superficially co-operative, but not really taking any responsibility for her considerable problems. Thus apparent co-operation is not of itself enough to lower thresholds of risk for children: direct evidence is required of changes in parenting. Critics of western child protection systems have argued that clients refuse services mainly because of the 'limited repertoire of services' now on offer which do not satisfy consumers because they are dominated by forensically driven, authoritative protection practices to the exclusion of more benevolent forms of family support (Parton, Thorpe and Wattam, 1997). Thus in this view the services need to change if better outcomes are to be achieved. As this book has shown, the system must be reformed to make it more child and family friendly. However, this leaves out the client's contribution. It is hard to imagine that more could have been done to try and engage with the vulnerable mother in this case. But for reasons no doubt connected to past adversities in her life she was not able or willing to truly engage and do the necessary work on herself. While there was (perhaps too much) attention given to alcohol addiction, not enough systematic professional attention was focused on assessing and working with the trauma arising from childhood sexual abuse, reception into care and the possibility of what Herman calls 'complex post-traumatic stress syndrome' (Herman, 1992). There was not enough 'original pain work' (Bradshaw, 1988) that appears necessary to heal the underlying wounds which drive addictive, destructive behaviour and lead to serious problems in forming healthy, nurturing relationships with children and others. The kind of intervention that can promote healing of the underlying trauma that worked so well in Case-study 140 (see Chapter 7) never really began. In many respects, the intervention was, if anything, too benevolent and lacking in the setting of boundaries. There is also the painful fact that that there may be not enough time to allow some very vulnerable parents to heal without damaging their children. The key point is that professionals need to become more skilled at assessing the impact of trauma, the possibilities for recovery (Herman, 1992), the motivation and competencies of 'toxic parents' (Giddens, 1992), recognising the process of *meaningful* engagement, and working with them to promote whatever change is desirable and realistic within the bounds of child-safe practice.

What is striking is the ambivalent attachment (Howe et al, 1999) and the degree of 'closure' around herself and her children that Anne maintained through her avoidance of helping services. Such closure enables an emotional and physical boundary to be maintained between the family system and professional system, enabling the client to maintain control. A key pattern here was one of 'disguised compliance' (Reder, et al, 1993). Anne appeared to have significant unmet dependency needs, having been sexually abused as a child and spent time in care, and was still experiencing violence from her (ex)partners. Professionals seem to have got overly drawn into attempting to meet those dependency needs to the exclusion of attention to the children. Thus, no one was really focusing on the children and *their* dependency needs, and no attention whatsoever was given to the mother–children or father–child relationships. The closure seemed to fragment the efforts of the professional system to grasp the case, with a resulting scattering of information which was selectively passed on to different professionals by Anne, resulting in the children being moved around, never seen and so on. Such was the power of these systemic energies around closure and fragmentation that as researchers we found this an extremely difficult case study to reconstruct, processes that were further mirrored by our own failed attempts to engage with Anne, who agreed on two occasions to meet for an interview, but who, without explanation, did not turn up.

It might be argued that it is unfair to criticise professionals in a mainly low-risk, borderline child welfare/protection case which took a dramatic new direction with suspected NAI in such an apparently unpredictable way. Care does need to be taken about the inappropriate use of hindsight. Yet, this takes us to the core of the crucial issue of the system's accountability, or lack of it, in cases of this kind. Professionals *were* sufficiently concerned about the 'neglectful' parenting to try and connect the mother into a number of services, which surely means that work should have been put into the children's safety and welfare. It is not acceptable for the whereabouts of a child in a substantiated neglect case, identified as not receiving adequate care and protection, to be unknown or for an assessment not to be made of the degree to which the child's needs will be met through the change of care. Such practice derives from a lack of clarity about who the primary client is, confusion over professional roles and communication, and uncertainty about the type of approach required for effective child protection and welfare work. And, as already suggested, it also has its roots in the complex dynamics and systemic processes which draw professionals away from focusing on children's needs. Practice is by its very nature invariably on the edge of irrationality and uncertainty and the sheer complexities of the lived experience of child protection must be grasped if children are to be kept safe.

This chapter and case study show that the real issue is not always, and perhaps less and less frequently, lack of resources, as the case received many services. But resources need to be used in a focused, child-centred way, especially in work with resistant parents. Thus, even when NAI was suspected there was a palpable lack of safe child protection practice in this case. Despite the high level of suspicion of NAI and other grounds for concern, no systematic risk assessment was made with respect to the father and the children of the new relationship. Social workers saw such an investigation, if carried out, as the gardaí's responsibility, but the latter did not feel able to intervene until the medical NAI investigations were completed. Thus, once again (see Chapter 5) we find ambiguity arising here from the structural problem of role confusion. The 'criminalisation' of child abuse through the 1995 gardaí/health board procedures has created a routine role for the gardaí in child abuse investigations which enables social workers to divert that part of their role to them. The selectivity here is striking in that the level of 'proof' in a referral required by social workers to initiate a routine investigation is, as this book has shown, generally quite low, with a minimal filtering out of referrals. Yet, when a suspected high-risk NAI situation arises in a case already known and now framed as high risk by the health board, the law and a much higher threshold of forensic evidence are invoked by social workers and gardaí as a means of avoiding immediate direct action. The health board needs to clarify the precise investigative responsibilities of social workers and how these relate to the role of the gardaí under the *Child Abuse Guidelines*. The protection needs of children rather than the status of information and stage of a case in terms of possible criminal offences should determine when investigations occur and who should perform them.

Notes

[1] Two of these referrals relate to one family.

[2] The 26 per cent re-referred physical abuse cases were not necessarily re-referred as physical abuse—this also applies to the other categories.

[3] This figure includes two referrals (Cases 290, 278) made to the social work team during the initial sampling period which were treated as a separate 'case' in that social workers, as requested, completed a separate research form on every referral regardless of previous involvement. Treating these two referrals sseparately in the analysis so far was necessary as the response to *each* referral was being examined. However, for the purpose of the analysis here, these two referrals are treated as one 'case' in terms of assessing how the protection and welfare needs of the *children* were met. Hereafter, these two referrals are treated as one 'case'.

[4] Case 290 is included in this figure which, as already outlined, is being treated here as

one case. The initial referral in the sample (278) was not notified to the DCC, however, the second referral during the sampling period (290) was notified, hence this case is being considered as both a notified and substantiated case. In all of this analysis, non-notification refers to the initial referral, other than in the qualitative sample of case studies, systematic information was not gathered on the notification of re-referrals.

[5] Excludes Case 290.

[6] The GP did not wish to be interviewed for the research, stating he did not have a lot of contact with the family.

11 Defining 'Safety' and Promoting Welfare: The Complexities of Child Care and Protection Work

The central research question explored in this book was the extent to which the elements of a safe, good quality child protection service are in place in Ireland. This was explored through a case-study of the Mid-Western Health Board region. We have identified examples of best practice, where the safety and welfare of the children involved was promoted, as well as significant gaps in the system. In this concluding chapter we draw together the findings ,which show the complexities of child care and protection work and the need for an adequate definition of 'safety' and the promotion of welfare for children and vulnerable families.

Defining 'safety'

The research was designed not only to evaluate intervention into child abuse, but to provide an analysis of how the child protection and family support aspects of the Child Care Act 1991 are working in practice. Contrary to the impression given by the child abuse inquiries and some aspects of the debate on mandatory reporting, the system appears quite 'successful' in the narrow sense of identifying children and intervening to protect them from abuse. Although there are still problems with the system, it is clear that huge efforts are put into information gathering and investigation, child care and abuse problems are treated very seriously, and the level of accountability is high. These efforts deserve to be fully recognised.

A key marker of the 'safety' question is how often previously known and substantiated abuse cases come to light again and give rise to further concern for the children—the re-substantiation of re-referred substantiated cases. As shown in Chapter 10, further substantiated concern for already known at-risk children was a feature of 15 per cent of the sample. As argued in that chapter, it would be unfair to label such cases simplistically as 'failures to protect'. Giddens (1990) argues that expert systems fail for two main reasons: first, because of what he calls 'design faults', where problems are built into the very fabric of the system; and, second, because of 'operator failure' in practice in the system, either individual or collective. Social workers and other professionals seem very aware of the ambiguities involved in providing safety for children, but public pressure, arising from child abuse inquiries, for some abstract or idealised notion of safe practice, and avoidance of 'dangerous' practice, creates great strain. Anxiety and a new 'risk conscious-ness' also arise from the need to avoid being responsible for children suffer-ing protracted abuse or death which has become a key dimension of social workers' identities (Ferguson, 1997a). Social workers have heavy caseloads involving extremely complex, often intractable problems for children and families, their resources are often overstretched and their working condi-tions poor and they receive routine threats to their personal safety from hostile clients.

Any definition of system safety which can provide a realistic baseline for policy and practice needs to take all of these social conditions into account and must begin from the realisation that the provision of safety for children can *never* be guaranteed. 'Safety' is a concept and practice riddled with con-tradictions, for example, when the abuse of children occurs in the very care system that they entered for protection. One fourteen-year-old girl in this study, who was in care, alleged abuse by care staff, yet still insisted in the research interview that the health board had 'saved my life'. Her mother, meanwhile, was immensely angry and disillusioned with the response the family had received, and felt excluded from decision-making, especially with regard to the planning for her daughter in care.

Three types of 'safety problems' can be identified from the evidence pre-sented in this book. The first concerns the further harm experienced by some children despite the system's intervention—that is, the recurrence of substantiated abuse—in cases where the outcomes were regarded by all in-volved, parents and children included, as generally *good* in terms of the pro-motion of the children's welfare. This was illustrated in in Case 140 (Chapter 7) where, although the child was bruised following a beating by her mother, the overall outcome in the case was extremely positive. In these instances, the real measure of 'safe' practice, despite incidents of substantiated re-harm, is the extent to which the assessed level of risk to the children is decreasing over time and the welfare of the children is being promoted. It is important, therefore, to be clear about where (isolated) *incidents* of re-harm fit into the overall *process* in the case.

A second type of safety problem arises from risks taken by the profes-sional system, for example leaving children at home rather than taking them into care. The concept of safety needs to include an understanding of the *ythms* of cases and child protection. This is particularly relevant where decisions were made to leave children at home when it would have been easier to take them into care sooner; early care provision is generally not regarded as best practice when working to promote the welfare of the child under the terms of the Child Care Act given the requirement that children be brought up in their own families whenever possible. This pattern was evident in Case 138 (Chapter 6), where huge risks were taken, albeit through the 'protection' of a supervision order, to keep the children in the family, recognising the difficulties of meeting the needs of a large group of traveller children in care. Thus the concerns about further harm to children expressed in re-substantiated re-referrals are a reflection of the very high risk already known. The pressure to remove the children from home increases as they suffer further neglect, harm or injury, or the key worker carrying the bulk of work and responsibility can no longer tolerate the risk of leaving the children at home (see also Case 109). Thus, further incidents of known harm to children occur within a downward process in the trajectory of the casework. Risk-taking in such scenarios is to some degree structural, deriving from the 'liberal compromise' in which family privacy and parental freedoms are balanced with the demands of protecting children's rights (Dingwall, et al, 1995).

Thirdly, and perhaps most importantly for health boards in the light of child abuse inquiries, the research has identified dangers the system creates *for itself* through its own practices. This is a form of 'manufactured risk' (Giddens, 1994) which has its roots in the sophistication of advanced expert systems. 'Manufactured risk' is apparent, for instance, in how, as was shown especially in Chapters 4 and 5, the health board CPN system and garda notification system can slow down decision-making and create communication problems which *delay* the response to some children at risk. The very rationality intended in the creation of a uniform, bureaucratic response to children actually stops workers from responding quickly in the manner intended. This is a classic design fault in the system which is not reducible to flaws in human action.

Problems also arise from the way the system defines cases and the types of responses which flow from such definitions. We explored the relationship between the concepts and practices of child 'welfare' and 'protection', where what are essentially welfare cases become contaminated by the principles and practices of protection; and the dangers involved in a welfare response to protection concerns. With respect to the latter, serious safety problems can arise from the initial framing of cases. As shown in Chapter 2, instances of grave risks to children may not even *become* referrals if the concern is not accepted as legitimately communicated and investigated. There are also situations where information about children leads to a primary definition of the case which is not appropriate to the safety needs of the child. Specific harms to children are suspected, yet, as Case 234 in Chapter 4 showed, the case is framed in welfare terms, with a resulting absence of authoritative child-centred intervention. Children end up not even being seen, never mind engaged with, as suspected victims of abuse. Meanwhile, because the case is defined as welfare, with the emphasis on children 'in need' rather than 'at risk', the suspected perpetrators are never engaged with about the behaviour which is placing the children at risk.

While there is evidence of inappropriate notification to the CPN system of some welfare referrals, there is less evidence of inappropriate protection responses to what are essentially welfare concerns. We have shown that in determining such matters it is crucial to examine the outcomes of cases rather than concentrating on categorisation issues ('protection' vs 'welfare') which have dominated so much of the literature (for instance, Parton, Thorpe and Wattam, 1997). The research for this book found that, unlike in other studies, (Gibbons, et al, 1995; Department of Health, 1995), only a small number of families in substantiated cases were left with little more than an investigation into child abuse with no attempt to meet the needs of the children. This is reflected in the very low level of screening out of referrals without investigations as 92 per cent were directly investigated. While 23 per cent of all referrals received an investigation only, in a significant proportion of these the decision not to provide post-investigation services was entirely appropriate as there was no substantiated need or risk in the case.

Such findings go against the grain of much of the existing research and commentary on child care and protection in Ireland. In the early 1990s, Irish research suggested that greater proceduralisation and accountability in child protection had resulted in cases being screened out at every stage through the system so that only a small proportion of children reported to health board community care teams received services of any kind (Buckley, 1996). This finding was consistent with international research (e.g., Besharov, 1985; Gibbons et al., 1995; Parton, Thorpe and Wattam, 1997; Thorpe, 1994) which found that referrals were being defined prematurely as protection and children in need were being screened out of the system having received little more than an investigation, and referrals that did not fit the abuse categories set by the agency were not even investigated. Some researchers have argued that similar patterns of system response are evident in Ireland (Buckley et al., 1997; Thorpe, 1997). Our research does not bear this out and we suggest that such arguments rely too heavily on frameworks for understanding child protection that were developed outside Ireland, and do not take into account the dramatic changes that have taken place in child care services in Ireland since the early 1990s.

It is possible, of course, that the work of the Mid-Western Health Board on which this study is based is not exactly replicated across every health board in the country. Indeed, we have seen that variations in practice exist even within the three community care teams of the MWHB. Nevertheless, the broad patterns of cases and practices and commonalities across the region are striking, and we suggest that the findings from this study are broadly generalisable to the country as a whole. Moreover, the safety problems and best practice issues identified in this study have international relevance in terms of deepening understanding of child care and protection systems and practices. Media commentary and anecdotal evidence since the 1990s has increasingly emphasised 'crisis' in Irish child care in terms of such things as resource problems resulting in unallocated referrals/cases and how the dominance of child protection allegedly results in the neglect of family support (see, for instance Holland 2000). A general sense of pressure and of services being stretched to the limit does exist as the system strains to respond to increased demands (Lavan, 1998). What is striking, however, is the lack of analytical rigour and detailed attention in such commentary to the dynamics of filtering practices and the child protection process as presented in this book. The very nature and meaning of 'child protection' has been taken for granted, when in fact, as this book has shown, its meanings are socially constructed.

The concept of 'child protection' now operating in the Irish system embraces a notion of family support not present to the same extent in many other Western welfare systems (Ferguson, 2001a). There is a need for greater critical awareness of the differences between welfare regimes which are operating within different cultures. The Irish system reflects, in part, the importance attached to the integrity of the family both culturally and in Irish social policy. Thus we have seen that significant attempts are made to define referrals as 'welfare', to the extent that 28 per cent of all referrals in this study were placed in non-abuse categories. As Chapter 8 in particular showed, the levels of adversity for children in such welfare cases is often no less than that in high-risk protection cases. The relative importance of protection is evident, however, in the way those 'welfare' cases which also contained 'abuse' concerns generally received more services over a longer period of time. Thus the central notion of a 'child protection concern' is quite elastic, permitting children at risk and in need of a broad range of services to enter the system. While there remains considerable room for improvement, significant services, relatively speaking, are now being offered under the rubric of child protection in substantiated cases. This is a product of changing views of child welfare and the system development that has occurred following the implementation of the 1991 Child Care Act. We have seen that there is now a complex division of labour in the provision of post-investigative services, with social work having a core co-ordinating function. As Chapter 7 showed, in 40 per cent of substantiated cases social workers either have no active role at all or simply a case-management role, while the primary therapeutic and support work is done by other professionals. Nevertheless, social workers continue to provide meaningful protection and welfare services in 60 per cent of substantiated cases, usually in conjunction with a range of other services which have developed significantly following the implementation of the Child Care Act, and the resulting increased resources.

Despite extensive service provision, the book has identified a 'service gap' of 26 per cent where, although referrals were substantiated, treatment/support services were not delivered. Thus significant problems of unmet need remain. This derives in some instances from the nature of the service itself, a particularly serious manifestation of which was identified in Chapter 5, of CSA cases receiving a narrow forensic, evidence-based response and generally poor outcomes for suspected abused children and non-abusing carers. The entire system for investigating and managing child sexual abuse cases requires major reform to make it work faster, bring more suspected offenders to justice and promote the welfare of children and their non-abusing carers. More generally, deficits in service provision have been shown to occur most often for cases of poor parenting skill and competence; this reflects the struggle to respond to the high level of need in the large numbers of neglect and child behaviour and control problems in the cases coming to attention. Surprisingly, the main reason for unmet need in substantiated cases was not the absence of services *per se* but lack of co-operation by parents and some children. The need to skill practitioners in the process of engagement of resistant clients has emerged in this study as crucial to effective child protection practices.

Particularly acute safety problems arise when workers and families get caught up together in complex processes of care and control and the family and professional systems need to be understood as one large interacting system (Dale et al., 1986; Reder et al, 1993). These processes result in professionals becoming enmeshed in cases in ways which lead to closure by the family, fragmentation in the professional network, breakdowns in communication, and restriction of access to and a loss of focus on the children at risk (as shown, for instance, in Case 290, Chapter 10). There is no easy solution. Frontline workers and managers can, however, be helped, through training and good supervision, to be aware of the problem by engaging in reflective practice so that these complex processes are recognised and adjustments made.

One-third of all the referrals in this study were re-referred at least once (and some much more often) within the following year, and a significant proportion of these had long-term histories of health board involvement. We have identified a pattern of long-term, multi-problem, multi-referred child protection cases which keep coming (back) to the agency's attention and are at the heart of the high-risk work being done. The health boards' professional systems are, in a sense, chronically enmeshed with certain types of cases and families and this poses particular challenges. The cases are typical of those coming to the attention of health boards, as shown in this sample: they tend to involve reconstituted families or lone-parents (usually mothers) who live in poverty, often suffering addiction problems, and other adversities such as a violent (former) partner who may or may not be the father of the children. As the children grow older and enter their teenage years, they tend to become out of control; they have to deal not only with the legacy of years of adversity and child abuse, but also with a view of them as threats to themselves and/or social order. Thus the often long history of health board involvement with a family may begin as a child protection case when the children were younger and move on to welfare work with challenging adolescents. Of all the findings and recommendations in this book the most urgent is the need for health boards to design a strategy for working with these cases, which are immensely demanding of energy and resources. Professionals need to be trained and well-supervised so that they may deal effectively with these often hostile, but invariably extremely needy and traumatised, parents and their children.

Promoting welfare and healing

Such a strategy requires a central change in the way child care services are conceptualised and delivered. The system needs to stop trying to fit cases into a 'child protection concern' frame and approach child welfare on the basis of assessed need, regardless of the presenting problem. Some commentators, writing in other jurisdictions, suggest that the best way to address the dominance of child protection is to rationalise services by defining cases more accurately at the referral stage into distinct 'protection' and 'welfare' categories and responses (Thorpe, 1996). This, it is thought, will prevent welfare cases being defined prematurely as 'protection' and gaining little more than an investigation into abuse, leaving needs unmet (Thorpe, 1994; Wattam, 1997). There are at least two reasons why such an approach does not fit the Irish situation, as shown in this book. Firstly, given that it is the norm for referrals to contain both protection and welfare concerns (as shown in Chapter 2) it is not only very difficult to define them as either one or the other, but it is not always in the best interests of children and their carers. As we have shown, a mixture of skills and services is needed to meet the safety and welfare needs of children on a routine, case by case basis, and distinguishing 'welfare' and 'protection' systems implies a false separation which endangers the provision of the full range of services needed in each case. The best way forward is to develop integrated services where workers and systems have the skills and knowledge to respond to the mixed protection and welfare needs evident in child care practice. Irish professionals already, in a sense, intuitively recognise this by forcing as much as possible into the category 'child protection concern'.

Secondly, and relatedly, given the complexity of children's and their carer's lives, welfare-type problems can cause as much adversity to children and young people as abuse. Thus, practice and assessment models need to focus less on categorisation of referrals and more on the needs of children, regardless of the source of adversity (for an example of such a model, see Howe, et al, 1999). The promotion of safety, welfare *and* healing needs to be at the heart of an integrated model of child care which takes the 'whole child' as its focus. As already suggested, this is already happening to some extent but in an ad hoc manner when what is needed is a properly developed theory and strategy which will be implemented in policy and practice. It is encouraging, then, to see the 'whole child' perspective at the heart of the first ever National Children's Strategy launched in late 2000 (DoH, 2000). At its best, the aim of intervention is to assist children and parents to move beyond traditional hierarchical forms of patriarchal relationships towards the creation of a 'democratic family' form (Giddens, 1998). Child care policy and practice should be about the promotion of such self-actualisation and equality for all family members so as to achieve effective child protection, welfare and healing (Ferguson 2001c).

The evidence presented in this book also raises crucial issues about adequate public representation of current child care work. At an official level, 'abuse' has not only become the key case definition which elicits a system response, but is also the new 'signifier' (Thorpe, 1997) of the receipt of public attention and resources. The Department of Health statistics on child abuse are a perfect illustration: there is no other 'reality' or way of officially recording other child care problems. The same appears to be true of data produced by health boards (such as the Section 8 reports produced under the terms of the Child Care Act). The fact that there are few other ways of categorising information further increases the organisational pressure to classify as much as possible as 'abuse' thereby distorting the nature of the real work and service needs on the ground. As long as the system only formally recognises 'abuse' there will be little organisational momentum to develop non-protection services.

In order to change this it will be necessary to provide public information on and accurate representations of 'abuse'/protection services, honouring the range of child welfare and support work going on. The public needs to know about the support as well as the protection work so that it can make informed decisions about the range of services available. Unless this happens, perceptions of child care will continute to be that it is little more than an investigative, at worst, punitive service more concerned with removing children into care than relating to the lives of those who are struggling to parent in difficult circumstances. Encouragingly, we have seen that mothers themselves make more referrals than any other group; making the public aware of this could lead to a more positive perception of the services so that increasing numbers of vulnerable parents and children will feel safe enough to come forward and look for help.

The Section 8 reports could usefully give more attention to the kinds of linkages between child protection and family support services set out in this book. Better still, the health boards, and the Department of Health, need to research and design information management systems capable of accounting for the range of work going on under the Act and of measuring outcomes. It is important to be aware of professional hierarchies in the value that is publicly (and privately) given to particular types of services. Bill Jordan has shown how, in the implementation of the 1989 Children Act in England and Wales, for all their talk of partnership and wanting to advance prevention, social work and health staff have had great difficulty sharing professional power with colleagues in support services such as day care centres (Jordan, 1997). Cases officially categorised as abuse through the CPN system have a better chance of receiving scarce resources. However, our evidence suggests that the service has developed over recent years in a way that retains enough flexibility in the system, and commitment to treatment and family support, for us to conclude that child welfare has a relevance under the Act. A balance of sorts is being struck.

The increased focus on child abuse does come at a price. The shortfall between referrals and the offer of services leaves some parents feeling alienated and does still occur because of the relative absence of longer-term coordinated treatment, counselling and preventive resources. It bears emphasising again that neglect is the most common form of abuse worked with and control and behaviour problems in children also loom large. Contrary to public perceptions, the numbers of referrals of physical and sexual abuse involving actual injuries or which end in children entering care are thankfully comparatively very low. Parenting difficulties, control and behaviour problems in children, neglect and addiction problems dominate, accounting together for 67 per cent of the referrals which end in children entering care. It is these types of problems that require the bulk of preventive and healing work. Developing parenting skills is the area of most need and more home- and community-based services need to be available to meet the challenge of promoting the welfare of such disadvantaged children and, ultimately, keeping them in their families. What such work can—and should—ideally look like was shown in Chapter 7 through an example of best practice of very effective family support in the context of very effective child protection. The best outcomes in such cases typically involve combinations of therapeutic (most often child psychology or psychiatry) and support (family support and/ or child care workers) services, in addition to social work, public health nursing and other community-based services. A mixture of child protection and welfare services is now the norm in practice and our language and concepts need to do more justice to the scope of the practical and therapeutic work now going on in their name. The language of practice needs to go beyond the limits of 'protection' and 'support' to account adequately for the therapeutic processes of self-redefinition and healing that can, and should, be promoted for children and parents through effective interventions.

In effect, the book has shown that outcomes for children need to be assessed in terms of the promotion of their general welfare. In a climate of anxiety about child protection, consideration of children's overall needs can too often be seen as secondary to that of their protection (Farmer, 1997). The findings support other work which has demonstrated how, without the benefit of therapeutic services, the difficulties of abused children deepen over time. On the other hand, some individual work with abused children, however modest, which relates to the abuse and its effects on them can effect some improvements in their situation (Howe, et al, 1999). Supportive visiting can be of some benefit to struggling parents, just as 'monitoring' can contribute to children's protection. However, as Chapters 7 and 8 in particular showed, the more direct services intervene with children's distress and provide direct assistance to parents in the care and management of children, the more children's welfare will be promoted and the ultimate goal of child safety and healing for parents as well as children will be achieved. Parents and children have their criticisms of practice, especially with respect to exclusion from planning and decision- making, as was shown in Chapter 9. Yet it can also be said with some certainty that many families value the child protection and family support services they receive in the name of promoting the welfare of children, and the more those services are developed the better the outcomes will be for the children, and for us all. Overall, in Ireland a huge amount of effort is put into processing and responding to referrals and into long-term child protection and welfare work. The level of accountability in the system is now high. The key challenge arising from this book is the need to harness that effort and (re)direct the good work that is being done to advance further the vital project of keeping children safe.

Appendix 1: The 32 Cases Selected for the Qualitative Sample

No.	Primary definition of case	Interviewees*
305	Sexual abuse:	Social worker, garda, school principal
234	Sexual abuse:	Social worker, home help, PHN
224	Sexual abuse:	Social worker, garda, father, mother, girl aged 14
310	Sexual abuse:	Social worker, PHN
293	Sexual abuse:	Social worker, garda, PHN, mother
279	Physical abuse:	Social worker, two teachers, AMO, garda
290	Physical abuse:	Social worker, garda, hospital consultant, other hospital staff member, PHN, FSW, member of a voluntary organisation
275	Domestic violence:	Social worker
280	Domestic violence:	Social worker
311	Neglect/domestic violence:	Social worker, PHN, boy aged 13, boy aged 12
239	Neglect:	Social worker, garda, PHN
255	Neglect:	Social worker, foster mother
265	Neglect:	Social worker, mother
283	Physical abuse/neglect/domestic violence:	Social worker, PHN, two gardai, school principal, mother, three girls aged 15, 14 and 8, two boys aged 12 and 10
167	Sexual abuse:	Social worker, garda, mother
166	Neglect:	Social worker, PHN, father
109	Neglect:	Social worker, FSW, PHN
106	Neglect:	Social worker, FSW, PHN
115	Neglect:	Social worker, FSW, PHN
189	Neglect:	Social worker, school principal, teacher, PHN
190	Neglect:	Social worker, school principal, teacher, PHN
172	Neglect/child out of control:	Social worker, garda, FSW, school inspector, mother, boy aged 14.
173	Neglect/child out of control:	Social worker, FSW

183 Domestic violence: Social worker, school principal, CCW
140 Domestic violence: Social worker, school principal, FSW, father, mother, girl aged 11.
157 Domestic violence:Social worker, FSW, PHN, GP, garda, director of nursing, hospital consultant, nurse, mother
138 Physical abuse/domestic violence, emotional abuse: Social worker, school principal, garda, PHN, counsellor, father, mother, girl aged 13, boy aged 11.
3 Neglect: Social worker, school principal, PHN
53 Neglect: Social worker, GP, mother
16 Domestic violence: Social worker
51 Domestic violence: Social worker, GP, mother
32 Domestic violence: Social worker, PHN, garda

Note: In some instances the same professional was interviewed about more than one case.

Appendix 2: Source of Referral by Main Presenting Problem

Table 1   Source of physical abuse referrals

Source	%	No.
Anon.	9	2
GP	4	1
PHN	4	1
Hospital accident & emergency	4	1
Hospital antenatal unit	4	1
School	22	5
Social workers	13	3
Other professionals	4	1
Gardai	9	2
Parents	17	4
General public	4	1
Voluntary organisations	4	1
Total	*100*	*23*

Table 2 Source of neglect referrals

Source	%	No.
Anon.	9	5
PHN	13	8
Hospital paediatrics	5	3
School	15	9
Social workers	10	6
Other professionals	10	6
Gardai	10	6
Parents	7	4
General public	17	10
Voluntary organisations	5	3
Total	*100*	*60*

Table 3 Source of emotional abuse referrals

Source	%	No.
Anon.	9	1
Hospital Accident & Emergency	9	1
School	18	2
Other professionals	27	3
Gardaí	18	2
Parents	18	2
Total	*100*	*11*

Table 4 Source of sexual abuse referrals

Source	%	No.
Anon.	6	2
GP	6	2
PHN	6	2
Hospital paediatrics	3	1
Mental Handicap service	3	1
Hospital maternity	3	1
School	11	4
Social workers	11	4
Other professionals	11	4
Legal	11	4
Parents	11	4
Child him/herself	3	1
General public	14	5
Total	*100*	*36*

Table 5 Sources of domestic violence referrals

Source	%	No.
Anon	5	1
PHN	11	2
Hospital Accident & Emergency	5	1
Hospital paediatrics	5	1
Social workers	11	2
Other professionals	5	1
Gardaí	26	5
Parents	26	5
Lay sources	5	1
Total	*100*	*19*

Table 6 Sources of child-centred difficulties—behaviour/control referrals

Source	%	No.
PHN	3	2
GP	2	1
Hospital paediatrics	2	1
Psychiatry	2	1
School	18	11
Social workers	8	5
Other professionals	20	12
Gardaí	7	4
Parents	30	18
Child him/herself	3	2
General public	5	3
Voluntary organisation	2	1
Total	*100*	*61*

Table 7 Sources of parental difficulties referrals

Source	%	No.
Anon.	4	2
PHN	21	9
GP	4	2
Hospital paediatrics	2	1
Hospital maternity	2	1
Community psychiatric nurse	2	1
School	2	1
Social workers	4	2
Other professionals	9	4
Gardaí	4	2
Parents	36	16
Lay sources	9	4
Total	*100*	*45*

Bibliography

Adams, D. (1988), 'Treatment models with men who batter' in M. Bograd and K. Yllo (Eds), *Feminist Perspectives on Wife Abuse*, New York: Sage.

Allen, A. and A. Morton (1961), *This is Your Child: The Story of the National Society for the Prevention of Cruelty to Children*, London: Routledge.

Arber, S. (1993), 'Designing samples', in N. Gilbert (Ed.), *Researching Social Life*, London: Sage.

Beck, U. (1992), *The Risk Society*, London: Sage.

Besharov, D. J. (1985), '"Doing something" about child abuse: the need to narrow the grounds for state intervention', *Harvard Journal of Law and Public Policy*, 8, 539–589.

Birchall, E. (1989), 'The frequency of child abuse—what do we really know?', in O. Stevenson (Ed.), *Child Abuse: Professional Practice and Public Policy*, London: Harvester Wheatsheaf.

Bradshaw, J. (1988), *Healing the Shame that Binds You*, Florida: Health Communications, Inc.

Buckley, C. (1996), in *Dear Daughter*, RTE television documentary, February 26.

Buckley, H. (1996), 'Child abuse guidelines in Ireland: for whose protection?', in H. Ferguson and T. McNamara (Eds), *Protecting Irish Children: Investigation, Protection and Welfare*, special issue of *Administration*, Dublin: Institute of Public Administration.

—(1998), 'Filtering out fathers: the gendered nature of social work in child protection' in *Irish Social Worker*, 16, 7–10.

—(1999), 'Child protection: an ungovernable enterprise', *Economic and Social Review*, 30, 21–40.

Buckley, H., C. Skehill and E. O' Sullivan (1997), *Child Protection Practices in Ireland: A Case Study*, Dublin: Oak Tree Press and South Eastern Health Board.

Butler, I. and H. Williamson (1994), *Children Speak: Children, Trauma and Social Work*, Essex: Longman.

Clarke, M. (1998), *The Lives of Children in Care: Issues for Policy and Practice*, Dublin: Trinity Children's Centre.

Cleaver H. and P. Freeman (1995), *Parental Perspectives in Cases of Suspected Child Abuse*, London: HMSO.

Colwell Report (1974), *Report of the Committee of Inquiry into the Care and Supervision Provided in Relation to Maria Colwell*, London: HMSO.

Corby, B. (1987), *Working With Child Abuse: Social Work Practice and the Child Abuse System*, Milton Keynes: Open University Press.

—(1993), *Child Abuse: Towards a Knowledge Base*, Buckingham: Open University Press.

Dale, P., M. Davies, T. Morrison and J. Waters (1986), *Dangerous Families: Assessment and Treatment of Child Abuse*, London: Tavistock.

Daniel, B. and J. Taylor (1999), 'The rhetoric versus the reality: a critical perspective on practice with fathers in child care and protection work', *Child and Family Social Work*, 4, 209–220.

Department of Health (1977), *Memorandum on non-accidental injury to children*. Dublin: Department of Health.

—(1987), *Child Abuse Guidelines: Guidelines on Procedures for the Identification, Investigation and Management of Child Abuse*, Dublin: Department of Health.

—(1995), *Notification of Suspected Cases of Child Abuse between Health Boards and Gardai*, Dublin: Department of Health.

—(1996a), *Report of the Committee into Child Abuse in Madonna House*, Dublin: Stationary Office.

—(1996b), *Putting Children First: Discussion Document on Mandatory Reporting*, Dublin: Department of Health.

—(1999), *Children First: National Guidelines for the Protection and Welfare of Children*. Dublin: Department of Health.

—(2000), *Our Children—Their Lives: The National Children's Strategy*, Dublin: Stationary Office.

Department of Health (UK) (1995), *Child Protection: Messages from Research*, London: Department of Health.

Department of Health and Social Security (UK) (1988), *Protecting Children: A Guide for Social Workers Undertaking a Comprehensive Assessment*, (London: HMSO).

Department of the Tánaiste (1997), *Report of the Task Force on Violence Against Women*, Dublin: Government Publications.

Dienhart, A. and D. Dollahite (1997), 'A generative narrative approach to clinical work with fathers', in A. Hawkins and D. Dollahite (Eds), *Generative Fathering: Beyond Deficit Perspectives*, London: Sage.

Dingwall. R. (1989), 'Some problems about predicting child abuse and neglect', in O. Stevenson (Ed.), *Child Abuse: Public Policy and Professional Practice*, Brighton: Wheatsheaf.

Dobash, R. E. and R. P. Dobash (1992), *Women, Violence and Social Change.* London: Routledge.

Doherty, D. (1996), 'Child care and protection: protecting the children—supporting their service providers', in H. Ferguson and T. McNamara (Eds), *Protecting Irish Children: Investigation, Protection and Welfare*, special issue of *Administration*, Dublin: Institute of Public Administration.

Edwards, J., (1998), 'Screening out me: or "Has mum changed her washing powder recently?"' in J. Popay, J. Hearn and J. Edwards (Eds), *Men, Gender Divisions and Welfare*, London: Routledge.

Edwards, S. (1987), 'Male violence in feminist theory: an analysis of the changing conceptions of sex/gender violence and male dominance' in J. Hanmer and M. Maynard (Eds) *Women, Violence and Social Control.* London: Macmillan.

Egelend, B. (1988), 'Breaking the cycle of abuse: implications for prediction and intervention', in K. Browne, C. Davies and P. Stratton (Eds.), *Early Prediction and Prevention of Child Abuse* Chichester: John Wiley.

Fahy, B. (1999), *Freedom of Angels: Surviving Goldenbridge Orphanage*, Dublin: The O'Brien Press.

Farmer, E. (1997), 'Protection and child welfare: striking the balance', in N. Parton (Ed.), *Child Protection and Family Support: Tensions, Contradictions and Possibilities*, London: Macmillan

Farmer, E. and M. Owen (1995), *Child Protection Practice: Private Risks and Public Remedies*, London: HMSO/Chichester: John Wiley.

Featherstone, B (1996), 'Victims or villains? Women who physically abuse their children', in B. Fawcett and B. Featherstone, J. Hearn and C. Toft (Eds) *Violence and Gender Relations, Theories and Interventions*, Sage: USA.

—(1997a), "'I wouldn't do your job!" Women, social work and child abuse' in W. Holloway and B. Featherstone (Eds) *Mothering and Ambivalence,* London: Routledge.

—(1997b), 'What has gender got to do with it? Exploring physically abusive behaviour towards children', *British Journal of Social Work,* 27, 419–433.

—(1999) 'Taking mothering seriously: the implications for child protection' *Child and Family Social Work,* 4, 43–54.

Featherstone and Trinder, (1997), 'Familiar subjects? Domestic violence and child welfare', *Child and Family Social Work,* Vol. 2, 147–160.

Ferguson, H. (1994), 'Child abuse inquiries and the *Report of the Kilkenny Incest Investigation*: a critical analysis', *Administration,* Vol. 41, No. 4.

—(1995a), 'The paedophile priest: a deconstruction', *Studies,* 84, 247–256.

—(1995b), 'Child welfare, child protection and the Child Care Act 1991: key issues for policy and practice', in H. Ferguson and P. Kenny (Eds), *On Behalf of the Child: Child Welfare, Child Protection and the Child Care Act 1991,* Dublin: A. & A. Farmar.

—(1996a), 'Protecting Irish children in time: child abuse as a social problem and the development of the child protection system in the Republic of Ireland', in H. Ferguson and T. McNamara (Eds), *Protecting Irish Children: Investigation, Protection and Welfare,* Dublin: Institute of Public Administration.

—(1996b), 'The protection of children in time: child protection and the lives and deaths of children in child abuse cases in socio-historical perspective', *Child and Family Social Work,* 1, 205–217.

—(1997a), 'Protecting children in new times: child protection and the risk society', *Child and Family Social Work,* 2, 221–234.

—(1997b), 'Women protection, child protection and the implications of the Domestic Violence Act, (1996)', a paper based on the findings of a research study commissioned by the Mid-Western Health Board.

—(2000), '*States of Fear,* child abuse and Irish society', *Doctrine and Life,* Vol. 50, No.1, pp 20–30.

—(2001a), 'Ireland', in B. M. Schwartz-Kenney, M. McCauley and M. Epstein (Eds.), *Child Abuse: A Global View,* Greenwood Publishing: Westport, CT.

—(2001b), 'Promoting child protection, welfare and healing: the case for developing best practice'. *Child and Family Social Work*, 6, 1–12.

—(2001c), Social work, individualisation and life politics', *British Journal of Social Work*, 31, 41–55.

Ferguson, H. and P. Kenny (1995), 'Towards an integrated system of child care services', in H. Ferguson and P. Kenny (Eds), *On Behalf of the Child: Child Welfare, Child Protection and the Child Care Act 1991*, Dublin: A. & A. Farmar.

Ferguson, H. and T. McNamara (Eds), *Protecting Irish Children: Investigation, Protection and Welfare,* special issue of *Administration*, Dublin: Institute of Public Administration.

Ferguson, H. and P. Synott, P. (1995), 'Intervention into domestic violence in Ireland: developing policy and practice with men who batter', in *Journal of Administration,* Vol. 43, No. 3, 57–81.

Gelles, R. J. (1975), 'The social construction of child abuse', *American Journal of Orthopsychiatry*, 45, 363–71.

Gibbons, J., S. Conroy and C. Bell, C. (1995), *Operating the Child Protection System*, London: HMSO.

Gibbons, J., S. Thorpe and P. Wilkinson (1990), *Family Support and Prevention: Studies in Local Areas,* London: HMSO.

Giddens, A. (1990), *The Consequences of Modernity*, Cambridge: Polity Press.

—(1991), *Modernity and Self Identity*, Cambridge: Polity Press.

—(1992), *The Transformation of Intimacy*, Cambridge: Polity Press.

—(1994), *Beyond Left and Right: The Future of Radical Politics*, Cambridge: Polity Press.

—(1998), *The Third Way: The Renewal of Social Democracy*, Cambridge: Polity Press.

Gilligan, R. (1995), 'Family support and child welfare: realising the promise of the Child Care Act 1991', in H. Ferguson and P. Kenny (Eds.), *On Behalf of the Child: Child Welfare, Child Protection and the Child Care Act 1991*, Dublin: A. & A. Farmar.

Gondolf, E. W. (1993), 'Male batterers', in R. L. Hampton et al, (Eds), *Family Violence: Prevention and Treatment*, New York: Sage.

Hallett, C. and O. Stevenson (1980), *Child Abuse: Aspects of Interprofessional Co-operation*, London: Allen and Unwin.

Hanmer, J. and D. Statham (1988), *Women and Social Work*, London:

Macmillan.

Harris, T. (1993), 'Surviving childhood adversity: what can we learn from naturalistic studies?' in H. Ferguson, R. Gilligan and R. Torode, (Eds), *Surviving Childhood Adversity: Issues for Policy and Practice*, Dublin: Social Studies Press.

Hawkins, A., S. L. Christiansen, K. Pond Sargent and E. J. Hill (1995), 'Rethinking fathers' involvement in childcare: a developmental perspective', in W. Marsiglio (Ed.), *Fatherhood: Contemporary Theory, Research and Practice*, London: Sage.

Herman, J. (1992), *Trauma and Recovery*, London: Pandora.

Hogan, F. (1998), 'Soulfull storytelling with men: an invitation to intimacy', *Feedback: Journal of the Family Therapy Association of Ireland*, 8, 12–17.

Holland, K. (2000), 'Major review of childcare services urged to cope with crisis', *The Irish Times*, 19 September, 2000.

Howe, D. (1992), 'Child abuse and the bureaucratisation of social work', *Sociological Review*, 40, 491–508.

Howe, D., M. Brandon, D. Hinings and G. Schofield (1999), *Attachment Theory, Child Maltreatment and Family Support: A Practice and Assessment Model*, Basingstoke: Macmillan.

Humphrey, C. (1999), 'Avoidance and confrontation: social work practice in relation to domestic violence and child abuse', *Child and Family Social Work*, 4.

Irish Catholic Bishops' Advisory Committee (1996), *Child Sexual Abuse: Framework for a Church Response*, Dublin: Veritas.

Irish Society for the Prevention of Cruelty to Children (ISPCC) (1956), *First Annual Report*, Dublin: ISPCC.

—*Annual Report*, 1974, Dublin: ISPCC.

Jordan, B. (1997), 'Partnership with service users in child protection and family support, in N. Parton (Ed.), *Child Protection and Family Support: Tensions, Contradictions and Possibilities*, London: Macmillan.

Keenan, O. (1996), *Kelly: A Child is Dead, Interim Report of the Joint Committee on the Family*, Dublin: Government Publications Office.

Kelleher and Associates with O'Connor, (1995) *Making the Links—A Study Commissioned by Women's Aid*, Dublin: Women's Aid.

Kelly, A. (1995), 'A public health nursing perspective', in H. Ferguson and

P. Kenny (Eds.), *On Behalf of the Child: Child Welfare, Child Protection and the Child Care Act 1991*, Dublin: A. & A. Farmar.

Kelly L., (1996a), 'When does the speaking profit us?: reflections on the challenges of developing feminist perspectives on abuse and violence by women' in M. Hester, L. Kelly and J. Radford (Eds), *Women, Violence and Male Power* Open University Press: Milton Keynes.

—(1996b), 'When woman protection is the best kind of child protection' in H. Ferguson and T. McNamara (Eds), *Protecting Irish Children: Investigation, Protection and Welfare*, special edition of *Administration*, Vol. 44, No. 2.

Kempe, C. H., F. N. Silverman, B. F. Steele, W. Droegmuller and H. K. Silver (1962), 'The battered child syndrome', *Journal of the American Medical Association*, 181, 17–22.

Kennedy Report (1970), *Reformatory and Industrial Schools System Report*, Dublin: Stationary Office.

Kenny, P. (1995), 'The Child Care Act, 1991 and the social context of child protection', in H. Ferguson and P. Kenny (Eds), *On Behalf of the Child: Child Welfare, Child Protection and the Child Care Act 1991*, Dublin: A. & A. Farmar.

Kenny, P. (1996), 'Child protection: messages from research—a review essay', in H. Ferguson and T. McNamara (Eds), *Protecting Irish Children: Investigation, Protection and Welfare*, special issue of *Administration*, Dublin: Institute of Public Administration.

Lavan, A. (1998), 'Social Work in Ireland' in S. Shardlow and M. Payne, *Contemporary Issues in Social Work: Western Europe* Aldershot: Arena.

Maynard, M. (1985), 'The response of social workers to domestic violence', in J. Pahl (Ed.), *Private Violence and Public Policy*, London: Routledge and Kegan Paul.

Mayo and District Branch NSPCC (1938; 1955), *Annual Report*, London: NSPCC Archives.

Milner, J. (1993), 'Avoiding violent men: the gendered nature of child protection policy and practice' in H. Ferguson, R. Gilligan and R. Torode (Eds), *Surviving Childhood Adversity: Issues for Policy and Practice*, Dublin: Social Studies Press.

— (1996), 'Men's resistance to social workers' in B. Fawcett and B. Featherstone, J. Hearn and Cl. Toft (Eds), *Violence and Gender Relations, Theories and Interventions*, London: Sage.

McElwee, C. N. (1996), *Children At Risk*, Waterford: StreetSmart Press.

McGinley, M. (1995), 'A programme manager's perspective', in H. Ferguson and P. Kenny (Eds), *On Behalf of the Child: Child Welfare, Child Protection and the Child Care Act 1991*, Dublin: A. & A. Farmar.

McGrath, K. (1996), 'Intervening in child sexual abuse in Ireland: towards victim-centered policies and practices' in H. Ferguson and T. McNamara (Eds.), *Protecting Irish Children: Investigation, Protection and Welfare,* special edition of *Administration* Dublin: Institute of Public Administration, 57–72.

McGuinness, C. (1993), *Report of the Kilkenny Incest Investigation*, Dublin: Stationary Office.

McKay, S. (1998), *Sophia's Story*, Dublin: Gill and Macmillan.

McKeown, K. (1999), 'Evaluation: a guide to its language and logic', *Administration*, 47 (1), 50–77.

McKeown, K. and R. Gilligan (1991), 'Child sexual abuse in the Eastern Health Board Region of Ireland in 1988: an analysis of 512 confirmed cases', *Economic And Social Review*, Vol. 22 No. 2, 101–134.

McKeown, K., H. Ferguson and D. Rooney (1998), *Changing Fathers? Fatherhood and Family Life in Modern Ireland*, Cork: Collins Press.

Mid-Western Health Board (1997), *Review of Child Care and Family Support Services*, Limerick: Mid-Western Health Board.

Moore, C. (1995), *Betrayal of Trust: The Father Brendan Smyth Affair and Catholic Church*, Dublin: Marino.

Mullender, A., (1996), *Rethinking Domestic Violence: the Social Work and Probation Response,* London: Routledge.

—(1997), 'Domestic violence and social work, the challenge to change' in *Critical Social Policy*, Issue 50, Vol. 17 (1) February.

Murphy, M. (1996), 'From prevention to "family support" and beyond: promoting the welfare of Irish children', in H. Ferguson and T. McNamara (Eds.), *Protecting Irish Children: Investigation, Protection and Welfare,* special edition of *Administration* Dublin: Institute of Public Administration, 73–101.

Nelson, B. (1984), *Making an Issue of Child Abuse: Political Agenda Setting for Social Problems.* Chicago: University of Chicago Press.

North Western Health Board (1998), *The Report of the Inquiry into the West Of Ireland Farmer Case*, Manorhamilton: North Western Health Board.

O'Connor, M. (1996), 'Protecting abused women and their children: the Irish context', in H. Ferguson and T. McNamara (Eds), *Protecting Irish Children: Investigation, Protection and Welfare*, special issue of *Administration*, Dublin: Institute of Public Administration.

O'Hagan, K. (1997), 'The problem of engaging men in child protection work', *British Journal of Social Work*, 27, 25–42.

O'Morain, P. (2000), 'Judge still fighting for troubled children', *The Irish Times*, 18 October 2000.

Osborne, D. (1999), *The Intimate Abuse of Young People in an Adult World: A Qualitative Study*, unpublished Ph.D. thesis, National University of Ireland, Cork.

Owen, M. (1996), 'Child protection and research: understanding the messages', *Child and Family Social Work*, 1, 255–259.

Parton, N. (1985), *The Politics of Child Abuse*, London: Macmillan.

—(1991), *Governing The Family: Child Care, Child Protection and the State*, London: Macmillan.

—(1997), (Ed.) *Child Protection and Family Support: Tensions, Contradictions and Possibilities*, London: Macmillan.

Parton, N., D. Thorpe and C. Wattam, C. (1997), *Child Protection, Risk and the Moral Order*, London: Macmillan.

Raftery, M. and E. O'Sullivan (1999), *Suffer the Little Children: The Inside Story of Ireland's Industrial Schools*, Dublin: New Island Books.

Reder, P., S. Duncan and M. Gray (1993), *Beyond Blame: Child Abuse Tragedies Revisited*, London: Routledge.

Richardson, V. (1999), 'Children and social policy', in S. Quinn, P. Kennedy, A. O'Donnell and G. Kiely (Eds), *Contemporary Irish Social Policy*, Dublin: University College Dublin Press.

Ruddle, H. and J. O'Connor (1992), *Seeking a Refuge from Violence: The Adapt Experience: A study of the Needs and Characteristics of the Users of the Adapt Refuge*, Limerick: Mid-Western Health Board.

Skehill, C. (1999), *The Nature of Social Work in Ireland*, Lampeter: Edwin Mellen Press.

Stanley, N. (1997), 'Domestic violence and child abuse: developing social work practice', *Child and Family Social Work*, Vol. 28. No. 1.

Stark, E. and A. Filtcraft (1996), *Women at Risk: Domestic Violence and Women's Health*, London: Sage.

Stevenson, O. (1996), *Child and Family Social Work.*

Task Force on Child Care Services (1981), *Final Report*, Dublin: Stationary Office.

Thoburn, J., A. Lewis and D. Shemmings (1995), *Paternalism or Partnership? Family Involvement in the Child Protection Process*, London: HMSO.

Thorpe, D. (1994), *Evaluating Child Protection*, Milton Keynes: Open University Press.

— (1996), 'Categorising referrals about children: child protection or child welfare?', in D. Platt and D. Shemmings (Eds), *Making Enquiries into Alleged Child Abuse and Neglect: Partnership with Families*, Brighton: Pennant.

— (1997), 'Regulating late-modern child rearing in Ireland', *Economic and Social Review*, 28, 63–84.

Trinder, L. (1996), 'Social work research: the state of the art (or science)', *Child and Family Social Work*, Vol. 1, No. 4.

Waterhouse, E. and J. Carnie (1991), 'Social work and police response to child sexual abuse in Scotland', *British Journal of Social Work*, 21, 373–379.

Walsh, T. (1999), 'Changing expectations: the impact of child protection on social work in Ireland', *Child and Family Social Work*, 4, 33–42.

Wattam, C. (1997), 'Can filtering processes be rationalised?', in N. Parton (ed), *Child Protection and Family Support: Tensions, Contradictions and Possibilities*, London: Macmillan.

Winston, N. (1999), 'Social policy evaluation' in G. Kiely, A. O'Donnell, P. Kennedy and S. Quinn, (Eds), *Irish Social Policy in Context*, Dublin: University College Dublin Press.

Wise, S. (1995), 'Feminist ethics in practice', in R. Hugman and D. Smith (Eds), *Ethical Issues in Social Work*, London: Routledge.

Index